ONE PEOPLE MAYOR

A Journey

Sebert Graham
in conversation with Ian Mulder

H
HANSIB

First published in Great Britain in 2005
by Hansib Publications Limited
P.O. Box 226, Hertford, Hertfordshire SG14 3WY

Email: info@hansib-books.com. Website: www.hansib-books.com

ISBN 1 870518 38 1

Cover design by Graphic Resolutions, Hertfordshire, England

Design and Production by Books of Colour, Hertfordshire, England

Printed and bound in Great Britain

Foreword

EVERYONE'S VOICE IS UNIQUE. THE VOICE OF SEBERT GRAHAM, heard in this book in dialogue with Ian Mulder, is distinctive: warm, reflective, humorous, calm. It tells a compelling story – of how a boy born in Jamaica came to be the first citizen, so to speak, of a town in a far-away country.

But though everyone's voice is unique, it also participates in a wider conversation. Sebert Graham was born into a world in which most people didn't travel far, and in which the United Kingdom contained only a small number of people born abroad. He moved to this country, eventually became the first Mayor of High Wycombe and Buckinghamshire from the African-Caribbean community, and now lives in a Britain which draws strength from being both multi-ethnic and multi-cultural.

Sebert's story is thus part of a wider tale – of how modern Britain came to be what it is. It's a story told with modesty, insight and much goodwill. I was struck particularly, in reading it, by his generosity towards those who, during his first years in Britain, were prominent in demanding immigration control.

It isn't necessary to share all Sebert's views to honour the contribution he continues to make to High Wycombe – and thereby to the wider community. He writes of being told by one person, when he became Mayor that he had become "one of the sons of High Wycombe". I know Sebert less well than many of the people who appear in this tale. But I know him well enough to appreciate that the compliment was well deserved.

Paul Goodman
Member of Parliament for Wycombe

Acknowledgements

I FEEL A GREAT DEBT OF GRATITUDE TO THE MANY PEOPLE IN High Wycombe and elsewhere who have supported and assisted me in the years covered in this journey. They had faith in me, they helped practically, they encouraged me when I needed it most. Thanks, colleagues, friends and family! You know who you are.

Thanks also to High Wycombe's local newspapers, *Bucks Free Press*, *Midweek* and *Star*, through their Editor, Steve Cohen, who has given permission to use archive material, both text and photographic.

But most of all I want to express my thanks for the presence, through thick and thin, year in, year out, of my partner, Beaulah, who also made a most gracious Mayoress, appreciated wherever she went, and whose continual and enduring support means everything to me.

S.G.

Contents

Preface

SEBERT HAD BEEN SEEKING A COLLABORATOR TO WRITE HIS story. I was uneasy about "ghosting" an autobiography, and the publisher in any case told us emphatically that he did not approve of such a deceit. We got round it by doing a story in two voices. Mine (Ian's) is in italics. Sebert's is in normal text. Other voices are shown framed in black lines. They are extracts from press cuttings, letters and other materials.

His life story is a particular example of the experience of Black people in England over forty-five years. Such a tale could be told differently by every black immigrant and every Black Britisher born within these shores. Our country is famous for its hospitality and embracing diverse cultures, but the younger generation may think this arose naturally and without effort. They may take our peaceful coexistence for granted, without seeing anything precious. The older ones amongst us on the other hand may fear immigration as a threat to our established way of life. But then they might fear new technology or changing social customs just as much, for the times are always a-changing, and every generation looks back to its own golden age.

The wellbeing of the community at any particular time does not come about by accident and owes its quality to the efforts of many who work mostly in the background, as volunteers, for the sake of public service. Sebert Graham is one such citizen. His life and work is a living demonstration that immigration can enhance our traditions, breathing new life into ancient rituals and linking a provincial market town in England's Green Belt with the wider human family.

It's his tale, told his way. But first, a little background.

High Wycombe has a unique ceremony for the Mayor-making. Other towns in England make Mayors, but no other in the world, so far as I know, weighs them in. That is only done with boxers before a big fight. Well, as a young Army recruit, Sebert Graham did learn to box with gloves in a ring and won a number of bouts, as he will relate.

But here he was, dressed in robes from another age, swinging on a weighing-chair, in this town once famous for making chairs, on account of the hardwood beech trees that grow naturally in these parts. This town of High Wycombe has been weighing in its Mayors, some say, since an unfortunate incident in 1678, where one of them disgraced himself with drunken behaviour.[1] (There are several accounts of the origin of this custom and we will encounter others.) It was an affront to the townspeople that he should act badly in front of them, and at their expense too. Ever since then,

Mayor Making Ceremony
Order of Procession
from Guildhall

Police

Beadle

Town Clerk   Mayor's Chaplain

Macebearer

Mayor   Mayoress

RAF   Army

Hon Burgesses

Counsellors

The Town Crier

New Mayor weighs in

There were plenty of cheers for new and old mayors as they banished their bashfulness to sit on the scales and reveal their weight to the public.

The ceremony dates back to Queen Elizabeth I who noticed that Wycombe had an extremely overweight citizen.

From *Bucks Free Press*, 24.05.96

The incoming Town Mayor will be invited to:

- Sign the Declaration of Acceptance of Office
- Take the following Oaths:
  Oath of Allegiance
  Oath of Mayor of the Market
  Judicial Oath
- The Incoming town Mayor will be invested with the Chain and Badge of Office and the Robe by the retiring Town Mayor
- The retiring Town Mayor will hand over the regalia, i.e. the Mace, the Small Mace, the Chain, the Mayoress's chain and the Silver Stick
- The incoming Town Mayor will present an Ex-Mayor's Badge bearing the High Wycombe Arms to the retiring Town Mayor and an Ex-Mayoress's Badge to the Retiring Mayoress
- The incoming town Mayor will express thanks for his election, appoint his Chaplain and invest the Mayoress with her Badge of Office
- (continues with ceremonies relating to the Deputy Town Mayor)
- then there is the Weighing-in Ceremony (46 people weighed, starting with the new Mayor)
- then the Quarter Peal of Parish Church Bells

Lest the Quarter Peal of Parish Church Bells sounds like short-changing the Mayor—"Why not the whole peal?"— a quarter-peal takes about 46 minutes.

The newspapers seem to agree that it was Queen Elizabeth I who passed through the town on a revenue-collecting tour and noticed that the Mayor was rather too fat. But Sebert told me it was Queen Mary I and who am I to doubt him. The idea of the Monarch going through the land personally to collect taxes seems to indicate something long ago, and Mary was longer ago than her younger sister Elizabeth. When times became more civilised, the Monarch trusted others to collect taxes on his or her behalf, "On her Majesty's Service" as the envelopes from Inland Revenue used to say.

A beadle is a kind of forerunner to the town policeman, with responsibilities for law and order, workhouses and protection of official property. I am not sure what the Wycombe Beadle does officially these days when he is not in processions.

the weighing-in is a "sobering reminder" that an individual may take on the mantle of glory, but is not beyond being watched, measured and judged. You may well imagine that Councillor Sebert Graham was watched even more closely during his term in office.

And why were these ceremonial accoutrements bestowed:—the cocked hat, the fur-trimmed red gown, the Mayoral chain, processions with mace-bearers and beadle, a peal of bells rung at All Saints Parish Church? Perhaps tradition and pomp play an important part in cementing the nation together, like royalty. The Mayoralty is the focus of the town's civic pride in itself, almost a regal symbol, someone to represent impartially the entire community. It lets us enact, in pageantry endlessly repeated, the giving and receiving of gestures of respect. Mayoralty, Royalty—even the words are similar. But unlike the King or Queen, the Mayor is elevated from amongst the people, and reverts to ordinary life a year later. It is like the tale of Cinderella, where her elevation and finery lasts only till midnight. Is it an empty role, the comic out-dated ritual of a settled population, celebrating their democracy and undisturbed development over centuries? It could be so, but the role exists for the incumbent to make something of it. It is an improvised pageant rather than a fully scripted Shakespeare play. We shall see how Mr Graham played this role.

"I'm happy and proud for you all," says Mayor

Wycombe's first black mayor hopes his year of office will lead to other black people following in his footsteps.

Cllr Sebert Graham says that the district's Afro-Caribbean community is 'elated' that he is the new mayor.

The 56-year-old production operator officially took over from Cllr Alan Hill last night, when he was officially weighed in under High Wycombe's Guildhall.

Sebert (Lab. Bowerdean and Daws Hill) told the Bucks Free Press: "I am the first African-Caribbean person to be elected a mayor in Bucks. And I think that is extremely important for race relations in this community.

"I think the whole community is quite elated, and I am extremely happy and proud for them. I would like to think the younger generation will be inspired by there being a black mayor."

. . .

He recalls: "I had been through High Wycombe on the way to Oxford and remember seeing the Rye and Kingsmead. Those green open spaces reminded me of those in Jamaica. So I decided to make the move."

Sebert's political aspirations were fuelled after becoming involved with the Race Equality council, and finding the council wasn't providing it with enough satisfactory answers.

He said: "Nowadays, the council is so much more approachable."

Excerpted from *Bucks Free Press*, 24.05.96

The Mayoral weighing-in ceremony.

But how did he wake up one day to find himself appointed as this dignitary who outranks everyone else in the town? He had left school and joined the tide of black immigrants who took whatever jobs were offered and sometimes faced crude racism in the Fifties and Sixties. How did he get to a position of mingling with professors and Ambassadors and Head Teachers and wide-eyed schoolchildren? Having served in the Jamaica Regiment, without even making it to lance-corporal, how did he become socially on equal terms with an Air Vice-Marshal?

His opportunity came from through the legacy of centuries of tradition. We know the names of every mayor in High Wycombe since 1285 AD. Someone has to do the job, and, par excellence, he fulfilled the criteria. I wonder if the 220 Mayors before him each asked themselves the same question: "Why me?" Perhaps some of them had other and bigger claims to fame. Perhaps they felt it was their due. Perhaps they were part of a family tradition, and their grandfathers or great-uncles had been Mayor before them.

But Sebert was born in another valley, on the other side of an ocean. Instead of beechwoods and rolling wheatfields, he was surrounded by tall breadfruit trees, sugar cane, coffee, bananas. The traditions into which he was born could hardly have been more different, though Jamaica revered England as the Mother Country. They shared the same language and institutions. The names "Sebert" and "Graham" are both from the Anglo-Saxon. His birthplace of Enfield, in the parish of Westmoreland, echoes English place-names.

If you had gone back seven hundred years, in the place where he was born, you'd have found quite the opposite of unbroken traditions and peaceful development. A people called the Arawaks had lived there. And where are their descendants now? All gone, slaughtered, leaving few traces. The island of Jamaica had been repopulated with men and women from West Africa, forcibly taken there, under the cruellest conditions you can imagine. They had been hand-picked for their strong physique, to work on the plantations for the white owners. Only the fittest survived.

There is significance that a man descended from slaves was chosen to enact a proud ceremony, in the land of "Rule Britannia, Britannia rules the waves. Britons never never never shall be slaves." He accepted a chain gently laid over his shoulders, but his ancestors would have had a chain roughly clamped to their ankles. It was no token gesture. Let Sebert tell the story.

I.M.

NOTES

1. *Weighing-in:* see also page 78 for another explanation of this custom.

CHAPTER 1

A country childhood

I WAS BORN IN THE PARISH OF WESTMORELAND, JAMAICA, IN the District of Enfield[1]. My parents, Hubert and Almena Graham, were also born in Westmoreland.

I am the third of my mother's nine children and the eldest of my father's six. My father spaced us out well—what skill!—because we were born approximately two years apart: myself on 5th January, 1940, Derek on the 10th September 1942, Roy on the 5th January 1944. Notice that Roy and I share the same birthday, without being twins. There's precision. [Laughs] I wish I could do the same. Then my brother Dudley was born on the 17th January 1946, followed by my sister Myra on the 12th February 1948. Finally there was the last young man. He was a real surprise to my mother, as I can remember very clearly—she thought she'd be free from children now that the rest of us were growing up! My youngest brother Albert arrived on 27th September 1950.

What about your older siblings?

My father treated my two older brothers and one sister just the same as the rest of the family, but they left us quite early. My sister Icyline, eight years older than me, and my brother Astley, five years older, went to live in Kingston. My other brother, Joshua, two years older, went to live with his uncle in Trelawney. Then from time to time, in later life, they would all come back and we would have a big reunion. My elder sister would always call my father Poppy. I've got a great respect for my sister, in fact all of us do. The first time I ever tasted the delights of the city was when my sister came from Kingston, and came to see us in the country places. She brought popcorn, sweets and other things I had never seen before. Those were exciting times! We loved her more, because of those goodies. That popcorn! Memories like that never leave you.

Our home was a place of kindness and discipline and love, all in plenty; and above all, it was a Christian home. How well I remember the banter between my father and mother: "Mina! Is me dinner ready?" "You think you have any servant here, Papa?" "Wha you mean, Ma?"

Now we all have televisions and radio, but back in those days our entertainment was a gramophone with a horn. You didn't need electricity— we didn't have any!—you could just take it anywhere and wind it up. In fact in the entire nineteen-forties I never came across electricity. [Laughs] I remember passing my cousin's house—we had a very close relationship— and I remember him playing his gramophone, and one of the songs he was

singing to his daughter was "Miss Caroline, around the singing machine".
His daughter's name was Caroline.

My brothers and I were quite a unit—in fact we have stayed very close
to this day. I know I'm one of those who can't stop saying how well off the
children are today, in terms of material things. But in those days we would
make our own entertainment. We used to improvise and make small carts
with wheels. We call them hand-carts in Jamaica.[2] Or we would make a sled
from the rubbery stalk of a buba tree—that's a kind of palm tree. Imagine a
hot sunny day. You climb up a small hill, and this thing slides down the
bottom of the hill like a bobcar—

As in that movie "Cool Runnings"![3]

[Laughs] Cool Runnings, Ha ha! Yes, you see how these Jamaicans can
improvise, and how they can make things happen. As you say, *Cool Runnings*.
Those boys had never seen snow until they went to Canada. And yet, they've
done extremely well. I'm surprised they haven't carried on and progressed.
But Jamaicans have got real aspirations and initiative to get on and do things.
They are people who know how to get up and go.

But we were talking about my relationship with my brothers. Yes, we
had our improvisations, making our own entertainment. But we also had
our dreams, even before we had started school. We were going to be
businessmen. Roy was very much orientated towards commercial things.
We were going to buy trucks, and have the family name written across
them: G R A H A M. My brother Derek, he was a sports boy. From a very
early age, he was a man who wanted to sing, to perform—he was that
type of person. However as the years went on he changed, in the direction
of Christianity. In his late teens he had decided he was going into the
Church, to study for ordination as a minister. Poor man, he never lived to
complete his studies.

It was simple things that carried us through, a simple country life. And,
as for my father, he was my friend too. We walked together. My father and
I would get up in the morning to milk the cow—her name was Dina. Then
Roy and Dudley would start catching the chickens around the yard. In the
night, they would sleep in the trees, but in the morning they would have to
be caught and put in their place. My brothers would tie some of them to
prevent them from wandering off to interfere with the neighbours' land. If
we let them go off, they might dig up the corn that the neighbours had just
planted in their fields. They'd put the others in a big cage to keep them safe
till it was night. And so we would all have our responsibilities. My father
and I would go to milk the cow, then it would be my job to bring back the
milk. Meanwhile our mother would be making breakfast and we'd come
back for that, and then some of us would be taking some milk over to give
to our granny—our grandmother who lived a little distance away.

A typical Caribbean breakfast is quite heavy. It's a cooked breakfast.

You could have boiled banana, with salt fish and ackee, or even with calaloo[4]. On the other hand, you might have roast breadfruit[5], with some fried pork. Sometimes it would be cornmeal porridge. Corn is very versatile and is used in Jamaica in many ways. To make porridge it is ground and boiled with milk. It's very nutritious and fills you up, so that you don't get hungry very quickly.

In those days we did not have piped water or drainage. My mother used ponds to do the washing. Some ponds were good clear water, so we would go there to collect our drinking water. Others were called slop ponds. You could go there and swim. They are not big, like lakes. Some are man-made: they've been dug out originally. Others happen naturally because Jamaica is full of little valleys and these are natural catchment areas. The water can flow down the hills and gets caught in the low-lying land, helped by the impervious clay soil. In some cases, ponds are the result of natural springs. And that is where you could have your bath, or swim. And in Jamaica we also have many rivers, and we would use those as well.

But back to the subject of washing. My mother would go there with some of the children, from a very early age, and encourage them to learn how to wash the clothes. And this is what you would find in Caribbean life. You'd find that most Caribbean men can wash and cook. They can even sew. Because that is instilled in you by your mother. She'd say that when it was time for you to leave home, or if she died, you'd be able to look after yourself, without depending on anyone. This was the environment in which we grew up.

Our home was always open-house to friends and well-wishers. For example, Zachariah Coke, a family friend, would drop in. We thought of him as the Encyclopaedia of the district: he knew everyone's age and all about them. At some stage, after food and drink, they would start a friendly game of dominoes or cards. Then the thing would be to get Zack going. My father would say something like, "Well, Mina, you are older than me." That was enough to get Zack going and the laughter would never stop.

I would say that of the two, my mother was the stronger personality. Father was hard-working but easy-going, though you would do well not to misjudge him. She would be the disciplinarian and he would be the peacemaker. And they remained very much in love.

And I said that my father was also my friend. I meant that. We walked together. We would share things together And that's my memory of my family life.

When I look at life now, I think that Caribbean people are absolutely brilliant, because they have grown up in a very poor environment. My pre-school education was given to me by my mother. We had no nursery education in those days and we didn't start school till six years old. Our mother taught us ABCs, she taught us to form letters at home. She taught us how to hold a pencil. Actually, we used slates. You'd have this small black slate with a frame, for writing with chalk. Some of us had this good start, that even before you went to school, your mother would have taught you your letters at home. In her long day, she had time to do a lot of things. She would go out and wash the clothes. Sometimes she would go out to my father and take his lunch to him. Of course nowadays, children sit and watch television in the evenings. We didn't have that luxury, not even radio. We would have family evenings. You'd sit out on the verandah till mother would call time. She was the head of the house. Father would be there with us. We'd look up to them. They would talk with us. We'd play games.

Father wouldn't be too tired from his day's work?

No, he would sometimes have come home in the middle of the day. And then he would work in the fields until maybe 4.30. And then on the way home, he would wash himself in the pond. He'd come home, shave, change from his dirty working clothes into something more comfortable and clean for the evenings. Then we would have our dinner. Afterwards we'd sit there with Mamma. She'd read to us. Father would sometimes go and play a few domino games in the shop.

A shop in those country places was where you would get your food provisions and your rum. A shop was general, it would sell everything. And you could sit at tables, they would serve you whatever you want. So these were the pastimes. No television. When they finished these few games of dominoes, it would be back home to the family.

I can remember very clearly a particular day. It was 6th January 1946, the day before I started school, on a Sunday. I went to look for my grandmother. I should mention that by this time we had left Enfield for an adjoining area: Bigwoods. The village was called McDonalds District. My father was born in Enfield, but we all moved to take up residence near my mother's relatives. I was out looking for my grandmother and some of my other relatives—aunts and cousins. In the evening, I went to my aunt Gertrude's home—she's my father's sister. And so when I got there, one of my elder cousins was there: Mr Ules Elvin —he's here in the United Kingdom now!—and another distant relative, a third cousin down the line. This was a friend of Astley's and my cousin Ules. His name was Desmond Ferguson, and we were the same age. These two elder relatives tried to have us fight a contest! [laughs]

We found out in the course of talking that Desmond would also be starting school on the next day. Same class, both of us six years old. And so we met at school, went into the same class, and by nine or ten o'clock, it was time for recess. That's when they give you a break and you go out for fifteen minutes to play before going back in for the next class. We went out and straight away we got into fisticuffs. Ha ha ha ha! All exciting fun. And I remember at twelve o'clock, we had another break, for an hour. That was the real crunch-time. We had a big punch-up! To this day, Desmond Ferguson and I remain the best of friends. I went to Jamaica and saw him in 1973, and then again in 1998. We still feel that bond of friendship and every time we meet, the conversation returns to that fight. There was no harm. It was all good fun. But those are the things you tend to remember.

NOTES

1. *Source:* this and the next nine chapters are the edited transcript of conversations which took place on Feb 6th, 13th and 20th, 2005. The editing was to assemble the content chronologically and to ensure clarity, whilst maintaining the easy conversational flow.
2. *Home-made hand-carts* are still employed in Jamaica to take goods through the streets, or for hawking produce and wares.
3. *Cool Runnings*, movie comedy (1993) based on the real-life Jamaican bobsled team's entry in the 1988 Winter Olympics in Calgary.
4. *Jamaican breakfast:* the bananas used for boiling are small unripe ones. Ackee is Jamaica's national fruit, originating from West Africa, not eaten much except by Jamaicans. It has a savoury flavour and is somewhat poisonous if not gathered and cooked properly. Calaloo is a green vegetable akin to spinach.
5. *Breadfruit:* imported to Jamaica as a staple food for slaves by Capt. Bligh of *Bounty* fame from its original home in the South Seas. The large heavy fruits are roasted over direct fire.

CHAPTER 2
School and after

I THINK SCHOOL LIFE IS SUCH GREAT EXPERIENCE. I HAVE SUCH an urge to tell this to young people—I even tell my own children the same—the best time of your life is your schooldays, and all of your early life. I think until you are sixteen, most of it is play. You don't start to think of it as serious. It never seems to sink in, what teachers are saying, in those early years. For me, anyway, it was always a time of fun. When you are 16, 17, 18, you begin to see the more serious side of life. You begin to see the seriousness of what was put to you when you were 10, 11, 12. You can see things more clearly. Life is one great tree of learning. Learning never stops and with increased understanding comes a higher-quality experience. It's rather like planning a pension.

The thought of joining a pension scheme, to people of my age, at twenty, was a big joke. We had another thirty years before we'd want to think about it! But thirty years isn't too far away: it seems to come up on you suddenly. And so by the time you start to realise, "My gosh, I need to put away some savings," it's already a bit late. The younger you are, the easier it is to take steps to secure your life will be secure. At the younger age, those insurances will be cheaper and you need not even put additional money into it. To preserve their value when you are old and infirm, you have got to learn not to touch them, and never be discouraged from putting away what you can. At the end of the day you'll find the benefits of your savings. But it's hard to say these things to young people. I'm just giving an illustration of how you learn when you're older, and try to tell younger people. Some take your advice and some don't. It's a long process.

You were saying that at 10, 11 or 12 a child doesn't take things seriously but they do later on at 16, 17 or 18. Do you think it is right that in this country pressure is being put on children at an ever-younger age to achieve, and to perform well in tests?

My personal view is that Governments are with us to make some decisions. I believe that Government will lay out a guideline for hospitals and schools, for example. Having laid out the guideline, it should be left to professionals to see it through. I think it is the responsibility of the teachers to monitor the child from a very early age. Every child has got a potential and a limit. Teachers should be left to measure those children's strength, and to find appropriate standards. Take the National Curriculum, for instance I would have hoped it would do something good. As I understand it, just as in Jamaica, your child could leave Buckinghamshire, and go to live in Birmingham, but their lessons in their new school would follow exactly the same pattern, and so when I heard about it, I embraced the idea. But it's not working that way. Each local authority has their own system: to me that's wrong.

There are some of us who will never attain the high standard of learning that is expected of us. Some of us are going to be good at doing things with our hands. Some are going to be more articulate and capable of becoming lawyers. And this is where teachers and other professionals, like the school inspectorate, should be able to have a look at the child's work, and make an honest assessment of where in society this child is best going to fit. Failure to take this approach has led to so many shortages in the fields of carpenters or bricklayers. We have a shortage of toolmakers and aircraft fitters. I saw yesterday in the *Bucks Free Press*[1], that an Arab country was advertising in the UK for aircraft fitters. Now if we had some skilled people here, there would be an opportunity for people from here to go and do jobs in those countries.

I know I'm digressing here, but immigration can work both ways. You have people coming into the United Kingdom. You have other places calling on the United Kingdom for some advanced skills. And there is a free exchange these days, as we were discussing. Younger people—and everyone else—have got to open up their minds. Politicians have got to be honest with people and stop talking about "the pressure of immigration". That has always been with us, people are always migrating. But the world has now become a global village and everyone has got free access from their village to your village, and we're going to have to live with that. What we need to do is to educate our people into the skills that are going to be necessary for them to go to other countries, or be skilful enough to be able to do all the jobs that are already available here in the United Kingdom.

The schools have got a great responsibility. We should have the schools as they used to be in the Caribbean, where boys were taught to do woodwork once a week. Girls would be doing Home Economics instead. All, right, I'll grant you, we have a bigger set of options now. But why did we stop apprenticeships? Government should be investing in institutions that offer apprenticeships, so young people can go and learn skills of value. Some of the things you learn in school are useless. I have learned things in my day which have absolutely no value after you leave school. They were quite useless, and have never had meaning for me. You couldn't get a job outside of the school environment, with those skills.

Can you give an example?

Well, for example I learnt a lot of Geography, useless to me: teachings about where is Mount Sinai, and Egypt, and Galilee, and the courses of great rivers, which have no meaning in this life. We spent so many hours learning those things. I would put learning algebra in the same category. It's not all of us that are going to use algebra when we leave school.

What I am saying is, the teachers should be left alone to make an honest assessment of children, to measure where they are going to fit, in life. That's my belief, anyway.

I admire the great men and women from the Caribbean, I mean those people born there. I would call them pretty brilliant, in a way. My own children started school here in the United Kingdom, at four or five. They had a good start, with the advantage of being taught by someone trained at an early age. But people like me who were born over there, we've experienced an imbalance. Some had already obtained good qualifications and developed their careers in the West Indies. Yet on coming to this country they found it extremely hard to get a job appropriate to their skills. It's an odd thing because many of the teachers over there had been professionally trained in the UK, and the education standards were supposedly linked. After all, we were a protectorate of the UK. We were under that banner. But it is fair to say that the nonsensical books that we were given to read in the Caribbean—*Brer Anancy*, *Mother Hen*, *Miss Tibbs*—they were foolish books. It was a robbery! I think it is fair to say that the education standards must have something to do with the failures of people, in the context of Caribbean people. The kind of books that were handed to us for use in our schools there were unlike anything I have seen handed out in the UK.

Are you referring to books teaching children to read? So what should they have been like?

Well, if you look at the kind of materials we use in schools here now, they are much more intelligent. A child can actually match it up to something, make sense of it. Or the person teaching you will help you with it, because they know what it's about. The child is intelligent enough, the book is intelligently enough written, the pictures relate to the words. All in all, they can make sense of it.

I'd say that the colonial style of teaching has been a major factor in the under-education of people. I give praise to those like Dr Eric Williams of Trinidad and Tobago, to Michael Manley[2] and to Norman Manley[3], his father, who went to Oxford on a Rhodes Scholarship, and came out with flying colours. He got the very highest marks. They must have been absolutely brilliant, to get the highest marks in the United Kingdom.

So there is no doubt in my mind that some of these high flyers from the Caribbean, they are as brilliant or more brilliant than their English peers. My experience of how the world works and how education is perceived—not only for blacks but also white children—tells me that education is set up primarily for the benefit of, say, 30% of children. Therefore, for those people who come from the Caribbean, to come here and go to Oxford or Cambridge, and come out with those high standards, not to mention possible prejudice and racism, to come out with flying colours, it shows they were so brilliant it couldn't be hidden.

I was starting to tell you about my early life at school, and then we digressed to the value of school education in the overall learning process. But let's get back to school life. There are I think advantages and disadvantages in the Caribbean and also here. When I talk about how we don't take our schooling seriously enough, believe me, I speak from experience! There were three of us, all friends, Desmond Morris, Elliston Stuart and me—all bad boys at school [laughs]. Well, we were certainly mischievous. We'd do things like getting behind someone and flicking their ears.

Did this disrupt the class?

Not in a big way, but it may have distracted the other children a bit. And sometimes we were caught, because as you can imagine, a teacher would turn her back to write something on the blackboard, then suddenly she would turn around and see a little girl crying, so she'd want to find out what happened. And that's where the discipline would come in because we were brought up, whether at home or at school, to strict discipline. And if you broke any code of conduct, you'd know you were in trouble, most likely a little bit of spanking. I know that in the United Kingdom these days, even in Jamaica, we are against corporal punishment. But it has its deterrence. You do something naughty once, and you will not do it again, because you know what will happen when you get caught. Punishment would be handed down to you very heavily—sometimes almost unfairly.

We had a teacher who would say, "You're going into the Hot Room". That's a room where you'd be confined, to stand in there till the end of the lesson. That was a harsh discipline. Otherwise you might find a teacher who would say, "All right, will you go and pick up the mail from the Post Office?" Because unlike in the United Kingdom and other developed countries, we didn't have post offices close by, and they didn't deliver to your house. We had to go and get the mail. At times, for me, it was the freedom of getting out of the school.

It doesn't sound like a punishment!

For me, it was not a punishment, it was the chance to have a good run and then enjoy a lovely lunch at my teacher's house, when I got back.

Sounds like you were such a nuisance that the teacher wanted to get you out of the class, sometimes!

Well, you weren't allowed to be in the class for that period, so it was a way of giving you something else to do. But it wasn't something that your parents would have appreciated. And in any case you can't go back to your parents to tell them it was a punishment for being naughty. And so looking back, you can see how very stupid it was. But in those years, it was more fun.

Looking back now, do you think that sometimes the discipline was too strict?

Well, what I recognise now is that the teachers may have taken advantage of a situation, which would be illegal today. Suppose when he sent me to the Post Office I had been knocked down in an accident? Nowadays we look back and see that the teacher was being irresponsible, but that sort of thing was overlooked then. Not only did he deprive you of a lesson that you were entitled to, but he put you at risk without informing your parent.

But I have really enjoyed my school life. Though I would say that in those early years, at school in Enfield, I lost a lot of time, all the same I did have two outstanding teachers.

One was Mrs Arnott, a brilliant teacher whose spoken English was beautiful, as good as anything I have heard in the UK. She taught me to speak properly. For instance, in our English classes, I'll always remember the way she demonstrated the way to pronounce "th": "I threw three thick things through the window." [Laughs] I find it difficult to say this even now, but when you speed it up three times, your tongue becomes tied. But she would insist on correct pronunciation, and after a while, it became the norm.

The other teacher was Arthur Henry Leroy Miller. He taught us maths, history and poetry. A brilliant teacher. He taught us to recite with feeling:

I vow to thee, my country
All earthly things above
Entire and whole and perfect
The service of my love;
The love that asks no question,
The love that stands the test
That lays upon the altar
The dearest and the best.

I think I may have missed something there, but that was his way of exciting his pupils to recite with feeling, almost in a Shakespearean style— ha ha—but he was an excellent teacher. In a way, he had a very short fuse. If you stepped out line with him, you'd know what would happen. Very firm, but fair. Though I think he always had a preference for the girls over the boys anyway. [Laughs]

So what would happen? What kinds of punishments?

Well we have talked about corporal punishment. He wouldn't hesitate from pulling the strop, to somebody who persistently interrupted his class. That is when you would get the strop, or be put in the "hot room", where you would miss part of the lesson.

Can you describe the strop?

It was about 18 inches long and an inch and a half wide, leather, two millimetres thick maybe.[4] You'd get two strokes, on the palm of your hand. Yes, he was that type. Nobody likes to be hit. As I have told you, there's got to be some kind of discipline in the schools. Without it, the teachers would not be allowed to carry on with the class properly, and I think it would be less easy for the children to take their lesson seriously. So the strop acted as a deterrent to anyone interrupting the class. In any case, it never harmed me, either from my parents' scolding, nor at school. Within limits it should be all right and instil a discipline for life.

It doesn't seem to have got in the way of your respect for him.

Certainly not. One would have appreciated it was one's own fault. It's the system and you don't bear a grudge. You've already been taught at home to know right from wrong.

Yet even though he was fair and a good teacher, I wasted some time in his classes. He got to like me in a way. He had a pet name for me. As I was saying to you earlier, in the Caribbean we like to over-ride your official name. He used to call me Sadas. He explained that it was because I looked like one of his old schoolmates. And I remember that in 1957, when I was leaving to join the Army, I went to see him, and he said to me stuttering as he used to do, "S-Sebert! Never let me down. Never let me down." I said, "I am not going to let myself down, Teacher, and therefore I will never let you down." That's the last time I ever saw him. I looked for him when I went home in 1973, but he had retired to his own home in the parish of St Elizabeth, and on making enquiries, I discovered he had died there. But the memories of all those teachers have stayed with me over the years.

Was he the one who used to send you to the Post Office?

[Laughs] Yes, he was the one. He was probably trying to do me a bit of a favour, sending me to the Post Office and letting me miss some of those arithmetic lessons that I disliked so much. Well, I forgive him for all those things—those were learning years. I hold no malice. It was good at the time. It was innocent enjoyment, even though in retrospect, I wish I had taken it more seriously.

My first work experience, apart from helping my father around the farm, was when he sent me to learn carpentry with Freddie Harvey, one of the most noted carpenters in McDonald district and around Darlaston. I used to accompany him on Saturdays. In the Fifties, many boys aspired to the study of agriculture at university. Others wanted to be mechanics, carpenters or masons. I thought carpentry would earn me good money to support a family, wherever I went. But just as today, youngsters would tend to change their minds as we grew older.

Then I went to the next school, at the secondary level, Darlaston School. It was in 1954. I was only there for a short time, but it was valuable all the same. You see, in that same year I went to Kingston to live with my grandfather, Robert Graham, whose house was no. 1 Whitfield Avenue, off the Maxfield Avenue. I was then enrolled in the Whitfield Town Secondary School, under the watchful eye of headmaster Carey, whom my grandfather knew well. Yes, he had his beady eyes on everything that was happening in that school. He too had a "hot room". It must have been a characteristic punishment in Jamaica in those days. It was a very disciplined school—again lovely teachers. If I had spent more time at the

Whitfield School, and less at Enfield, I think I would have learnt more. Just like here in the United Kingdom, the teaching standard in the big cities seems to be a bit above that in the outlying area.

Education is very much treasured in Jamaica. When I went back recently to Montego Bay, I was very struck by the roadside signs everywhere: "TAKE CARE OF OUR CHILREN. THEY ARE OUR FUTURE". The motorists are taking that on board too, and reminding themselves.

Let me tell you how it was for a country boy from Westmoreland to come to Kingston, and go to school amongst Kingstonians. They considered themselves as rough boys and me as a country bumpkin, but that did not wash well with me. You know from our previous conversation that I was ready to stand up for myself and would not tolerate being called names. In a city, you've got to be street-wise, or else you will get sat on. [Laughs] Speaking with boys of your age, you've got to be forceful with them and make sure they understand you, and don't push you around and treat you like a toy. There was Alan, and there was Shaggy—we called him that because he was very scruffy. Yes, I am happy to give their names, then if they read about themselves, they might look me up and we could meet up for a drink, and I am sure they would confirm the truth of what I'm saying. My best friend amongst that crowd was Vincent Cargill. And so I had to put Alan in his place, and also Shaggy who was a bully. But over time, we became friends, so I had gained their respect. No more taunting with "country bumpkins" because they got to see I could be as tough as those Kingstonians. But sadly, I've lost touch with Vincent. When I went back to Jamaica in 1978 I looked for him but his mother had died and he had gone to join his father in the United States.

Our Whitfield Town school used to have this rivalry with a school in Trenchtown, that part of Kingston that Bob Marley made famous, rather full of roughnecks. Our school used to challenge theirs at sports, that kind of thing, and there would be confrontations with those boys—

You mean off the field?

Yes, we had some good fun there. [laughs]

Can you explain that?

Well, Vincent Cargill was very articulate and he was also very high-spirited, and would love a fight as well. But unfortunately he cannot fight. So either Alan or myself would have to end up defending him. [Laughs]

Vincent would start the fight—

And we would have to finish it! So I don't want people to misjudge me and assume I've been the one to seek out a fight. It wasn't that. I was a defender of the truth. And if someone is being taken advantage of, it's my belief that you have the right to defend that person. But those times were good fun. And we Jamaican people have a special way of doing things, which is to say that you know what will happen if you cross the line. For example if you start making comments about a person's mother—not actually knowing his mother—you can bet your life there's going to be some problems there.

And might you have done that to someone, if you were ready to pick a fight with him? Said something about his mother, I mean?

No. [Laughs] I would only do something when someone had provoked me first.

Would you let Vincent start fights for you?

[Laughs] No, it wouldn't be like that. Sometimes the first we'd know about it was when he'd start calling out for our help. So we had to be there. Wonderful years.

Then it must have been 1956 when I finished school.

Did you leave school at the normal age?

Yes, at 16. I could have stayed on, but I decided to leave and work for my grandfather. Actually it was his decision not to support my education any longer. Since I had already made a start in carpentry, he felt that he would now pass on his skills to me.

Those years in Kingston were pretty good ones for me. I learnt a lot. My grandfather was a member of a kind of Masonic Lodge. It was called The Royal Benevolent Society No. 1. He was a disciplined, abstemious man. He wanted me to join and take over from him, so he nominated me to join when I was 21. But of course I never stayed long enough: I moved on.

We were great friends, my grandfather and I. He was a committed Socialist. On a Sunday morning I had to read the editorial of *The Gleaner*[5] to him. At certain points, he would stop me "Hold it, son," he would say. Then we would have a debate. It was not that he couldn't read. He told me that when I would read to him it allowed him to analyse the situation more clearly.

Anyway, he used to go to his meetings on a Wednesday night. That was the night I would be able to slip out, quite unknown to him, for a night out in Kingston. There would be films, with Errol Flynn or John Wayne. There was *Gone with the Wind*[6], with Clark Gable, for example. Excellent film even by today's standards. I had to be back always by 9.30, because that was when my grandfather returned from his Lodge meetings! I was indoors when he left, and that's where he expected to find me when he came back. [Laughs] It was a hell of a race against time. Some nights I'd get home just minutes before I heard his key turn in the door. He'd come in and find me snoring away. Those were good times.

Sometimes we had to stand in a long queue, just as here in the United Kingdom, to get through the cinema door. One time Vincent was ahead in the queue. Alan, Shaggy and I gave him our money so he could buy our tickets. But when I reached the door, the doorman would not let me in because Vincent had not bought my ticket! I waited outside so long for him to come out. Eventually I got back to my grandfather's house just in time.

So you were mad with Vincent Cargill for that?

He paid. He paid.

How did he pay?

Well, we had a few hard words. [Laughs] Ah yes. [Long pause.]

You say you went to work for your grandfather.

Yes, he had worked for a time in Cuba, and had learnt the trade of shipwright. That's someone who works for example at the bow and the stern end of a boat, where the most difficult cuts have to be made: bits of wood to fit into certain shapes. He had also worked on housing projects. He was an excellent carpenter, and undertook contract work. Now that I had left school, he decided to take me under his wing and complete the training in carpentry that I had started in Enfield.

Well, I started and made some good progress, but although I was doing a lot of very heavy work, I was being paid too little. In fact I got fed up with the way I was being treated. You see, my grandfather won a big contract to build an extension to the old Foundry in Darling Street and renew the roof, for his old buddy Mr Dailey. So he called in his old friend Sam, a good carpenter who was to be my foreman. Mr Sam was a man that I just couldn't tolerate. When my grandfather wasn't around, he would exploit me and make me do almost everything. I had started to get pretty good at my job. In Jamaica a carpenter would be able to do everything from the foundations up. There weren't the specialised roles in carpentry like we have here in England. He would do the doors, the roof, the shingles, everything. I was doing a lot of work, but the reward was not enough for what I was putting in. Sam and I seemed to be getting on for a few weeks until I found out what he was earning. My own earnings had increased well beyond the initial five or ten shillings a week, but I resented the fact that as the younger man in the team I was doing most of the hard work. It culminated with a big argument with Sam and my grandfather didn't like that.

So I decided to go back to my parents' home where I could easily get ten shillings a week without having to work for it. Everyone yearns for the environment that they know best. It was a great feeling to be reunited with my brothers and sisters in Westmoreland, but after a little while I felt the urge again for the bright lights I had known in Kingston, in such contrast to the dull dark country life.

So I went to stay for a few months with my brother Astley in Montego Bay. Not that it was anything like Kingston. This was in October 1956. In a country like Jamaica you can go somewhere and there will always be someone there for you. And they'll be ready to help out. It wasn't bad for me in those days.

NOTES

1. *Bucks Free Press*, local newspaper covering the High Wycombe area.
2. *Michael Manley*, Jamaican socialist politician who served as prime minister (1972–1980 and 1989). A leader of the Jamaican trade union movement, he advocated Caribbean solidarity and worldwide redistribution of wealth.
3. *Norman Washington Manley*, 1893–1969, prime minister of Jamaica (1959–62); father of Michael Manley. Of Irish and African descent, he was educated at Oxford and became an internationally known lawyer. He founded the moderately socialist People's National Party in 1938, and, with his cousin, Alexander Bustamante, dominated Jamaican politics for several decades. He served as chief minister of Jamaica (1955–59) before being designated prime minister.
4. *Strop:* i.e. a razor-strop designed for sharpening a straight or "cut-throat" razor.
5. *The Gleaner* is Jamaica's oldest newspaper.
6. *Gone with the Wind:* It must have been a re-release. The film was made in 1939.

CHAPTER 3

I join the Army

ONE DAY MY FRIEND LESLIE—HIS PET NAME WAS BRIGGS—showed me an advertisement he'd seen in *The Gleaner*, recruiting for the Army. "Let's join," he said. I was already in the Boys Brigade, and attracted to uniforms. I went home very excited and told my mother and father about my desire to go and be a soldier. They said, "All right, yes", and gave me their blessings.

So Briggs and I went to Kingston. It was January 1957, a few days after my seventeenth birthday. We went for our interviews and medicals. I was accepted but Briggs failed. I felt awful about that, but he was happy for me.

The Army was a huge experience. This is where you learn the real discipline of life. In fact from comparing notes with people I would say that it is more disciplined than the Navy or the Air Force.

You might have answered back to your parents, and been cheeky to the teachers, but in the Army there was no answering back. You do what you are told. I found Army life exciting but hard.

I was assigned to Bravo Company. Bravo just means "B". Two of us, MacIntosh C. and Graham S.—that's me—were called the "baby soldiers", because we were only just 17 when we joined. But we had passed our physical and educational tests, and there we were. Normally you had to be 18, but they were short of recruits and they took us on.

Every day it was the bugle call for Reveille at 6 o'clock, then a morning run, sometimes for 3 miles. Then return to barracks, have breakfast. Then get the barrack room and all your kit ready. In case of inspection, everything must be spotless and your blankets must be folded in a certain way, just so. You must polish your brasses and your boot caps must be so shiny you could comb your hair in the reflection. It teaches you pride and discipline. And it gives you some training too. You could learn motor mechanics or clerical work—typing and so on. After I'd moved to Charlie Company I trained as a signaller. I learned Morse code, and could tap out messages. I was under the leadership of an Englishman, Lieutenant Shaw, from Worcestershire. The Worcestershire Regiment had been posted to Jamaica. There was a Jamaican sergeant-major under him and we had a Scottish RSM—Regimental Sergeant-Major Gibson, very strict, very tough, as all RSMs are.

The Army not only gave us discipline, it taught us comradeship, regardless of what is happening outside the team. You always look out for your comrades and support one another. I can easily understand the difficulties that the British and the American armies have been going through in Iraq. It cannot be easy with a real enemy. We were only pretending to capture those British soldiers, in our war games. But what about those in Iraq? They may see their best friend killed, or their brother. Then you may capture some of the enemy and it must be hard to stand by the Geneva Convention on how to treat prisoners of war. Despite all the discipline, it must take something extra-special not to retaliate. I have every sympathy with those men. They've been trained as killing machines. I almost find it incomprehensible that they've been tried and pushed out of the Army[1]. I know what they are accused of is very wrong. But my feeling is that it's not easy for them. I don't think they just did it sadistically. In their imagination, they'd be seeing their comrade being mutilated or killed. You have a strict code of practice to go by—

But the army is about more than killing. There are political repercussions.

That's right. And maybe they were, as they said, obeying orders. As a soldier you're not going to defy your commanding officer.

But the officers at least should have been politically aware.

Well, the officers are human too. They too can be aroused to passion by seeing their men killed. And they could take the view that they had come to help the Iraqi people, and did not deserve to be treated as an enemy. I am not condoning the wrong that they have done, but I have sympathy for those soldiers. It's a pity that they have to be disgraced for doing their job.

Anyway, back to the story—

Yes, the story! I was paid thirty shillings a month when I joined, but then of course I got free board and lodging, free uniform and free medical care. I was all set to make the Army my full-time career.

It was the first step towards an adult way of living for me. Though I had asked my parents' permission to join the Army, the decision was one that I freely made. It was also the first time that I was able to do something to look after my parents. Most of the time I was able to send them my complete earnings.

Training was hard, for example three-mile runs. And this puts me in mind of our athletes, when people say it's easy. Sport is hard. I did my first proper boxing— with gloves on—whilst in the Army. When I look at professional boxers, doing fifteen rounds in the ring—it's not easy. But what I would like to say to medical people and critics of the danger of boxing, is this. They worry about blows to the chin or to the head. But it's the blows to the rib-cage or the stomach that you feel the worst. Trained professionals have various ways to harden their bodies, so to them it's not as barbaric as it may look. It's like anything in life. If you are adequately trained, the hazards are minimal.

And was your amateur boxing career successful?

Oh yes, they didn't hand out medals, but I won many bouts. It helps to have recognition as a good sportsperson as you work your way up. Yes, I had a good time in the army.

So why did you leave?

One of my peer-group had been made up to lance-corporal. We didn't get on. Promotion went to his head and he used the chance to push everyone around.

Did you wish that you had got the promotion instead of him?

No. I've never been like that. Where someone else makes progress, even today, I wish them well. I don't wish it was me. I strive to do what I am doing to the best of my ability. If I am recognised for it, so be it. If someone else gets it, I don't begrudge them their good fortune.

So for Barry and me, it was almost a personal thing. "He's been made up and now he is the one who's pushing us around." Some of us didn't like that.

And there was nothing much you could do about that.

Right, he had the upper hand. If I spoke back to him and didn't obey him, then all he had to say was, "Private Graham, you *will*." There was no argument. You could be charged under Section whatever-it-was of the Army Regulations. And you would be confined to barracks. You lost your right to take leave.

Therefore Lance-Corporal Barrington Hill was one of my reasons, and then there was Sergeant Hibbert. There was a standpipe in front of the barracks, that we used for attaching hoses to. The tap was dripping. And Sergeant Hibbert calls out to me and says, "Private Graham! Go and turn off that tap." I must say that when I am spoken to in a certain way, I do not like taking orders. Everyone should be treated with proper respect. And that's what was missing on this occasion. He came up to me. But I just carried on and went off to the canteen for my lunch. Then three or four soldiers came for me, Barrington being one of them. They told me to stop eating. I carried on eating. Then I got a "regimental order" to stand up and move. [Laughs] They marched me straight to the guardhouse and I was put away. I was sentenced to fourteen days' CB—Confined to Barracks. That was for disobeying an order from a senior NCO. It was a little bit harsh. You have to go before the Commanding Officer. You stand stiffly to attention. He asks you some questions, and as far as he is concerned, you have broken the rule, and you deserve what you are going to get.

For me that confinement wasn't too bad. You have to answer every call of the bugle at various times in the day from 6 in the morning to 10 at night. Plus you have various duties, for example you might have to scrub the barrack room.

But if you are treated with respect, I think the price of being in the Army is worth it. Since I have to show them respect, they should show some for me as well. If I had been that sergeant, I would have gone about it in a different way.

So I took the view then, that if I've got to live with Sergeant Hibbert and Lance-Corporal Barrington Hill, then the whole of Jamaica will be too small for us. One day we'd be on the rifle range, with live bullets—and there might be a dreadful "accident". They knew it as well. I could not continue with those two, if they carried on with that sort of behaviour.

But I had a golden opportunity to get out, and I took it. The regiment was regrouping. When I joined, it was the Jamaica Regiment. But now it was becoming the First Battalion of the West India Regiment, and I had a choice whether to join it. In fact they were renaming it back to what it had been in the first place, years previously.

I've still kept my testimonial from the Army. It gives me very high marks for my achievements—my wireless skills and so forth.

I had also been one of those who would be selected for a scout patrol, where you creep up behind enemy lines, to find where they are and their movements. That's a serious job. And I was the number one man on the Bren gun. I used to like that. We'd take a Bren gun and we'd go very close at times, and we'd go back and we'd report how many "enemy" we had seen, what they were doing, how many lorries they had and so on. And there was map-reading with Lt Shaw. Yes, I did enjoy it. But it was just those two men who put a damper on it for me.

But wasn't it part of the Army's intention to break down your sense of personal dignity to an extent?

Well, there was another member of my intake, Crombie, The sergeant-major used to pick him out to humiliate him. I can understand why the Army does this. Don't forget also that it was different in the Fifties. You were using more manpower. You have to be tough in the Army. It isn't for the faint-hearted. Those drill-sergeants are the ones who will make you or break you as a soldier. I've seen some that didn't make it. They had to go through six weeks of basic training—drill and the like—before being passed out. Some dropped out long before that. They couldn't take it.

The sergeant-major used to look at this fellow Crombie and call out to him: "You darling! You whipping-puff!" [laughs] But we weren't allowed to laugh. We had to stand to attention with straight faces. But having said all this, it's a great place. The Army is not for the faint-hearted. Your comrades' lives may depend on you. The Army needs strong people, mentally and physically. People of strong character. I could understand the way things are done. I think the Army is the backbone of all the Services. I think they are great.

So what were your thoughts on leaving? Regret? Anxiety for the future?

No. Certainly not. There's no decision that I have made in my life without careful thought. I had no regrets about joining, and none about leaving either. It taught me discipline and that is something that has always stood me in good stead.

As for the future, my time in the Army gave me a certain badge of respectability in seeking other jobs. But as I have said to you before, the high unemployment in Jamaica and that part of the Caribbean in those days made it difficult, despite all good intentions and despite my glowing testimonials.

We'd been told that as ex-servicemen, with all our discipline and training, people would look up to us. We were valuable citizens who had put our lives on the line for the public good. But there was no job forthcoming. Unemployment in Jamaica was very high. We had a young population. And from 1940 to 1960, the priority in the various Jamaican governments was to gear up for independence. Jamaica was talking of freedom and the United Kingdom was listening. Prime Ministers had to be worthy of their votes. Government was under all sorts of pressure to make many changes in society and create a new nation. With all this happening, a strong economy, with full employment for young people like me, dropped down in the scale of priorities.

So I went and made lots of job applications, only to get the most patronising letters back. "We regret we are not able to offer you employment at this time. However we will retain your application on our files, and as soon as there is a job opportunity, we will contact you further." They knew damned well there wouldn't be an opportunity because in the forties and fifties, if you had a paler skin there might be a chance once in a while, but if you have a darker skin type like mine, there would be a much longer wait. [Laughs] You knew very well, if you go to the wharves and the factories, there'd be no chance in hell of getting a job. You might get a job in a hotel as a dishwasher or a bellhop, carrying suitcases for guests, but even there it was hard, because of the sheer numbers applying for any job that was going.

What kinds of places did you apply for jobs?

I tried at Grace Kennedy[2], various shipping companies, Dennoes and Geddies on Spanish Town Road—they made the Red Stripe beer—big tyre companies, all sorts of places.

Nothing came up for you?

Nothing, that's right. I must have applied to fifteen or twenty places in all.

Over what period?

It was about two years, and during that time I had plenty of support from family. During my time in Kingston after I left the Army I was staying with my dear Aunt Ivy and—bless him!—her husband Mr Byfield. My aunt gave me ten shillings a week. She had her own home. Mr Byfield worked at the railway station and my aunt ran a shop. As I have told you before, a shop sells everything. So she was well off. And for her to give me ten bob a week was wonderful.

And did you help out there at all?

Oh yes, the only thing I need do was when my aunt went out I would keep the place clean; and if there were any dirty dishes I would clean them, so that the place was all neat when she came back in.

And the rest of the time was yours?

And the rest of the time was mine. [Laughs heartily]

So when not applying for jobs, how did you spend your time?

Well we would go swimming, at a beach called the Olana, in Greenwich town: Vincent, Alan and I. It was just us three, always together. If anyone had reported seeing me, to my Aunt Ivy, except in that group of three, she would not have believed it. We wouldn't drink beer at our age, but nip stout, in a small bottle. The old boys would be drinking their rum. And I got the taste for port. You could buy a glass of port for one shilling. And if we got hungry, there was a restaurant opposite the central police station, where we would buy patties. So ten shillings could go a long way when you were getting your bed and food at home. And when you went to those bars or places where they sold ice creams or patties, maybe a girl in there might like you, and buy it for you.

You were quite popular with the ladies?

[much laughter] Well, it wasn't everyone who was an ex-soldier.

Was it that? How would they know?

Well, if you had been there before, when you were in uniform, and now you were revisiting your old stamping-grounds, they would know who you were. And you'd explain that now you were a civilian, and had time on your hands.

That's Kingston.

So when Alec was telling my parents that in England he was getting twelve pounds a week, you can see what I was talking about! That's when I moved back to Westmoreland, to my own district of Bigwoods. And from there, Derek and I went around a few times to visit other relatives. And— this would be 1959—I went back to Montego Bay, to spend a little time with my brother Astley, and then back to my mother's district in Westmoreland. I was 19. My brother Derek was already a junior teaching assistant, at the Darlaston school. He did very well there, becoming a right-hand man to his teacher, Mr James.

That was very young, he was 2 years younger than you!

That's right. He became the leader of the school in woodwork, and was able to take a class. He was an excellent cabinet maker. And so when I went back to Westmoreland and met up with him again after I left the army, we used to go around with some of our friends. I remember going to a sports day with him in Bluefields. It's about 8 miles from Darlaston across country. And those were such good times—unbelievable. We had grown together, as brothers, and now, as "big men", our closeness and friendship was quite unique.

I had left the army and was now trying to get a civilian job. The only places actively recruiting were the army and the police force. Had I not come to the United Kingdom when I did, I'm sure I would have joined the police force.

NOTES

1. *Soldiers on trial:* American soldiers had been convicted of offences at the Abu Ghraib jail in Baghdad, and at the time of the recording, a court-martial against British soldiers accused of similar offences was continuing.
2. *Grace Kennedy* is a Jamaican conglomerate, food products being amongst the most well-known of its many divisions.

CHAPTER 4

Emigration

BUT AROUND THAT TIME, AT THE END OF THE FIFTIES, SOME OF my family had already emigrated to the United Kingdom. My cousin Alec was one. We were close though he was a little older than me. Anyway the family structure in the Caribbean is such that there is great respect for family members. He wrote home and told his father about life in the United Kingdom: a place where there were plenty of jobs. I remember the day very clearly when my great-uncle Tassy called in one day to talk to my father and my mother. And he said to them, "Why don't you let your boy go to England? I heard from Alec and he says there's a lot of jobs going in the United Kingdom. Conditions are not too bad." And then my father said to me, "Well, Sebert, what d'you think? D'you want to travel?"

It was the first time that my father had ever said that to me. It was the first time travelling abroad ever came into my mind. I had never ever thought of travelling outside of Jamaica, though many young men had gone to the Unites States, for jobs like apple- and orange-picking.

But before you left for England, you got married. How did that come about?

Hilda Williams and I met in Westmoreland. We had been to the same school. It was my brother Derek who reintroduced us. At that time my father had a little shop and her family used to come and buy groceries from the shop. And it was my brother Derek who set me up, saying this girl likes me. And so we got chatting and we formed a relationship. Her father and my father were also very good friends. Hilda and I got engaged, but I was not allowed to take her to my house before we were married.

Hilda's father knew then that we were in friendship. And there was a child on the way too. And my father asked me what we were going to do about it.

Did he put any pressure on you?

No, we were just talking reasonably. And I said that sooner or later I would surely be getting married to someone, so I might as well do it now. Which was an honest thing, because regardless of what has happened in my life, I have followed the principle that every man should make sure he looks after his child. So we got married on the 21st February 1960, just seven weeks after my 20th birthday. It was a big step.

And you didn't even have a job.

Right, but this is the strength of the family, the unity and the love. I remember my mother said to my sister then, "See, Sebert beat you. He is younger than you, but he is the first to get married." I got married before my elder brothers and sisters. I seemed to be the first in most things. My parents were very proud of me, and so were my sisters and brothers. They all used to say, "You've beaten me to it."

So where did you live then?

Well, I had the choice of two houses. I could stay in my mother's home, or with Hilda's parents. I was not always around there. I had the luxury of my sister Icyline's place as well, where I would go and stay and look after my nephews. I would move between them. Because I was unemployed and was not amongst those who went out into the fields to work. We were under no pressure, and could float between.

And this was about the time that my uncle James came to tell my parents about England. Well to be honest, emigration was the last thing I had on my mind at that time. But my father told me to think about it. He said that if I decided to go he would help me with the fare. After all I had a wife and an unborn child to support now. I got my passport and other relevant travel documents ready. By August, I received a departure date. I was to travel on the 9th September, leaving Kingston on the *SS Iripina*, a Spanish ship. I had booked that date so that I could at least be there for the birth of my child.

But as the date of the voyage drew near, the child was still not born. It was too late to change my booking. And in fact Hilda spent only a year with our daughter Cherry, because when she came to England she left her with my parents. And as my sister Icyline lived more or less next door, she was spoilt in a way. I heard that my father wouldn't put her down. [Laughs] They seemed to adore this child. Unfortunately she died when she was three years and three months. It was one of those fevers, an infection like typhoid.

So you never saw her?

I only saw photographs. But I remember you asked me at one time what was the hardest experience I ever had to endure. It was when I learned of the death of my brother Derek. That was harder to take than when I heard of my own daughter's death. I had never met her. Derek and I grew up together, walked together, swum together. We walked to school together, we had conversations. That was the hardest blow I have gone through, even to this day.

When did he die?

It was the 21st June 1965, when he was 24. The date is recorded in my Bible. He died of a brain haemorrhage. He was studying to be a minister. He got a nosebleed. They took him to hospital. It was quite sudden.

And you were here. Did you go back at that point?

No, I couldn't go back. In those days, it wasn't easy. I had a family and I didn't have enough savings. That was the hardest thing in my life. We'd corresponded in letters, but we'd not been able to keep up that feeling, that touch. That was a horrid experience.

You look back on life, and you see how immigration can be destructive, in a way. It's useful for economic purposes, but that's about it. These days, it's different. You can make short visits to places.

But if immigration is a problem, then there's a proper answer to it. Just develop the country that people are coming from. You can stop a lot of world problems at the same time. People migrate because they think the grass is greener on the other side. They don't really want to leave their homes. But if we could help make their lives just a little better in their home country, I am sure that all this mass migration would be greatly reduced. People would feel so much better at ease in their own country, as long as their standard of living is tolerable. If I could have found money in Jamaica I would never have come. If only the Jamaican Government in that instance, and so many other instances today, had been able to organise things so that the produce of my country could have been grown and exported to the United States or the United Kingdom, which had need of it, then the available raw skills and land could have been put to a proper use. Instead of taking the human labour force, help the developing country to build its factories, produce its own things and distribute them. There must be a way, whereby the resources can be evenly spread to the benefit of all.

I sense that looking back on those years, you are feeling what an enormous price you had to pay by leaving all that you knew and loved, and coming here.

It has been a price. And I think it would be the same for a white English person, if they had emigrated to Australia or New Zealand, in those days, for economic reasons. And then perhaps their grandmother, or their father, died over here. And if they had not been there long enough and had not saved money yet, it would have been also impossible for that person to have raised the money to go back and attend their grandmother's funeral.

It's not that I regret coming here. Since then, life has improved for me. But the impossibility of coming back to bury my brother, to look at him for the last time, it's something that you feel very sad about. But on the other hand I had outlined in a letter to my brother the conditions of life here, and it was his choice not to come. Maybe that's a good thing, because if it was actually his destiny to get that brain haemorrhage anyway, and he'd had it in the United Kingdom, I would have been the only one of the family here. Neither my mother nor my father would have been able to come— he was one of those old-fashioned types who wouldn't fly—the great majority of my family wouldn't have been able to come. They would have never had—how shall I put it—the satisfaction of seeing him properly buried and being able to go and visit his tomb. For me, it was a great feeling of sadness, but I got the comfort of knowing that my father and mother and family were there for him.

Overall I am not complaining about travelling. But I am saying that immigration, for black people especially, is something that divides the family. At least, apart from Derek, of course, whenever I went back to Jamaica until the early Eighties, my family would all be there. It's only recently that my brother Roy has emigrated to the United States. When I go back these days, that strand of my family is not there. I took a special trip to the United States to see my nieces. Roy has only managed to produce girls, beautiful as they are—when he reads this, he'll know I am laughing at him. It's been left to Dudley, Albert and me to hold up the Graham line by ensuring we have some boys.

But this is to show you my feeling about migrating. When I go back to Jamaica, almost all my family from my brothers, to my nieces and my grand-nieces—they're all there! Beautiful! The family remains there. I feel those bonds of unity. I feel those great feelings of pride when I go home and I met my family in that strong bond. And then I go back to the States and I visit my other family there, to link up with my brother Dudley's two sons. And then I've got my sister's two sons and one niece there too. But it just shows how migration scatters one's family. And hopefully all those children who are studying over there in the States, their intention is to go back to Jamaica.

But what about the children born of immigrants in the UK or the States. They have the same number of relatives "back home", but won't their feeling about Jamaica be quite different?

Very interesting question. For the generations of children born here in the United Kingdom, it's going to be as difficult for them going there as it was for me coming here, if they go to Jamaica to take up positions there. The accents are so different. Imagine someone going there with a Mancunian or Brummie[1] accent. They won't understand one another, just as it was for me when I first went to different parts of the United Kingdom. They will say "What these people talking about? What the hell are they saying?"

There are young men born here who put on their own interpretation of a Jamaican accent!

Well that's true but there are so many ways that they would have to adjust, all the same.

****

I embarked upon my Atlantic voyage in the *Iripina* full of hope and expectations. I'd promised my parents to spend no more than five years in England. It was obvious to me that I would be able to earn a lot of money in that time, far more than if I stayed at home. Not only this, but I could improve my education. I had left school rather early and though I had learned a great deal in the school of life, I now felt ready to take courses and improve my command of English.

Alec was there to meet me at Southampton. We took the train to Waterloo and then another to Kew Bridge. When we got off there, it was a big surprise for me. When I reached outside I asked him if this was London. He said "Yes". I looked around and said to myself, "Well, there are a lot of factories around!" But actually they were houses. It was the smoke from the chimneys that gave me the idea. It was a very unusual sight for me—I had never seen anything like that. Then we went to number 1 Mortlake Road, where I was to live with cousin Alec and Aunt Gertrude. Being with them helped me feel at ease in this new, predominantly white society.

And in the morning, when I got up, and took a walk around, it was simply amazing. Here I was in London. Often I had been to the cinema in Jamaica and seen the Pathé news, and seen places like Holborn, Piccadilly, Oxford Street. They never showed places like Acton, Chiswick, Shepherd's Bush—you know, places that were not so posh. But it did not take me long to settle down. I had met plenty of white men in the Army whilst I was at Uppark Camp, so they were not entirely strange to me.

And it makes me think that if I was Prime Minister of Jamaica now, you know like the time when they showed the University Hospital, what was happening there, I would not have allowed journalists to come and take photographs in my country unless they were authorised to take them in certain places. You may call it censorship, but as I learned later, what the cinema had shown me was the best parts of the United Kingdom, and that is what had influenced a lot of us to migrate here—because we really thought we were going places!

What I found, though, was a hard, dirty place, especially in the winter months—nothing like England as portrayed in the cinema. The food was utterly appalling. The winter was damp as well as cold. Night fell early and it had brought a sad lonely atmosphere. But these drawbacks were things to overcome with ingenuity and acceptance. This was the environment, and you just had to get used to it.

But having said that, it was an experience and I came to see that the United Kingdom is not a bad place. People who left Jamaica came here with very high expectations and some were disappointed. And I think there were three fundamental notions which persuaded Jamaicans to come to this country. First and foremost, the employment situation was bad back home, and so people wanted a better life. Secondly, some of them wanted to further their education. Some have fulfilled those dreams, and some haven't. The third notion—it was common to most of us—was to come here for five years only. The five years has now become forty-five years. Most of them have lost the dream of returning, but some still hold on to it. But if they haven't fulfilled it now, I think they must have resigned themselves after all this time to stay in the United Kingdom with their grandchildren. That five-years dream died long ago.

Why could they not have returned after five years? What stopped them?

That's a good question. First, the money wasn't coming to them as fast as they were expecting. Alec had told me he was earning £12 a week or so. We had pounds, shillings and pence in Jamaica too, so we could make the comparison. He would have made £4 or £5 in Jamaica. But then, in Jamaica, he wouldn't have had to pay income tax, National Insurance, heating, electricity—and he'd have got most of his food free. And over here, he would have had to send money to his family back home. What was there left over to save? And people who came here had often borrowed their fare to come here. So it wasn't a big gain.

NOTES

1.   *Mancunian:* of Manchester. *Brummie:* of Birmingham.

CHAPTER 5

Early years in England

CAN I ASK HOW MUCH OF YOUR WAGE YOU WERE ABLE TO SEND
home to your family in Jamaica?
    When I came over, I was one of the lucky ones. Some of my countrymen
had great difficulty finding work. I was lucky and I got a job a couple of
weeks after I arrived, to work in Kew Botanical Gardens as a labourer with
some carpentry skills. I was working for J. Garrett and Sons, builders from
Fulham. It was a nice job and I was not spending a lot of time out in the
cold. I think I was getting about £6 per week. Don't forget if you are working
in a job like that, such as on a building site, you are sent home in the afternoon
as it gets dark early in winter—the days are shorter. But I was living with
my aunt and her family at the time there. I used to give them small amounts.
I used to pay them about £2/10/- (that's £2.50) as rent. Then from the rest I
would buy my food and maybe I could send back £1/10/- (that's £1.50) or
£2 to my mother and my wife. Well, it was a help.
    But looking back now on my life then in the UK, the second problem
about the five years, that became more than forty in the end, was that most
of us came as young men. The next thing you knew, you had a family. And
when you have a family, the rest of your dreams are put on hold.
    My wife came over to join me in July of 1961 leaving our first child
behind with my mother and father, and she started working too for a while,
but the next thing we knew she was expecting another child. This perhaps
more than anything put an end to my dream of five years of saving and
improving my education before returning to Jamaica.
    When the child was born, we lived in an attic room at Thornyhedge
Road, in Chiswick. Now I am not especially tall as you can see, but when I
stood at one end, I would bang my head on the sloping roof. It wasn't very
satisfactory but these were circumstances almost beyond my personal control
at the time. Where the ceiling was low, we had to use that end just for
storage. But I must be thankful anyway, because in the 1960s, when you
looked for accommodation in Chiswick, Acton and such places, familiar signs
would confront you: "ROOMS TO LET: NO BLACKS, NO IRISH, NO
CHILDREN". And it was similar when you looked for work. It was difficult.
    I would phone up: "Good evening. I have seen your advertisement on
the board with somewhere to let. Is it still available?" "Oh yes! Still
available," [speaking in a very polite voice]. "When will it be convenient
for me to come and view?" "Well, you can come any time between 4.30 and
5." "OK I'll be there at 5 o'clock." "OK, see you at 5."

So I went round at the time and rang the bell. When she answered the door and saw the face of a black man she said to me, "Oh, I'm very sorry, just after you called, someone came and I let it." I laughed. And she said, "Why do you laugh?" I said, "Let me put it to you. When I spoke to you on the phone you didn't realise that I was a black person. Now that you see me, and you don't want a black person in your home, you find a convenient way of telling me—a *polite* way—of telling me 'Look, I don't need you'." She said, "Oh, no, no, no." But I know and she knows that this is the truth. And there are many instances like this.

If it hadn't been for the Polish people, as willing landlords, the situation of the black immigrants would have been in even greater plight. The Polish were the ones more than anyone else who had the feeling to offer accommodation to the black people and took them in, and allowed them to live in their houses.

No black people had been in the country long enough to buy their own houses?

Exactly. The greatest influx was in 1959-1960. There was no great number of those already settled, no established route. But by 1970, that situation had changed. Jamaican people knew they'd find their own in Brixton, in Birmingham, in Manchester. These were the places where by that time Jamaican people were buying their houses, because this is something ingrained in black people, well I can at least speak with some authority for Jamaicans: the first thing that a man wants, is his home. He wants his own place. And so when he came, that was one of the priorities: to get a house, because he needed to send for his family as well. So they always work hard, to buy their home. I think it would not be an exaggeration to say that 65 percent of them acquired their own houses. That's what they do. They buy a house and share it—which of course is a way to make money too. That's the way it goes.

Something you have consistently said is that you did not personally feel victim of any racism at any time, though you are well aware of others who have suffered in this way. You have been successful though you might argue that had things been different in certain ways you could have been a lot more successful.

That is very true and I would not try to deny the existence of racism in this country and in the world more generally. But it is true that I have not personally come across any racial abuse from anyone, going back to the time when I lived in London in the early Sixties, when they had Teddy Boys[1] roaming the streets. We have talked about what it was like looking for rooms and jobs. I would go into pubs, and there I was treated with respect.

Did you never feel, "I am in the wrong pub, I am in the wrong district"? As if people were trying to indicate that this was a no-go area for black people?

No. I lived in Shepherds Bush and in Richmond and in Hammersmith, where there were lots of Irish. We had no problem with the Irish.

As for Richmond, in Surrey, you would think that was true suburbia, where shall we say some of the better-speaking English live. That is where you might have expected a bias. My cousin and I were living in Mortlake Road. When we went to these Richmond pubs, we were not allowed to buy a drink.

You mean they refused to serve you?

No, they treated us! They would not let us buy our own. It seems like in those days we were real objects of interest. There were very few black people in that area, unlike Shepherds Bush. They were friendly, and the older men used snuff, and invited us to try it. "It will clear your head," they said. They wanted to see how we would react. Well, it brought tears to my eyes.

I know that the younger generation of black youths often have trouble in their relations with the police, but I can tell you that when I first arrived they were most helpful. If we were lost we would always ask directions from a policeman. They were so kind and courteous, and gave us a lot of guidance. You would have thought those would have been the most difficult times. We came with a poor command of the English language and unused to the customs of the country. But it is the opposite of what you might have expected. And honesty compels me to tell it the way it was.

So it started good and got worse?

Things in a way got worse.

But in those early days there was no law against the colour bar. I am wondering what happened to race relations after the Race Relations Act was passed.

Well I suppose at first there was the rarity factor, and there was curiosity. The worsening of relations as time went on must have been to do with how we developed. When we first arrived there was a need. There were plenty of jobs. We came and we were prepared to do the menial jobs, the jobs[2]—

—that nobody else wanted.

That's right. But then as the immigrants started to progress and make a little money and start to integrate more into society, and go for better and more desirable jobs, and buy their own homes and cars—

Over the years, when you look at the advancement in Britain, as I have told you before, race relations in Britain have improved. But let me tell you about the improvement in the country first. We have mentioned housing conditions. When I came here, Britain was just coming out of the war, more or less. A lot of places were very derelict and in very poor condition. And as I mentioned there was smoke coming out of the chimneys, and it caused smog sometimes. But young people these days, sometimes they complain about how things are hard. It's really easy now, for all of us. Because in those early days, opportunities for blacks were not easy to find. Today, more or less, Government provides accommodation for people. It was under the government of Harold Wilson that things really began to move here, for black people. Taking away the stigma, and all those racist comments. It was made unlawful to put up those signs.[3] We felt relief from that. I remember those long years. It's no wonder that I and people of my race used to vote for the Labour Party in those years. The Labour Party—let's pay them their due—they were the ones who stood up for getting such things outlawed. It must be a good feeling for everyone in this country today.

So, Britain has moved on. And now immigration is once more an issue. And I am not against a lot of the things that are currently being said about it. Because I honestly believe there must be some form of control on immigration. For us to live harmoniously together, we have to make sure that our race relations law is strong and fair. We cannot allow some of the people in Europe, and I am going to say some of the people from Germany, France, Spain and certain other European countries, who have fascist leanings, to come to the United Kingdom and upset this standard that we have already set up. For it's been established now that people of different ethnic background here can live together, and work together, in a very harmonious way. People coming from Europe must know that we are a multicultural, multiethnic society. They've got to accept that. And therefore I hope that regardless of what the EU say—even if they say we can't legitimately place such restrictions—we will insist that people coming here declare themselves not to be racist. If they were to break these laws, when they get on this soil, then they would have broken a contract and would be deported.

It's for everyone's good in this country, that we have a harmonious way of living. And in fact it has taken more than 40 years for the people in this country to really accept blacks. Are we really accepted? We are very much integrated into society now. Everybody knows a black family now, more or less. I don't think there is any county in England that you will not see a black face. In the Thirties or Forties, that was unheard of. You'd have seen a few in Liverpool, or Bristol, or London. That's about it. In this leafy Buckinghamshire, I don't think there would have been any black people. We want to maintain what we've got now, no matter what it may cost.

I'm suddenly reminded of Enoch Powell's "Rivers of Blood" speech in Birmingham in 1968.[4]

Ha, yes, Enoch. You know, I'm aware of his story and I hold no great malice against him. He was a nationalist. It was his country! A lot of people would have been thinking the same thing. Maybe he was just one of the few with the strength to say what he said. He allowed people to give voice to their feelings. But the Government of the day was also strong, and in the end, it led to the Race Relations Act. They said, "You may have your views. You are allowed to express them. But do not incite others to do what you are doing." So I have no serious quarrel with Enoch. What he did enabled the government to tidy things up. It's easy to look back and to say, "He was wrong," but he spoke his mind. I have a feeling that many more would want to say what he said.

We talk about Europe and we talk about Enoch and I would say that in comparison with the United States, we have a certain education problem[5]. Now we West Indians mainly came from the English-speaking Caribbean— Jamaica, Barbados, Trinidad. We spoke a dialect and with a certain accent, so it was hard sometimes for people to understand us. So when we came over here, and were being refused jobs that we were well-qualified for, this provided a ready-made excuse. "You're speaking too fast. We don't understand you. Pardon? Pardon?" I found that a little disturbing. And the system of education, the books that we'd read, that we'd been taught with at school. Now you can look at them and see that they were quite nonsensical really. They had no relevance, either in teaching about today's world or in helping to develop a child's mind. Even in the Sixties, if you compare the books used in schools here, with those used in the Caribbean—ours had been a waste of time. Given that we were under British rule for 250 years, it should not have taken them that long to get used to us living here. Many of them had been to Jamaica themselves. They could have come back here, and shared their experience. And the greatest injustice of all is in the books, in schools and libraries, failing to tell children of the black writers, and poets and designers—people who do things and make things happen, not just growing bananas and so forth. It should be in the schoolbooks, so that everyone can see what we have contributed to society, that we are useful to the society in which we live. That is unfair.

Compare this with America. I have every respect for America, but it does not make me want to run down England across the board. There are still things about America which I find abhorrent. There are things about their society which they need to do something about. But I went to New York. It is a complete mix of backgrounds and there is no one group that can say it belongs to them. No one can say, like Enoch Powell, that "This is my land". The Africans who came there to provide labour, amongst other things, had been driven there forcibly. The American Indians, who were born there, were being pushed out of the way. And it was made up also of Europeans, from England, France, Germany—from everywhere in fact.

And one thing I liked about America, when I went to New York, they have an Immigration Museum at Ellis Island with the story in photographs of all those people who came to that country—where they came from, what they did, how they got there. And they have an Immigrant Wall of Honour. They celebrate their immigration, and that is something we do not do here in Britain! But we could do it. They could describe our background, how our ancestors were slaves. Our story could be told in a Hall of Fame somewhere in the United Kingdom. Let the British all know how long people have been coming here, and what they were. We can trace it back even to Africa, where they had the first kings.

Africa is a huge continent with a broad array of history. It's not that Africa was some wild place as was once taught. Africa is a vibrant continent, but it has sometimes been portrayed in such a misleading way. Even today many people still think of Africa as a country. The film *Tarzan* has always upset me. [Laughs] This European type of boy, born in Africa, lost his mother, lost his family, and there he is with the animals in the jungle, who take him, and nurture him. They don't eat him or hurt him. But you never see a film in which a black man can do that—whistle to the elephants and they come to him—oh no, you see them running away, unless they are going out to kill for food. You would expect that if anyone could be able to tame the animals, it would be the black Africans who had lived there for thousands of years.

There is so much misinformation that has gone out into the world. Who is it benefiting? What is its purpose? It seems nonsensical when you consider that here we all are on one planet. We are losing the elephants in Africa, the tigers in India. So who will lose out? All of us in the next generation. Meanwhile, if we all work together as one human race, and put out the historical truth, then all of us would benefit by understanding each other. It may be a simplistic way of looking at things, and readers might not all agree with me, but I think the world would be a better place if we had more truthfulness. And if we put less emphasis on the individual and more on the community.

And the community is what?

The community is the world. None of us is going to survive on our own. We are so interdependent that if you are suffering, I am going to suffer. We should feel as strongly about each other's feelings and each other's welfare as about our own. That's what would make the world a better place.

And are we getting there? Or should I say, what direction do you think we are going?

Ha ha ha! I look back and I look forward too, and this is what I feel. I won't be here in 30 or 40 years' time. I have a lot of feeling—I'm *wondering*, what is going to be happening in 50 years' time. I think our world is getting dangerously close to mankind itself bringing the world to an end. I think we are heading towards a disastrous situation where it might get out of control.

You said that the United Kingdom is now your home. Can you look back and pinpoint when you started to accept it as such?

I would say that the transition took place after Harold Wilson's government[6], after the racism and caricatures of black people had been exposed and fought against. I mean the *Black and White Minstrel Show*[7] was good. But why have them in the abstract, when you can have them as we are in person?

Ha ha ha!

So we removed those kinds of nonsensical plays and things like that. Now, if you want Black and White Minstrels, you can set Lenny Henry[8] alongside Jimmy Tarbuck[9]. Perfect. We can take the mickey[10] out of one another right on the screen, rather than in other ways.

So in that time, some things were removed and life was made much more easy for us. And following on certain laws being put in place, there was a gradual change in people's behaviour, and that was good for all of us.

So yes, my first home is Jamaica, because it has given me life, and that is where I started my education. And then the United Kingdom is now my home from home. How else would I look at it? I spent twenty years in Jamaica. I've spent forty-five years in the United Kingdom. This is my home. I have the same rights here as anybody else. I've been here longer than most who were born here. As I have said before, these young people don't know how lucky they are. We've cleaned up the country. We've made things happen. We've brought about changes—for the better. And so, I have no regrets about coming to the United Kingdom, and I would not swap this country for any other—unless it were Jamaica. This will always be my Number Two country, if not my Number One.

Everyone talks about racism. Everyone is a racist, in our own ways. I do not like every Jamaican or every black. I don't like the way some of them behave. You can call it prejudice. And so when I was deeply involved in race relations I had difficulty sometimes in the interpretation of what people saw as being racism. I am not going to say that it doesn't exist. It does. But some of the things that had been put down as racist behaviour, I would put it down like this, that because some people found themselves not socially accepted in certain places, they would call it racism. But it's up to each one of us to choose who we want to be our friend. You can't invite everybody into your home. And you will not always speak nicely about everybody regardless of their colour.

When you were Mayor you were a prominent citizen who could go everywhere and be respected. But have you ever felt, apart from that, excluded from anywhere, or treated in a negative way because of skin colour?

I have never come across that and I have never encouraged it. I was taught in Jamaica to be proud, to know who you are and where you want to go. I know who I am and I hope others would know who I am. If they do not know who I am then it's for me to tell them. I've never had any inhibition about going wherever I wanted to go. I had the opportunity of working with people from England before I came here. I was alongside the Worcestershire Regiment in Jamaica, and I was under the command of Lt Shaw, whom I told you about earlier. In fact if I had Lt Shaw's address, when I came here, most likely I would have gone to see him because he'd said to me in Jamaica, "If you ever come to England, look me up." We were like friends. Yes, there is prejudice and there are racists, but it's not everyone that's like that.

Jamaicans might not like to hear this but there is a certain amount of class structure in Jamaican society. But we have had no uprisings against one another, and we have very diverse cultures. We've got Chinese, Indians, Africans, Syrians, Jews—you name it! That is a truly multicultural society. And Jamaica's motto is "Out of many, one people".

NOTES

1. *Teddy Boys:* young men in the Fifties and Sixties notorious for: their style of dressing ("Edwardian") with oiled longish hair combed into a quiff; their style of hooligan street behaviour which combined languorous posturing and vague menace which frequently terrified the vulnerable such as old ladies or ethnic minorities; their espousal of rock 'n'roll.
2. *Menial jobs:* Sebert also told me that all the emigrants on his ship were given a leaflet with advice to take the first job offered.
3. *Race relations laws:* Both Conservative and Labour Governments in the Sixties passed laws to control non-white immigration from Commonwealth countries. A Race Relations Board was set up in 1965, to monitor instances of a "colour bar", i.e., racial discrimination in jobs and accommodation. The 1968 Race Relations Act finally made discrimination illegal. Thirty years later, Jim Callaghan, who had been Home Secretary at the time, admitted that he had bowed to pressure and failed to outlaw racial discrimination in the Police: a mistake which has cost the country dearly. A number of bodies were created, including the Community Relations Commission, which became the Commission for Racial Equality (CRE) with local Community Relations Councils locally including Wycombe. In more recent years the local name has changed again: what was the Community Relations Council is now the Wycombe Race Equality Council. It is funded by the CRE, the County Council and the District Council.
4. *Enoch Powell:* After this recording, I (Ian) went to check the full text of Enoch Powell's famous "Rivers of Blood" speech, to see what he had actually said. What struck me most forcibly was not Powell's quote about seeing the river Tiber foaming with blood, but his report of a conversation with a middle-aged ordinary man in his constituency. The man had said: *"In this country in 15 or 20 years' time the black man will have the whip hand over the white man."* It was a chilling but surely unconscious reference to slavery, and a fear of the black man's revenge. The whole speech would be illegal today.
5. *Education problem:* See also Appendix A, "West Indian calls for fairer education".
6. *Harold Wilson*'s first Labour Government lasted from 1964 to 1970 and saw the introduction of two Race Relations Acts. The one in 1965 banned discrimination in public places and the publishing and distribution of material intended to stir race hate. The one in 1968 made it unlawful to discriminate on grounds of colour, race, ethnic or national origins in housing, employment and the provision of services.
7. *Black and White Minstrel Show:* "With around 14 million viewers, the blacked-up singing and dancing routines of the Black and White Minstrel Show ruled BBC One's weekend schedule for 21 years from 1957 to 1978.
    "To its devoted viewers it was 45 minutes of harmless, glamorous escapism. To others it had less palatable connotations and in one of the most extraordinary turnarounds in broadcasting history, the once top-rated show was banned from the small screen." (From the BBC's Press Office website.)
8. *Lenny Henry:* Black British comedian who has made comedy from black stereotypes without racism. He was discovered at 16 on a talent show, and actually did appear for years on the Black and White Minstrel Show as – "the only one of 'em who doesn't need make-up", though looking back he says "It hurts thinking about it now. I think the term 'ill-advised' could be bandied about here." (Source: Lenny Henry's website.)
9. *Jimmy Tarbuck:* Old-fashioned stand-up comedian and compere, whose humour is based on working-class chauvinist attitudes, often confused with racism.
10. *Take the mickey:* English slang meaning "tease".

CHAPTER 6

How I entered politics

COMING TO ENGLAND AND BEING MADE A MAYOR WAS AN extremely important part of my life. But of course it was not easy to get to that position. I went through positions in community relations[1], where I was vice-chairman and chairman, over a number of years. I was aware of a problem in education at that time, that it was failing some of our children. And if you went to the local district council to discuss certain local issues, you were being fobbed off and referred to the County Council. You go to the County Council, they refer you back to the District Council.

So I came to a conscious decision, after working in race relations, and getting involved in various council meetings. One day I recall going up the stairs for one of these sessions, and coming across a former councillor for my ward, David Gladwin. I said to him, "You know, David, one of these days, that's where I'm going to go. I'm going to be a councillor here." That's what happened; and then I was in the place where decisions were made. I found out which body had responsibility for what, and I became part of that establishment. I had to stand three times before I won an election; it was when they had a by-election for Bowerdean and Daws Hill Ward. I remained a councillor in that ward for ten years, during which I spent a year as Mayor, becoming the first Afro-Caribbean councillor in Buckinghamshire and the first Afro-Caribbean to become a mayor in Buckinghamshire. That was an achievement which gave me great pride: to be able to share in the history of this country, and be part of a history in High Wycombe going back eight hundred years. So I entered into that history and that continuity of culture, not just for myself. It was extraordinarily useful, especially for the up-and-coming generation. When I went visiting schools, and they saw me walk in as their Mayor—I am not talking only of the Afro-Caribbean children, though I know that they in particular were in need of an achievement role model—I would ask them to put up their hands. "Who wants to be a Mayor? Who would like to become the Prime Minister?" And you could see the look on their faces, and their hands going up, black children, white children, all the same. This gave me great satisfaction.

And of course, I was not just a councillor for the black community but for all those whom I represented. All groups had given me their votes. We talk of prejudice and racism. Here in Bowerdean and Daws Hill Ward, we have some of the most expensive houses in the district. I was representing them too. And I stayed as their representative for ten years.

[At this point the conversation turned to the topic of local prejudice and

the existence of areas in High Wycombe in which one ethnic group predominated, sometimes making members of other groups feel uncomfortable if they lived in the same area. Sebert expressed his view that Government might have done more to encourage a fuller ethnic integration. All the same, he had sympathy with any people of whatever race who preferred being next to their own.]

I know that white people who feel close to the bottom of the heap might be offended if they find that black people are above them socially.

Yes, but then you can feel some sympathy with them. You know sometimes in Race Relations I had difficulty in distinguishing what is racism from what is a recognised social behaviour. You could understand white people saying, "Here I am. This is my country. I have always been here. I have worked hard. Maybe for some reason I haven't obtained what I should have had: a nice home, two cars, a nice family. And here are some strangers who walk in, and they have it all." And yes, it does seem unfair. And sometimes Government seems to recognise the achievements of one group in the community above another's. What Government needs to do is to educate people. As I said to you last time, it would help if at school they were to show us where people originated from; and that those people are achievers, and come from societies which have both rich and poor, educated and uneducated. And if you have had education, you are more likely to rise from the bottom. If people are left to feel inferior—and that could happen right across the board—they always look for someone to blame.

So let's think what's going to happen in an enlarged Europe. They will be free to come here of course. Germans are already very educated, so are Poles, so are those from Eastern Europe such as the Czechoslovak Republic. They will come here because we have a better health service and a higher standard of living than what they are used to. Suddenly a lot of our people here, both black and white, will be left at the bottom.

We have to have an education programme, and say to people, truthfully, that we can't all be at the top and there will always be someone at the bottom. It's easy to blame migration. But it's Government that makes decisions and they are there to be blamed.

But even in Jamaica skin colour is considered important. The Gleaner used to run features on "Black is Beautiful", aimed at women, earnestly trying to dissuade them from bleaching their skin to raise their value as objects of desire or marriage partners.

[I mentioned my anxieties about bringing my fiancée from Jamaica and wondering if she would be the victim of prejudice.]

The anxiety you mention is like a replay of how it used to be for us. In my culture, colour does matter. But we are trying to make the world a better place, so that one's complexion has nothing to do with the way we are valued.

Well, again, I am not going to blame society. I will say it is a matter of training. I'm in charge of a supplementary school that we are running at my community centre. It's mixed, it includes some white children. School starts at 10, finishes at 1. In the last 15 minutes, we bring the children together. And we tell them, "You have every reason to be proud of who you are, what you are, and where you are coming from. You must always be Number One. See yourself as the one who is an achiever." So what we are trying to do is wipe out all the negative feelings. If somebody feels less proud of you, or that your value is less, than what you think, that's up to them. It's for you to make sure that you are strong, that you have all the values that everyone else around you has obtained. We are training them to grow up with a very positive feeling. I've said to my own children, "Respect everybody, have good manners, because you can get through life with good manners. But don't show any special respect for anybody more than they will show to you." It's to do with teaching them to think positively.

And yes, there is a tendency nowadays to promote the girls. Yes, some of them are beautiful and you see them on the television and they make you wonder. But they must also not allow themselves to be devalued as people for the sake of their commercial appeal. Because those who are promoting the colour of one girl over another, where one is lighter, they are the ones that are humbugging the advancement, not only of black society but the whole of society. The effect is to divide people into certain groups. We need to take them for the best they can do: their skills, their education, how much can they put back into society. We are not here to say which one is better.

Are you saying some make a bigger contribution than others, so should be valued more by society? What about those who cannot do very much, perhaps through some form of disability?

Everyone of us has value, and every one of us can make some form of contribution.

So it's an individual thing, what we can do, and not something to be objectively measured by others?

Exactly. Look at the Paralympics. Who could ever talk those people down? They can do more than I can. Up at Handy Cross[2], I've seen some of them in wheelchairs, managing from that position to put the ball through the net when I could not do it even standing up. So I say, look at the person. Treat everyone fairly. It all goes back to proper education. We have different values and different abilities. But all of us help to meet the needs of society.

So I wonder if the influx of black people into this country, from forty years ago onwards, has opened our eyes, not just to the existence of racial prejudice, but all forms of prejudice, and to fight against the various types, for example gender, disability, age, sexual orientation[3]—though that has not yet happened in Jamaica!—

[They both laugh] Well, Jamaica is unique in a lot of things. As we've discussed before, we have more churches per head of population than anywhere else. Intolerance against homosexuality is still a big problem in Jamaica, I admit. It's not just the general population but the churches too, and I don't know how they will be able to overcome it. I don't know what it's worth but I think 90% of Jamaicans would call themselves Christians— even the armed killers amongst them. When there is so much Christianity in that little country, how come there is so much violence? Something is wrong fundamentally and the quicker we can find the solution, the better it will be, for all of us.

I found that in Jamaica, the churches were not conspicuous in preaching tolerance and unconditional respect for our fellow man.

Well, I have found that the United Kingdom is particularly tolerant. But respect is another matter, and in Jamaica I was taught respect at an early age and I think a lot of that attitude survives in that country. It derives from the family itself. We were taught to respect our elders and look after strangers. We were taught that in our early days at school as well: help strangers. What has happened in Jamaica in the Eighties and Nineties in particular is a problem which has arisen through governance. It's a failure of both political parties, and in consequence society has become a bit corrupt. Perhaps the police have been encouraged by Government to pursue certain lines and not others. And then promises by Government were broken time after time. All these things have helped diminish the level of respect in that country. People become disenchanted, and that helps create an atmosphere of intolerance in society. My feeling is that it doesn't come from the ordinary people.

The churches have become weakened. They used to be listened to. Here in the United Kingdom, churches have eroded the values that they used to stand for when I first arrived in 1960. We had been taught that the United Kingdom was a Christian country. But I used to see ministers here coming straight from the pub and then going into the church. That would have been unheard of in Jamaica, and yet the religious teachings were of the same kind. Society has changed. New translations of the Bible have been published—I hardly recognise the new readings. Things are being devalued. The old values have been progressively dismantled. We must not be surprised to see society getting more violent. People have been let down by the old certainties and now they make their own interpretations. Yes, there is less respect, and it saddens me to see what is happening in that country of mine. Now that both Edward Seaga and P J Patterson[4] are stepping down as the leaders of their respective parties, I hope that we will break the mould of the old style of politics there. And I look forward to a new breed of young Jamaicans that will take over. It is a very good sign that they are calling in help from the United Kingdom to modernise their practices. They have brought in some advisers from the Metropolitan Police—New Scotland Yard—to help bring in a greater transparency. There have been a lot of reshuffles with their senior officers. And as we move closer to a general election there, I hope there will be a policy of zero tolerance towards the kind of lawlessness that has been prevalent in some parts there. And then we will be able to get back gradually to the kind of respect and social cohesion that we used to enjoy in Jamaica. Jamaicans are resilient. The country is still highly respected. For a small country, it has a presence on the world stage still.

We do have a stable government there and that is a blessing. But we need a government with a new vision, that sets out clear guidelines, followed very transparently for Jamaicans to see and the world to see. Then it will be, with the people's support, once more a good and civilised society. I have faith in the Jamaican people. I am expecting to see those changes when I go back, in the next few years, or to read about them. That's how much faith I have.

I think you should go back and do a lecture tour, after the book has made you famous. You have such an optimistic vision and expatriates like you have a lot to offer.

[Laughs] Well, thanks for the invitation. Yes, Jamaica is such a versatile country. Look at Colin Powell, for instance. His parents were Jamaican. There are many of similar origin doing valuable jobs in the USA and Canada—and in this country. If these people, with all the qualifications they have obtained, and their humanitarian credentials, were to return home and pool their ideas, and focus on rebuilding that land—they could do something for it.

You have certain qualities, of caring. You are consistently community-minded, not looking for individual glory. I don't see you like other politicians whose real interest is to progress their careers. And it seems to me that the genius of Africa, the original home of your people, is to achieve a balance: to value those qualities that make us into a human brotherhood.

Yes. When I was first involved in community work in this country, or when I was asked by Mr Ray Whitney to join the Conservative party, I could have worked all out to win votes and get elected. It wouldn't have mattered that I had no degree. I am sure I could have become a Conservative councillor and in due course a Member of Parliament. I had backing from the Asians around here to stand as an MP, at one stage. But it worked out differently. I had to try three times before I was elected as a Labour councillor. And I was happy doing what I was doing, to help people at a local level, in local politics. Perhaps I would not have become an MP. But—if I had been a Conservative—I might have become Chairman of the Council, and then who knows. I know certainly I would have been able to go higher than Mayor.

And this is because where we live is a Conservative-voting area.
That's right, they are in power more often than the Labour Party. But I did not join a particular political party out of expediency. I joined it because I believed in what it stood for and to pursue social justice. I just love it when I see people lifted up, in a fair way. Yes, I care about the community. I have lost money being a community leader. I have missed overtime opportunities. I have accepted unpaid leave from Ford, for example to attend County Council meetings on weekday mornings. It wasn't for fun and games. I believed very strongly in what I was doing, and that continues. For example I am now in negotiations with the District Council to obtain a long-term lease for the Community Centre[5] of which I am Chairman. We want a lease of 30 years so that we can carry on regardless of any government policy changes. So when they have a commercial developer doing a new multipurpose development, they will make sure that there is a purpose-built community centre incorporated in it. You see, the Community Centre that we have at present is not secure. The land that it's on is liable to be redeveloped. And this will show the people who have contributed to this town over the last fifty years[6] that their contribution is recognised and that they are a part of the society. This will enable the grandchildren of these migrants—and of course the others too—to feel part of society. And that is what it should all be about. If you are part of a society, you must be able to feel it and see it.

NOTES

1. *Community relations* and race relations are almost used interchangeably in the UK.
2. *Wycombe Sports Centre*, in the Handy Cross area.
3. *Sexual orientation:* Jamaica has been notorious for the homophobic lyrics of performers of dancehall music, which reflect the widespread attitude of its society, where homosexual acts remain illegal.
4. *Edward Seaga, P J Patterson:* Opposition Leader and Prime Minister of Jamaica respectively.
5. *Community Centre:* The Hilltop Centre, often referred to in this book.
6. *Contribution over fifty years:* referring to Asian and Caribbean immigrants.

CHAPTER 7

My working life

MY FIRST JOB IN ENGLAND, AS I TOLD YOU, WAS IN LONDON, ON a building site in Kew Gardens, as a carpenter who had not almost but not quite completed his training. Then I worked on another site for J Garrett and Sons, at the Mount Pleasant Post Office sorting centre. We were building fixtures: shelves for placing letters. It was an interesting time. My wife was due to arrive in the United Kingdom so I found a room in Ravenscroft Road, in Chiswick. Then she arrived, and started working as well. At this time I started looking for work closer to home and also tried to get away from building sites.

The job I found was Norvik Electric Blankets, off Bollo Bridge Road in Acton, West London. When I was first looking for the place, I saw an old man—I suppose he was actually in his fifties!—walking his dog. I stopped him to ask the way. He happened to be the factory owner. He gave me the directions. I got the job, but the majority of people working there were from Eastern Europe, such as Poland and Yugoslavia. We really struck up a good relationship. There was only one English person, Bill Govaire. I struck up a good friendship with him.

After I had been there about eight months, I got a key position. In fact I learned so much about electric blankets that I could have gone back to Jamaica and opened my own factory.

You wouldn't sell any in Jamaica.

Well, that's true, it's warm enough there already. [Laughs] You see you have to work out, depending on the dimensions of the blanket, how many ohms of resistance to design into it, to balance heating and safety; and how many thermostats to incorporate, to regulate the temperature. The user can vary it to suit their need.

I stayed with them for several years, until they decided to move out of London. They moved up to Bolton, near Manchester, and as a key person I went up with them. But I did not like Manchester. It was too dark and dull.

They also obtained a place at Wardbrook, in Loudwater[1]. This was in late 1965. To start with, they were transporting people each day from London to High Wycombe, to train workers recruited locally. Now they had made me the Workers' Representative, because there were no trade unions in that company. But they had a Works Committee, and I was elected to serve on it. If any of the workers had a complaint, they would take it to me and I would speak on their behalf to the Works Manager. I have been lucky. My relationship with colleagues on the building site was always good. Then I moved to a completely different kind of job and was appointed as the workers' rep, out of at least thirty employees.

The person responsible for working out the ohm values and thermostats from the size of the blankets was a gentleman called Mr Singh, from Trinidad. He taught me the job, and I learned it well. There were four of us who did the job of moving the company from London to High Wycombe. The other three were Gregory Bourne, Dave Perkins and Terry Hunt. Then I was made supervisor of the section that repaired blankets, leading a team of eight. It was a busy section: customers would send back their blankets when something went wrong with them. Gregory Bourne was the main production foreman, and when he was not on the factory floor, I would take over that too. Dave Perkins was in charge of a new machine that we had which pressed together the outer material, the foam and the heating element. We were in competition with another company called Dreamland, but with this machine our product became the top seller. Those were exciting times. We were working from 7am to 7pm sometimes, or even 10pm. It was much better than the building site, a different atmosphere. In London it had been Polish and Yugoslav, but now it was a wider mix of people.

But as time went on, the blankets did not sell so well, so we diversified. One product we made was to keep babies' bottles warm, so a mother could get up in the middle of the night without having to prepare the bottle to the right temperature. We had also taken over another company in Wardbrook and started to diversify into electronics, such as computer components. The company changed its name to Ultra Electronics. I had left the blanket section and was now reporting directly to the production manager dealing with electronics in Wardbrook. My role was progress chaser. I had to go out on the ship floor each day first thing, before the Works Manager arrived, to check which machines were working, what jobs were ready, what commitments we had made for shipping today and what were still outstanding from yesterday. Then I would have to report all the problems to the Production Manager. It was a cushy time. That's what I would do in the morning. The rest of the day, I would check on the materials coming in, and go through the shop floor, making sure all was in order. I had a very pretty job at that time.

It sounds like it was a key role in the company.

Yes it was, but I had worked for them for eight years by this time.

In May of 1969 Ford Motor company started advertising: "Come and join us in building the big ones". What they were talking about was a new era of heavy-duty vehicles—big trucks. I took a chance and travelled out to Langley and had an interview. I actually applied for a job as inspector on the production line.

The personnel manager, having looked at my CV and my recommendations from Norvik, decided that that was not the job for me.

They gave me a job where I was responsible for the engineering releases. These were kept on paper and filed in various ways for easy retrieval.

Could you tell me what a release was?

They were lists of parts for the supervisors of what parts should be used on a vehicle. I will explain to you why we needed them. Suppose we were buying in some cross-members which joined together the two sides of a chassis which run the length of a truck. The chassis sides came with holes ready to attach the cross-members, but they might be out of alignment. This is where the superintendent would go to the engineers to get them to design a specification to work around the problem, and produce deviations from the original order, that is to say special parts that would match with the parts that we already had. The deviations had to be temporary, usually 30 days, exceptionally 90 days. When the time limit was up, it was up to me to tell the superintendent. You see, by the end of that time allowed for the deviation, the proper parts should have come through. So that was my job. It was very interesting.

Dealing with Ford Motor company gave me really good insights. I had real responsibilities. When I went out on the production line to tell the superintendent that the time was up for the deviations, there could be no argument. He would have been aware of it in any case because he would have had a copy of the deviations with him. If he had a problem with it then he had to go and see Chips Wood, the Chief Engineer. Or perhaps I would go and see Chips myself. You can see it was a very responsible job.

This was about 1970-71. Around this time there was a new set of vacancies, advertised internally and externally. I made an application for one of these— purchaser within the Buying Department. When I went to see the Personnel Manager, Peter Scott, he said to me, "Sebert, I have your application and also your recommendation from your previous company, Wardbrook, but we have asked for applicants to have x number of 'O' levels. I notice that you don't have any of these qualifications". So I told him: "When I first asked for a job, you were the one to tell me that my experience made me eligible to be in Quality Control, rather than the production line. And in this position, as you know, I have not let the company down. So," I concluded, "as to the job you are advertising now, I am absolutely confident that I can do it. All I am asking is for you to give me once more a chance to prove that I can do the job." Anyway, he gave me the job and said he would be monitoring me to see how I was progressing. There were two other superintendents interviewing people for the job I was applying for: Bill Williams and Eric Venner. After we had been recruited, Peter Scott invited them in to come and choose their men. Bill Williams came in and said, "I want you, and you, and you," picking me first for his team. I knew Bill already. Most people were afraid of him. He was one of the strictest managers in Ford. He was strict on timing and you really had to know what you were doing.

You were happy with that?

I was. Out of 22½ years at Ford, I must have worked 15 in that department. It was a job I enjoyed. Having worked as a progress chaser, my role increased enormously as time went on. At first I only had two people to report to: my immediate supervisor and my line manager. And if I was not happy with either of those I could talk to my union rep. Part of my job was to go and visit our suppliers, either with my supervisor, or on my own. One reason was to find out why they were behind schedule in supplying us with parts. They had to fulfil their contract to supply us with nuts, bolts or whatever it was. So we would find out if they had a capacity problem, a staff problem, or what. And we would also inspect their manufacturing process, for example if they had a clean environment. And perhaps most importantly, we would want to check whether they were giving their other customers priority over ours.

So we would report what we found, not what that supplier was trying to tell us. And whether our reports were verbal or written, our management would trust them.

So did you get to see people at different levels?

Yes, we did not just meet our own counterparts but their managements too. And we would get shown around the premises too—the shop floor and everything. We had specific quality issues sometimes with our suppliers: perhaps some of the bolts were unfinished and had burrs on them, or there was dirt left in the grooves. We were interested in how they handled their work in progress.

Were people surprised to discover you were black?

I had one experience like that. I used to have regular contact by phone with one of these companies. Some of them thought I had an Irish accent. Then I had to go and do one of these inspections. They were told that Mr Graham would arrive at a certain time, but of course we had never met face to face. So when I walked in and introduced myself the girl looked astonished. "Mr Graham?" I said, "Yes, Mr Graham. I've come to see Mr So-and-so." And they weren't expecting me to be like this. Anyhow, when I went to see those people, production managers and so forth, I was representing my company. I did not see anything that I would call racism or anything like that. I would just see the person that I was going to be dealing with. I was ready for anything. My attitude was, "You show me respect, you get respect. You want to be funny with me—it's down to you, because you'll get as much as you give."

So, for me, it's a positive way of looking at life. I am not saying all of us can be that positive or all of us will come out the same. We all have a different way of handling things.

You know, the wage levels at Ford were for many years used by successive governments as one of their yardsticks to measure inflation. And

Ford today is renowned for the quality of its products. The Ford Cortina used to be the most popular "poor man's car". Now the Focus has a great reputation. It's quite an outstanding company to give a person a good background in management and people-relationships—regardless of the adverse news about industrial relations that have hit the headlines over the years. It teaches you confidence. Norvik was a very gentlemanly company: "The customer is always right." We showed respect to people's position in the company by addressing them "Sir" or "Mr". But at Ford there was none of that. Every one was "Bill" or "Jim". It was as though we were accepted as worthy members of the team. When I presented a report, they would respect it and believe me. You were expected to be sure of your own skills, and not hide behind your rank.

I had 84 suppliers, not just in UK, but also France, Holland and Sweden. I could pick up the phone and talk to any of them. It was an excellent company to work for.

In my schooldays in Jamaica in the nineteen-fifties we didn't have to take regular exams, and I left with no qualifications. There were some who stayed on to take the Senior Cambridge examinations, which were equivalent to the GCE 'O' Level in the UK. I never went in for that at the time, because as I said to you before, by the time we started to realise the value of education, we had reached 16 or over. It's true that some of my cousins had taken the Senior Cambridge, and went on to study agriculture; but what we used to say at that time was, "OK you go off and study, and we'll look after the farm in the meanwhile, and when you get back we'll try and give you a job." [Laughs] So those were negative times and when you look back you say, "This was a mistake."

I don't understand what you mean.

Well you see, we would have been working on the land in the meantime, with money in our pockets. They would have a qualification but no money. It was negative thinking on our parts because we never thought of the value of their qualification. When I was sixteen or seventeen we thought of going to university simply as a way to have fun and avoid work. They were using up scarce money to have a good time. But now we are grown up and we see that our peers did the right thing. They went and pursued agricultural studies and that was a valuable and respectable thing to do.

So when I came to the United Kingdom I didn't want to people to think I had just done nothing. Around the time when my wife came to join me in I enrolled in further education at Chiswick Polytechnic with the intention to study English Literature. My ambition at that time was to become a crime reporter. But they put it to me that to begin with, I would have to do English as a foreign language. In the last few years they have begun to accept that the patois commonly spoken in Jamaica is a language in its own right, distinct from English. It is similar to English but not the same. Don't mistake me, you can also hear very good English spoken there, in fact my mother taught us to speak it, and my brothers were better at it than I. But I was unable to follow it through and complete the course. Work and family commitments took all of my time.

Before that as well, whilst still in Jamaica, I had taken a correspondence course from this country, to train as a Clerk of Works. This person would be the one to maintain liaison with the Town and Country Planners. His job would be to measure the building, make sure it's properly aligned, not straying beyond its boundaries, and conforming to all regulations. Again, I did not persevere with this till the end and so I didn't get the qualification.

But did these courses help you anyway?

Oh certainly! Everything that you study, everything that you read, gives you insight and experience. However I gave up the correspondence course when I decided to be a soldier. My interest just stopped at that point, when something else took over. When I went to Chiswick, I was thinking I would just be in England for five years and then returning. I had to focus my energies, but when our second child was on the way, I had to concentrate on supporting the family. I was earning £8 a week and had to find everything—rent and all—from that. I couldn't afford the time or the money for college.

More recently, I went to Amersham and Wycombe College, to do sociology, psychology and English. Being in local politics gave me a lot to think about, It seemed as if in each ten-year period the family structures in this country underwent some major change. At one time the concern was the spread in promiscuity. Then it was health risks—things like herpes, and how *that* impacted on the family. Or the way changes in legislation affected the family.

But then, you see, I was an elected member of the District Council. So I had a commitment to the people who elected me. I had to make a conscious decision: could I afford the time to continue this social studies course for three years, whilst working full-time and being involved in various community activities? So again, I dropped out! [Laughs] But in all three instances, it had given me a wider outlook on life. I learned something, so I have no regrets. Within my job—for example at Ford, where I spent the longest time—the absence of BSc after my name has been for someone else to worry about. I would have been glad to get a degree, but I have never let that hold me back, and I'm not letting it bother me now.

Now I am not saying that for others, a degree might not be easier than the path I have taken. I had a lot of luck in my working life, and learned discipline and self-reliance from an early age. A lot of employers might find it easier to use someone's certificates as an indication of the experience and the quality of the person, rather than give someone the chances they gave me.

Do you think, though, that your absence of degrees or other qualifications has affected your income?

Certainly. Yes, of course. At Ford, especially in the Seventies, the trend was for graduate recruitment. I've had the task of showing graduate entrants how to look at worksheets, that tell you for example what stock you have in hand, to complete your production schedules. Oh yes, they were highly trained in computer literacy, that is they thought what the computer said was right. But that's how they would often get you into trouble! There was a time that I had to say to my supervisor, "Without any disrespect, please don't send me any more graduates, because I cannot be held responsible for the mistakes they make when they fail to follow my instructions." We had 2,500 people on the production line. I had certain jobs like testing the pressure on the brakes, or building the Tilter-cabs on the trucks. If I told one of these graduates that we have not enough stock for tomorrow's jobs, and he must get some in, and he disobeyed, I don't want my manager coming to talk to me the next day about the problems caused. In short these graduates would have to do what I told them, or not work with me. I was respectful to my bosses, but firm. But yes, the paper qualification might have added £10,000 to my salary.

And yet your experience sounded more useful to Ford than those degrees.

Yes! [Laughs] In many cases. And after leaving Ford, I worked with a company called Vishay Vitramon, from Bourne End. They made electronic components for trucks, computers and especially mobile phones. And these people also found my experience useful. They also gave me a special responsibility. They were making these contacts, which I discussed with you before in some detail.

With the sand?[2]

Yes, and looking with eyes which had been trained by experience at Ford, I was able to make suggestions to the Production Manager and also the General Manager as to how he could improve output. He took it on board immediately and it saved the company a lot of money.

And that is the company where you were working when you became Mayor?

That's right, and I think he saw this as good publicity for the company. The Bucks Free Press were giving me a lot of column inches in their paper, as the first black Mayor in Bucks, and it wasn't till he saw my picture in the paper that my boss even knew I was a councillor! I hadn't told them anything about what I did in my spare time. I just went to work and carried out my duties. A few of the employees knew, because they were in the same community in High Wycombe, but I had never told anyone in management. So when they saw all these headlines about me, they were quite elated. And I had to tell them what it was all about. And they gave me the time off to do my Mayoral duties, and they even arranged a Golf Day to assist my Mayor's Appeal for funds to help the elderly.

Fund-raising: a brainstorm

- Collections tins in pubs
- Collections at theatre
- Cricket matches
- Company promotions
- Music at civic services
- Sunday league football
- Golf
- Slimathon
- Marathon run (sponsoring Steve Cohen)
- Fashion show
- Auction
- Sponsored events at the Sports Centre
- Arts show
- Race night (Lions)
- Bowling
- Caribbean Evening
- Wycombe/Marlow Mayors' event
- Charity market stall
- Street collections
- Antiques Road Show
- School sponsored walk opening of Chiltern Railway
- Wall chart
- Auction of cakes
- Mayor's Appeal Ball
- Photographic exhibition film "Our Heritage"
- Tea Dance
- Pig roast
- It's a Knockout
- Schools Mufti Day
- BBQ on the Rye

From the minutes of a meeting on the Mayor's Appeal, 22.05.96

Every Mayor selects a charity or good cause to support for the year, so I chose care for the elderly. You may remember some stories at that time, about old people found dead in their homes after several weeks, in London or elsewhere; and questions asked whether they could afford to keep warm in the winter. I was concerned about the elderly senior citizens in High Wycombe. I would not want to hear those stories repeated locally in our community. We raised £24,000 in my Mayoral year for the elderly, much of it through social activities organised by sympathetic groups, like my employers. Yes the company were very proud of that and they saw advantages.

Then I moved from Vitramon and went to another company in Aylesbury, called Airtec. You see Vitramon, a flourishing company in the Thames Valley—that people were comparing to Silicon Valley, because it has so many electronics companies—was taken over by Americans. Americans like to move in and exploit a market. Then they destroy the company by selling off most of it, keeping the best and then moving away. This is what they did with Vitramon. Part of it was moved to Israel and the rest to the United States, so this local firm unfortunately had to close down. Then I saw another job advertised in Aylesbury, Airtec, in the same industry. And I worked there for four years. Then the same thing happened again. The Americans moved in, telling us: "Oh this is a good company! This is where the future lies!" And they spoke about all their expectations for how well we would be doing under their management. But what they did was take the good bits of the company to Switzerland. We were sold out again. The remainder was moved to somewhere in the North of England. But our company down here was closed down.

I've always got a problem with multinational companies anyway. It seems to me that at times they have the power to overrule governments. I find myself sometimes very uncomfortable with that.

I don't understand how they can do that—overrule governments.

Well, take Tesco[3] as an example. It is now in a position where local authorities just have to listen. The size of the company is such that local authorities find it hard to turn down their planning applications.

Why is that? They make an offer that cannot be refused?

They have so much money to fight their case. But it is not just that. They promise to create so many jobs. Local authorities don't want to have a lot of unemployment. So the public usually welcome their coming. There is seldom reason enough to refuse their planning application. And they will offer to build some affordable housing too.

But there is another point. They have a vast monopolistic power. Government should put a cap on their monopoly power, because they are killing off smaller businesses.

Not just that but they use their power on the producers too. They can drive prices down till the farmers are almost bankrupted sometimes.

Exactly. And they are using this same power in Africa and other supplier countries. They have such a buying power that it exceeds the influence of other governments. They may even buy the land themselves and grow the produce themselves. They need to be controlled. We should try and save the local businesses in our community and not let them be forced out. Now Tesco is starting supermarkets in petrol stations. We should not allow it to happen.

It's true that Ford is a multinational company, but they have not been destructive to the interests of this country. We have derived good from their being here. The whole of Dagenham[4] depended on them at one time. They have put money into sport and other things here. I am talking about those companies who move in with a bunch of lies, when what they intend to do is to destroy the employment structure in a locality and then move out. I think Government should impose a penalty in such cases, or say that for companies acquired in this way, the buyer should keep it going for five years before they could close it down like this. Otherwise, they simply cause us job losses.

I have had a wide job experience but I have been quite fortunate. From the time I arrived in 1960, I have only been out of work for a short period. I'm thinking of that horrible strike at Ford in 1973 which lasted for nine weeks. It was a hard experience for me and I was not used to it. Though I was living in High Wycombe, I had to go to Uxbridge Road in Slough to sign on. It wasn't like now, when you have employment offices almost on your doorstep. You had to sign on for three weeks before they would consider giving you any benefits. At the end of that, they asked for my wife's payslip, and the family allowance book, that you used to take to the Post Office to get money for the children, that everyone was entitled to. It was very intrusive in the sense that everything that you earned had to be shown. I found it humiliating at the time. I found that even after providing all these papers showing the truthful information about the family's finances, there always seemed to be others who would just walk in and get a lot more money. I just couldn't understand how the system worked. I just wasn't used to being out of work

Even whilst we were on strike I found myself some work. I went to Bowyers, who made sausages and pies, in Amersham. It was just a part-time job, to tide me over until the Ford strike ended but there was a supervisor, Mr Wilson, who wanted me to come and work for them permanently. [Laughs]

So I don't know what you would call it. Either it is luck, or I have a knack for people liking me. I only came for a part-time job, but he wanted me to stay.

Well, you say you have been lucky, because you always got on well in each thing that you tried. But I wonder if in any of these jobs you used all of your potential?

Hmm, yes, I am not sure. If I had pursued higher education, I am sure I would have succeeded. If I had for example studied political science, I might have pursued a political career, and been successful, because that is a great interest of mine.

But then, I have achieved something, especially if I compare my life with some of those educated Caribbean young people who came over here in the early years, teachers, for example, and did not make much impact over here, despite their education. They did less well when they got here than they had done before. That is why I call myself lucky. Some people I know have come over here and been very bright, but have found it hard to hold down a job for any period of time.

I think that some of us have certain natural abilities which you can't learn even if you go to university. Perhaps it is not exactly luck, but I have been given the chance a few times to put some proposals to those in a higher position, which they have readily accepted. But if I had been to University, it could have been even better.

But you don't anticipate much higher education now?

No. That's right. I say that now, but I may still have another 25 years in my life. Who knows what tomorrow may bring? If the general public see this book, and decide it's readable, and that I have some more to offer, then we will be introduced via the book. Who knows what they might get out of me?

Well, yes indeed. Why not?

NOTES

1. *Loudwater:* A suburb of High Wycombe.
2. *Vitramon, sand:* in one of our conversations, Sebert told me how he invented a way of recycling the sand which was used to blast the contacts used in manufacturing the components, thus saving the company many thousands each year.
3. *Tesco:* British supermarket chain constantly opening new stores and adding new product lines to its core grocery business, such as insurance.
4. *Dagenham:* town in Essex once the headquarters of British Ford car production.

CHAPTER 8

The community

WE HAVE TALKED A LOT ABOUT MY WORK. BUT THEN THERE IS also all my community work.

Where did that start? Was it when you were the workers' representative at Norvik?

Yes, well they were indeed a kind of community.

And you as their representative acted on behalf of their welfare?

Yes, it started there, I think. And secondly it was when I had permanently moved from London out to High Wycombe, about 1973, and when I became actively involved with the Labour Party. And I have been also a worker with the young people, with the Youth Club. It started at the Multiracial Centre. They had a youth group which used to use the student union facilities of the Bucks College—what's now the BCUC, the Bucks Chilterns University College. Anyway it was the place where the young people would have their drinks and their evenings out. I was involved with that youth club and then they moved into the newly built Round House. I was very much interested in that.

How did you get involved in youth work?

When I came to High Wycombe, I got involved with the Community Relations Council[1].

And how did you get involved with that?

When I got to High Wycombe I was invited to meet Mr Webley, who was already involved with the Race Relations Council here. And part of that was the youth club. One of its members was young Fraser. We trained them in such a way that they could take over management for themselves, at a certain point: something which they did very well.

I also got involved with the Youth Training Scheme under the Conservatives, whereby they were trying to encourage young people to enhance their education and employment potential by learning new skills. I was there as the representative of the Community Relations Council to ensure the ethnic minorities children were offered the same opportunities. Various training centres were set up. Our nearest one was in Slough. My job from the Race Relations Council's point of view—this was co-ordinated through the Education Department in Buckinghamshire County Council—was to make sure that on these schemes young people from ethnic minorities were getting their fair share of this training.

Some of these young people, of whatever background, took this training very seriously. Others just couldn't be bothered with it. I spoke to you before about this, that if only young people would take up the opportunities laid before them, what a big difference it would make—to them and to the country too. Certainly there are opportunities. People are being paid to learn skills now. It's not cheap to pay them to learn, and it's not cheap labour either. But it was something to help those who had been looking for work for some time, or those who had been in work and then realised that they did not have enough of the skills that were wanted by the employers. If they didn't obtain the right skills they could only do labouring or some "dead-end" job. Doing this training, you get paid and it enables you to be independent of both your parents and the State. People should definitely take advantage. They might see it differently, but I see it as "windows of opportunity". What wouldn't I have done with that, in my time! But ultimately, they have to decide their own future.

But let's go back to the youth club and the Race Relations Council. These have enveloped most of my life here in this community, right up to this day. Having been involved in those early years—back in Jamaica—in the Boys' Brigade and Scouts, then coming here and doing this job, it's not something that I just jumped into from nowhere. And all the things that I've got involved with, I've enjoyed immensely.

But what I enjoyed more was to be able—when I was at the Council—to help people less fortunate. So when things like the Community Charge[2] were introduced, there were a lot of people who had been put through hell by it. Some could pay it straight off, but there were others—even sometimes professional people, if they had high mortgages and children—who were being harassed by the bailiffs sent by the Council. I am not blaming the Council so much: they were prepared to hand out guidelines. But the bailiffs were getting their own costs out of it, and this only added to the debts they went out to recover from the defaulting householders. It was hellish for those people, but in a number of cases I was able to intervene and say to them, "Hold on, don't worry about it. I'll get it sorted out." I was able to talk to the bailiffs, or sometimes I would go to talk to the Council department concerned. As their elected representative, I could go to the Council office and show that they were being harassed. They had paid a certain amount, say, and then their payments had fallen in arrears without them realising. And I would help negotiate, by getting agreement that the debtor would pay a certain amount per month, according to what they could afford, and get the bailiffs off their back. It worked! Because you see, when they are threatened with bailiffs, they panic and forget that they can talk to the Council about it. They'd just have this threat hanging over them, that in a week's time, the bailiffs would be coming round, to take away goods to the value of the amount owed. It caused havoc in their lives. Being able to take the pressure off their lives was something so worthwhile, and I don't know of any other position in which I could have

The Mayor visits a local school to open refurbished kitchens partly funded as a result of efforts by the Parent-Teacher Association.

done something like that. I have no regrets about the path I have taken through life.

And just as I learned a great deal at Ford, I learned so much as a councillor.

I know people complain about their councils. But there's a reason behind it all and if people took more interest, they'd understand. You find a hole dug in the road outside your house: "What's this?" But there's been a notice hung from a lamp-post for weeks, and you haven't bothered to read it. Every decision that they make, which will affect your life, has been published. And you have the right to complain formally too. But I didn't discover this until I got involved. It was an eye-opener for me to find out how everything worked, so that I could inform my constituents.

People have immense expectations from their councillor, and sometimes they are disappointed. The council gets misrepresented. But they need to understand how it works, how there are three layers of government: central, county and district. Central government passes across certain responsibilities on to the county council. And then the county passes down some of its responsibilities to the district. And that is how we end up having three tiers of government. So central government deals with the big questions: should there be capital punishment? Should there be a Green Belt[3]?

One of the County Council's biggest responsibilities is to carry through the education policies determined by central government. They are also responsible for the road network within the county. The local council is responsible for emptying your dustbins, and—together with the County Council—where you build your home, that is, making planning decisions.

It makes people cross sometimes, especially when they don't really understand how it works. When I was involved in the Race Relations Council at first, I couldn't find answers to many of the problems that arose. You'd go to the District Council, they'd refer you to the County Council—who would then refer you back again. It was frustrating from the outside, but when you get involved in local government, you can see the reason why. And when expectations are not met, politicians are sometimes seen as untruthful. That's not their intention. When you're in opposition, you have the right to make plans opposing what you see the government doing. But whilst you are in opposition, you're not able to see the accounts that the Chancellor[4] is maintaining. So you might make plans that you could not afford once you got into government. You might have to postpone your plan from Year 1 to Year 3. And it's the same in local government. As a councillor, you know what people want in your community. You have been listening to what people have been saying in the pub, in the road: "We haven't got anything for young people. We need a bowling alley." And then when you are campaigning to be elected you would put it in your manifesto. But then you might find it is not achievable after all: it might not fit in with other priorities. Sometimes the Council sends out a questionnaire, to see what people want. They might say they are more interested in crime prevention—more police. And it's likely that those who complain about non-achievement by the Council didn't participate in its surveys, didn't make their views known in that way.

I guess I am one of these people that you talk about. When I see the papers that the Council send to us—newsletters and surveys—I say look at how they are wasting our money now! It must have cost so much to print all this material, and all they seem to be doing is praising themselves.

Yes, well, you are not alone in that frustration, but if you take no interest in politics, you won't have an idea of what the Council does. And it is actually their responsibility to keep you informed, and to give you a free platform to air your views. It's true that I sometimes hate filling in questionnaires myself. It can take 20 minutes to fill them in. But look, at the present time, the Council is doing a major redevelopment of what they call the Western Sector[5]. The consultants are there, but the councillors are there to represent the people. The council officers have their own expertise too, to provide guidance. But this questionnaire provides real democracy so that the Council's Chief Executive can confidently say that "Yes, we want a cinema. We want a bowling alley," or whatever it is. And the developers will be told what to do, from this plan. They cannot build outside the wishes of the people. We are the ones who will be paying for it.

What about the new development at Wycombe Marsh[6]? Was there a consultation about that?

Oh yes, that's been on the drawing board for many years. So many plans have come forward and been thrown out. And what we have now, this mix of businesses and dwellings, is what the people actually said they wanted. And isn't it looking good? A little town centre outside the main one. So much consultation, and you end up with the people's wishes. It's a good example of how planning goes. You can see the big gain, for Wycombe and for the people in that part of town. Those people in Micklefield: I stood there for election to the County Council, and I promised them I would be pressing for amenities that they didn't have locally: a pharmacy and a laundrette. Actually I have heard that doctors are not in favour of a pharmacy there. But let's see what happens now, at the new centre. It will be good for those at the eastern end of town, those who don't have cars, and for those that do, it will reduce traffic.

So that's what local government is all about: participation. Looking back, I recall that being a councillor has been a great experience for me. I am grateful to the people of my ward at that time, Bowerdean and Daws Hill; and for the Labour Party who nominated me, to stand in that ward. It was back in July 1989 when I successfully captured the seat. It was a great pleasure to represent those people for ten years.

NOTES

1. *Community Relations Council:* see Appendix A, "Breakdown not break up".
2. *Community Charge:* known popularly (or should I say unpopularly) as the Poll Tax. Introduced in 1990 whilst Margaret Thatcher was Prime Minister, and contributed to her downfall.
3. *Green belt* is a specific planning tool, first introduced for London in 1938 but rolled out to England as a whole by a government circular in 1955. It urged local councils to consider designating green belts where they wanted to restrict urban growth. Green belts now cover 13% of England (around 1.5 million hectares). Wales has only recently begun its own green belt policy while in Scotland the concept is rather broader. (Source: BBC website.)
4. *The Chancellor of the Exchequer* is Britain's finance minister.
5. *The Western Sector* project in High Wycombe is a plan to replace a large surface car park and a grim 1960 bus station, in the space left from a Fifties slum clearance scheme, with a new town centre development.
6. *Wycombe Marsh:* site of a former paper mill. A major redevelopment of the site includes a mix of shops, restaurants and residential apartments.

CHAPTER 9

My political life

BUT TO BE THE FIRST AFRO-CARIBBEAN PERSON IN Buckinghamshire to be appointed Mayor, that was the icing on the cake. They have shown me so much appreciation for what I have been able to do. For me, it's wonderful to have shared in the culture of the people of High Wycombe, with its history going back a thousand years. Now I am part of that history. They have welcomed me, regardless of my origins far away. I have represented all the people of Wycombe, not just those from my part of the world. I don't suppose that I represented anyone else from exactly my home district of Lennox Bigwoods, in Jamaica. But in a different sense, I feel that I was representing my countrymen back home, not forgetting the place which gave me my start in life.

It's been good for me, it's been good for the children of all races. Apart from myself, the only other Mayor from an ethnic minority was Razzaq[1], from Pakistan. And once I got elected, I have had many Asian-British youngsters who have helped me in my work, for example distributing leaflets. I saw them grow up! At the Council elections in 1999, one of them came up to me and said, "I can remember you from when I was small. You were the only one I would approach. I had asked you how I could become a councillor, and you helped me. And now tonight, look at us!" Because on that night there were more ethnic Pakistanis elected than you could have imagined: I think five. I was moved by that. For I had not held office as Mayor just for the Afro-Caribbeans. My business was to serve the people—all of them. And it seems to me that that's what I've done. Of course people from my own Afro-Caribbean community particularly appreciated my being elevated to Mayor. All round, it has been a great satisfaction. When you ask around, you find that people don't think of the Chairman of the Council as being the top person, but the Mayor. I was lucky in my year. I had Councillor Betty Barratt as my Chairman. We were both in the Labour Party, and had no problems, in fact we pretty much worked as a team. It was a memorable year and the memory will remain with me forever.

Do you see signs of more political awareness amongst the Afro-Caribbean population?

Well, I am encouraging a couple of young people that are ready to join the Labour Party. I think in general the Afro-Caribbean population of this country are as politically aware as anyone else. We do have a few Members of Parliament. But I think they have felt a bit let down by Labour. In the Sixties and Seventies they were solid behind the Labour Party. These days it is not as straightforward. With some it is their Christian faith. They'll go out and vote but they are not prepared to join the Party and pay their monthly subscriptions. They are politically aware but they are not immune to the disenchantment that has affected all sections of society. It's not that politicians are lying—they don't go deliberately lying—

Not even to win an election?

[Laughs] It's like being a lawyer, you want to show the good side of your case, it's a matter of winning the argument. And this does involve being persuasive, and appealing to popular sentiment. So if I put a better vision forward, and you elect me on the strength of that, and then it happens that I am unable through circumstance to carry through that vision, you can't accuse me of lying. We all tend to be impatient. We want it now. Maybe sometimes politicians need to be more direct with the electorate.

So a Prime Minister owes it to the electorate to say what is deemed achievable in a timescale, and at the same time admit there is a cost to it. Nothing in politics is easy.

Take the Health Service, for instance. Health is not cheap. When I came here in 1960, I visited Queen Charlotte's Hospital, and later Aylesbury Hospital, when it was in its old state. They would smell intolerably of disinfectant. It's not like that today. You get a sense of cleanliness. And they use so much advanced technology, and monitor patients with so much close attention and all these machines. It is *expensive*. Has the Government put money in? Yes. Is that money being used to best advantage? Well, that is for the management at local level to answer. It's true that some has been badly spent because of political expediency at local level, both in hospitals and schools. The Government has a hard job to control it all. So then we have inquiries, and they are not cheap. It's your money and my money, which is being used. We need to inform our MPs of our experience and our views.

But if I were a young person listening to you, I would feel that politics is kind of boring. So much administration, the details of being fair and balanced. I would want something more exciting: to ban the Bomb, save a tree, put right some terrible injustice. In the old days, young people could see a role for themselves on the Left. I am not sure about now. There are plenty of injustices overseas, but not so many big ones left in this country.

Well, to answer your question, politics can be very exciting. When I was a councillor, I knew I had my chance to make a difference. I would take part in a big debate, and my supporters would be there in the gallery listening, and I would know I had a chance. There might be a big subject coming up, which you knew quite a lot about. And you would plan what questions to ask your opposition. It was quite exciting. The adrenalin would be flowing.

So how would I help make politics less boring for young people? In High Wycombe we have a Youth Council. They form their own debating bodies. I must give credit to Mrs Clarke. I think it was during her Mayoral year, that she introduced this young councillors' forum. And now they have a chance to come to the District Council. From their schools, they take their issues and discuss them as councillors. And they can pass them up to the real Councillors.

But it is not just in the realm of politicians. You could say everything is politics. Every decision we take is a kind of political one. Take fox-hunting[2] for instance. Families will be discussing it and the children will be having their say at home. So if the child can engage in the issues, I don't see how it will be any more boring to the adult than to the child. It's a matter of where our interests lie.

I think young people should take an interest in politics because they are the future. They can make a difference just as they did in the Sixties and Seventies, when the student unions were very vocal.

That's how Jack Straw got started. He was very active when he headed the National Union of Students. Everyone heard his name.

Well, I have observed myself that young people are less engaged in politics these days. Their values are a bit different from when I was growing up. They are more independent. They have social activities that take over their lives outside of full-time education.

It's as if they live in their own world these days.

Yes, they are so much less dependent on their parents than they used to be. The parents are better off and so are they.

What I have observed is that they get most passionate about "single-issue politics" as I suggested before. Some of them for example are attracted to the Green Party.

Ok, well let's look at this again. It's not that they have a simplistic view of everything. They do need to look a these issues in depth. Why is there hunger in the world, for example. We are not going to bring back CND. But they could construct an argument to tell the United States, "We are not interested in all this stuff about weapons of mass destruction. We want to see help given to prevent hunger globally." All these things will affect them, because the world is getting smaller. And if the polar ice-caps have a likelihood of melting, then that's a threat to them. They could mobilise themselves and talk to the United States and India and China, "Don't mess up our world." I certainly won't be around when those ice-caps melt and the water rises. This too is politics. High politics.

Young people need to engage themselves in political issues. Not in ten years, five years. They need to engage themselves in the issues now: in making a difference to the world and where we are going.

They often like to get engaged with pressure groups, like for example Amnesty International.

Yes. [Pause] These are groups that are useful. But sometimes they pursue the wrong people, as I read recently in *The Gleaner.* Amnesty had gone to Jamaica and spoken out about ill-treatment. I am totally against brutality against any person, in any form. But those persistent offenders who come out of jail only to offend again immediately—they need to be restrained, for the protection of society. Here in Britain, hanging has been outlawed. But if you take the Huntley case, where Mr Huntley murdered those innocent schoolgirls—I don't know the reason—that man has no right to live. There is no doubt he was the killer, because not only has he confessed, he has also clarified how he did it.

Criminality is indeed notorious in Jamaica. Innocent people there are at much greater risk of murder than they are here. The Jamaican Government has a duty to protect its people. Why should any outside organisation tell it who should or should not be hanged?

Aren't you talking about the Court of Appeal[3] here?

Yes, well that is another topic, but we are talking here about Amnesty, who have in common with the British Government that they are interferers. And in any case by publicising as they do, Amnesty are giving excuses to other countries to try to interfere in Jamaica's affairs.

Let me confess my own bias here. I have a correspondent on Death Row in Florida and I believe in the possibility of redemption for those who may have committed terrible crimes. But this is not about my opinions! And I think every human being should be treated with dignity.

And I respect your point of view. OK, I will put it clearly where I stand. Where it is proven beyond any doubt that the person is guilty of a dreadful crime, like Mr Huntley, then I will say without any reservations, that the person does not deserve the right to live. Period. But I do agree with you that anyone in prison should be treated well, with respect, and not abused in any way.

Now, you had mentioned the CCJ—the Caribbean Court of Justice[4]. Up to a point, I am in favour of it. The Jamaican PNP[5] and JLP[6] are looking at it together. I don't think the Privy Council should be allowed jurisdiction to determine whether Jamaica has a right to hang people[7]. Meanwhile prisoners are languishing on Death Row.

And no one has been executed for more than 20 years!

That's right. The resources for maintaining those prisoners could be better used for more positive purposes. But I must repeat that the death penalty must only be exercised when there is no doubt as to guilt.

Is this the main reason for the move towards the CCJ?

There are many reasons, this is just one. But another is this. We are an independent country now. Our judges are as good as any in the United Kingdom. It's true our law and parliamentary systems are on the British model, but we have the right of self-determination and that includes the independence of our own courts from external influence.

But let's return to the topic of human rights, and the Amnesty report. Jamaica has international respect as a country. We are very vulnerable as a small island caught in the middle of international drug trafficking that involves some extremely violent elements. We are a poor country and it is almost destabilising the Government. Even with help from the US and UK, the Government is under pressure trying to fight this international crime introduced from overseas. They used to have a sign there, when you arrived at Immigration. "Jamaica. No problem. Please do not be found with drugs." A very clear warning.

This kind of trade is chosen as an easy way out, to make a living but it has been jeopardising an entire society, that has been suffering from it over the last ten or twenty years. I am hoping that one day we will find Jamaica becoming again that haven that we used to know. All of us used to be rapping and understanding this concept of kinship and fellowship, as a great people.

NOTES

1. *Mohammed Razzaq* was Mayor of High Wycombe from 1988-89.
2. *Fox-hunting:* The ban on hunting foxes with hounds in England had come into force on 19th February 2005, the day before this conversation.
3. *Court of Appeal:* Though Jamaica is independent of the United Kingdom, the UK's Privy Council still acts at the time of writing as the final court of appeal for Jamaica's justice system, despite moves to replace it by a new body, the Caribbean Court of Justice (CCJ). The issue is controversial, particularly as the Privy Council has ruled in favour of a condemned man's appeal against hanging.
4. *CCJ:* See previous note.
5. *PNP:* People's National Party.
6. *JLP:* Jamaica Labour Party.
7. *Hanging:* there is an outstanding dispute as to the legality and scope of Jamaica's law in respect of the death penalty.

CHAPTER 10

Mayor

WELL, IAN, WE HAVE COVERED QUITE A JOURNEY OF MY LIFE so far[1]. Now I want to take you through how I became Mayor, the process involved. I have told you once about that visit to a class of schoolchildren, who all wanted to be Mayor, or even Prime Minister[2]. Well, at the age they were, and in a short visit, it was difficult for me to explain to them the processes of becoming councillor and then Mayor.

The first thing you would have to do is become a member of a political party, whether Conservative, Labour or Liberal Democrat. And then after you had been an active member for a while, they might call on you to stand as a candidate at the next Council election. That is stage one, to be nominated. If you were lucky and got elected as a councillor, then you would take up your position and attend the meetings in the Council Chamber. Then your party would invite you to serve on various committees. Actually being nominated as a Mayoral candidate is partly a matter of seniority. Both the nomination and the election are done by your "peers", that is the other councillors, rather than the electorate as a whole.

You are nominated by your own party? Who actually elects you?

Yes. It is put to the vote in a full council meeting.

So it is not like the election for the Mayor of London, where the public have a vote?

No, the election is strictly by your own peers. And this is an interesting way of doing it, because it is understood that you are going to be exercising your duties as Mayor in a non-political way. All sides of the Chamber will gladly give you their vote, in a general consensus.

Which party was in the majority when you were voted in?

At that time there was a Labour/Liberal Democrat coalition in power, with the Conservatives in opposition. I was elected unanimously. It was very humbling. In Jamaica I was accustomed to a similar system of government, based as it was on the English model. But Jamaica was more than four thousand miles away from the United Kingdom, with a quite different history and culture. From our perspective over there, the system of government and institutions of the United Kingdom had the highest possible prestige. What an honour to share in its history! High Wycombe, though a rather small market town, has its own very proud traditions. They told me here that even Londoners—from only thirty miles away—would stand out for not speaking the Bucks lingo, and would be seen as strangers. Yet coming from so far away, I was accepted as a local citizen, first as a councillor, then as a Mayor, to serve the people of High Wycombe.

One of my fellow-councillors said to me, in my opening ceremony, that I was now "one of the sons of High Wycombe". You could not get a better feeling than that. And to be sharing in such an ancient tradition, with all its ceremonies, was an eye-opener to all of us. The tradition had been going on for so long, but now, for the first time, they were seeing a black person involved in it as the leader of their town. It was an elevation for all of us, something pleasing.

"All of us" being who?

The people who live in High Wycombe: black people, white people. I have often said in Council, that no matter what may be said about race relations, in the United Kingdom, those of us who live in this district have enjoyed a special goodwill. We have so many groups and languages here – Italians, Irish, West Indians, Poles, speakers of Punjabi and Urdu – yet all of us seem to get on quite well. There might be the odd case of indifference, but you would find that anywhere you go. The different ethnic groups have got on pretty well. No one seems to be overtly racist. That is something to celebrate and I hope it carries on this way.

The role of Mayor needs a little clarification. In France[3] and Germany[4] the Mayor is the town's chief executive. In High Wycombe, our Mayor is more for civic and ceremonial purposes. He or she is expected to open schools or shops, attend civic functions. At certain times, we have our own civic service. I think it's every two months—

Church service?

Yes, church services which the Mayor attends[5]. The police and the Royal Air Force are invited. Invitations are also sent to selected members of the general public. This is an occasion where the Mayor dresses in the full regalia of office—red gown, gold chain and cocked hat—and will invite guests after the service to the Mayor's parlour.

The special service normally takes place at 10.30 at All Saints Parish Church. There is a formal schedule: we meet at the Mayor's Parlour for refreshments, get robed up—it is not only the Mayor who has special robes to wear—then we leave to join a procession which marches from the Town Hall up Queen Victoria Road, along the High Street and into the Church. At such times the police are deployed to close off these roads to traffic.

Then as Mayor you are invited to all sorts of functions, and in my case I was invited to the neighbouring towns of Oxford, Henley, Aylesbury by their respective Mayors. It is not always like that—I think an element of curiosity lay behind some of these invitations. They had heard about High Wycombe's black Mayor. They treat you with the utmost respect. These functions were normally linked to church services, with processions just as in Wycombe, the public lining the streets to watch. You did not see any dissent. No one was frowning at what they saw. They received you in a joyful way. So I saw that in all the surrounding regions, and not just in Wycombe, the office of Mayor is held in high regard.

Religious services and events attended officially as Mayor

*	Scouts Service
*	Women's World Day of Prayer
	Salvation Army Toy Service (at Salvation Army Citadel)
*	Mendelssohn Hymn of Praise (Choral)
*	RAF Freedom of High Wycombe Service
	Annual Convention at Church of God of Prophecy
*	Thanksgiving Service Godstowe School "UK's first and largest girls' preparatory boarding school"
*	Wycombe Abbey School Centenary Speech Day service (sermon by Lord Runcie, former Archbishop of Canterbury)
	Remembrance and thanksgiving service, Sue Ryder Hospice (at Nettlebed Parish Church)
	Mayors' Civic Service in Aylesbury
*	St Vincent and the Grenadines Association 17th Anniversary church service
	Carol Service at the Swan Theatre
	Town mayor's centenary civic service. Also attended by HM Lord Lieutenant for Buckinghamshire, Commander the Lord Cottesloe KstJ, JP, RN (Retd) (at All Saints Parish Church, Marlow)
	Chairman's Civic Service (at All Saints Parish Church, Marlow)
	A service of thanksgiving and blessing for the opening of Harleyford Golf Club (at the club)
*	Battle of Britain Sunday
	Licensing of team vicar (at Basilica of St Mary & St George, Sands, High Wycombe)
*	For all our babies and children
*	Mayor's Civic service
*	Remembrance Day service
	Salvation Army Christmas music (not sure of location)

Events marked with * were in High Wycombe's Parish Church of All Saints (Church of England)

In fact there is no one who carries out these functions quite in the way we do them in High Wycombe. It was my experience that when we went to places like Henley or Oxford, and the "Chain Gang" got together—that's how a group of Mayors is described[6]—we used to compare chains and ours was the proudest. Perhaps it was not the prettiest, but it was the most solid in the weight of its gold, and much admired.

Many other small market towns also have mayors. In the sixteenth century, Mayors were the main tax collectors for the central government. At a certain season, the monarch would drive through the town to take possession of the revenues which have been collected. The story has it that Queen Mary in about 1555 returned to Wycombe on one such mission and remarked on a phenomenon. She saw that Mayors were thin when they started the job but grew fatter as the years passed. She speculated that either they weren't working hard enough or they were eating too well at the town's expense.

Since then, the legend goes[7], each Mayor is ceremonially weighed in. And when your time reaches an end, you are ceremonially weighed out again. The townspeople gather in the market square by the Guildhall as they have done for centuries and if your weight has gone up they are ready to boo you out of office. All in good humour of course. In the year you are Mayor, you tend to watch your weight, as this private statistic becomes public property. We once had a visitor from the United States who was so impressed with our traditions he said he wanted to start a similar tradition in his home town. I don't know if it has been taken up or not, but apart from that, it's unique in the world.

A very close relationship has developed in the last few decades between our Mayoralty and the Royal Air Force[8]. We have given it the Freedom of the Town of High Wycombe. From time to time, the Mayors get invitations to the HQ at Naphill, and used to be invited to the base at Daws Hill[9], when there was a presence there. When a new Commanding Officer takes over at Naphill, they get an invitation to the Mayor's Parlour to be introduced to the Mayor and other councillors. It's a tradition that goes back. We have worked hand in hand with them. Every year, even though I am a former Mayor now, I still get an invitation there. They like to show how they work and to create links with the local civilian community. Before the Gulf War, I was privileged to be taken on a flight up to Scotland and the North Sea in one of their Jaguar[10] aircraft, to see how they refuel their planes. This was the RAF's way of keeping the local community informed.

For my inauguration, my brother sent me a congratulatory fax, which was read out at the Guildhall during the ceremony. It expressed the hope and the good wishes of the people of Jamaica.

This is what was read out:

```
                    C*O*N*G*R*A*T*U*L*A*T*I*O*N*S
Congratulations from Jamaica. We consider this to be a
historic and significant achievement in rising to the
rank of Mayor of High Wycombe. We share your joy.
    We are proud in knowing that a son of Jamaica will be
representing us as a worthy ambassador. The entire Jamaica,
and in particular the citizens of Bigwoods, Westmoreland
extend their sincere congratulations on this memorable
occasion.
    As you are called upon to serve in the position of
Mayor, we pray that you will serve not only from the
strength of your office but with humility.
    Your brother Dudley and his family regret that they
cannot be with you to share such an important event, but
our prayers as a family will always be with you.
    May God bestow upon you his grace, guidance and wisdom
as you perform your role as Mayor of High Wycombe.
From: DUDLEY GRAHAM AND FAMILY
```

Battle of Britain Sunday
Sunday 15th September 1996

Battle of Britain Sunday commemorates the great victory won by the Royal Air Force which saved Britain from invasion in 1940. As Sir Winston Churchill said, "The gratitude of every home in our island, in our Empire, and throughout the world except in the abodes of the guilty, goes out to the British Airmen who, undaunted by odds, unwearied in their constant challenge and mortal danger, turned the tide of the world war by their prowess and by their devotion. Never in the field of human conflict was so much owed by so many to so few."

From Order of Service

A CIVIC SERVICE TO COMMEMORATE THE GRANTING OF THE FREEDOM OF HIGH WYCOMBE IN 1971TO ROYAL AIR FORCE HIGH WYCOMBE

RESOLVED UNANIMOUSLY that in appreciation of the glorious traditions of the Royal air force, and in recognition of the long, friendly and close association with the Borough of High Wycombe, the council confer on the COMANDING OFFICER, OFFICEERS, AIRMEN AND AIRWOMEN OF ROYAL AIR FORCE HIGH WYCOMBE, the right, honour and privilege of marching through the streets of High Wycombe on all ceremonial occasions with swords drawn, bayonets fixed, bands playing and all colours flying: and that the Corporate Seal shall be fixed to an ornamental Scroll to commemorate the occasion."

THE CORPORATE SEAL of the Mayor Aldermen and Burgesses of the Borough of High Wycombe was hereunto affixed this ninth day of February 1971 in the presence of John Skipp, Mayor, N M Fowler, Town Clerk

From order of service

The Mayor and the Air Force

High Wycombe is the Headquarters of Strike Command, the "teeth of" the Royal Air Force. In today's England patriotic loyalty is not to be taken for granted. No one is criticised for opposing war. It is natural that the Air Force maintains close links with the local authority in a civic ceremony and invokes the Divine to remind itself of its purpose, to protect the people. The Battle of Britain is the best possible symbol of battle. The justice of the cause is unarguable. It was a battle that took place in the air, so everyone could watch. There were few if any civilian casualties. Many gallant young men on the British side sacrificed their lives against superior strength on the German side—and won. Had they not won, the Germans might have invaded. To a country which had not been successfully invaded for 874 years this was a victory worth celebrating annually. Where else but in Wycombe, the Headquarters of RAF Strike Command?

The figure of the robed and chain-bedecked Mayor as the elected ruler of the town, alongside the military men and women, symbolises the nature of our ancient land, the peaceful democracy that the armed forces exist to defend.

That these people should have chosen a Jamaican black man to be their symbol proclaims loudly, to those of all races, that this country stands for tolerance and opportunity and inclusiveness and brotherhood. These things are too easily taken for granted, but as this story shows, they should not be.

Having understood the above, that to the people of Britain there is occasion for sincere and God-directed thanksgiving for being saved from the hideousness of invasion by Hitler's Nazis, the other item on this page is still rather odd, unless you are accustomed to the traditional ways in which the military and the religious go hand in hand.

I have counted in Sebert's Mayoral year more than 20 special church services. But none could be so strange as this one: to have a church service to commemorate the right to march with swords drawn and bayonets fixed in the town's generally peaceful streets. I suppose that it symbolises the trust and affection which the civilian population place in the warlike garrison on their doorsteps: a trust which many countries might not easily understand.

It is hard for me to describe the very powerful emotion that came over me at that time, the feeling that fills you when one of your peers gives some testament to the services you have performed. You just receive it in humility.

So how did it happen? What was the mechanism of being voted in as Mayor?

Each year around February, they have to start deciding who will be the next Mayor, ready for the inauguration in May. Everyone is in there for the meeting, but you already know that you have been nominated.

OK, so how did the nomination happen?

It was at a meeting of our Labour Party group in the council. The leader, Ted Collins, stood up and said, "For this year, my party nominates Councillor Sebert Graham to be Mayor of High Wycombe." Then Claire Martin, the deputy leader, stood up and seconded the nomination. And there was a vote.

And you were at the meeting?

Yes, and it would also be discussed in a debate.

And you knew about it in advance?

Yes, normally they would come to you beforehand, to ask how you would feel about being nominated. So, there would be this discussion about it amongst the councillors. Most of them would have had something to say. That is the process.

In fact, it had happened before. It was in 1994 or 1995 that I was first proposed. But it didn't happen, because a more senior person had also been nominated. But usually, the nomination is unopposed.

It's not a matter of acrimonious debate.

No [laughs] this is one of those few events in politics that almost always run smoothly. And another point is the unwritten agreement that whilst you are Mayor, you don't use it for political advantage. You would certainly have the opportunity to do that as Mayor, because you get to see so much of what goes on, and you have a very public voice that would be listened to.

And you don't derive financial advantage from being Mayor?

No, there is no financial gain involved. You do get a subsistence allowance to help you through the expenses of the Mayoral year, but there is no money paid to you as a personal gift for doing anything. However as Mayor you nominate a charity of your choice and so you are the official recipient of donations from many quarters.

And this is carefully audited.

Oh yes. All the money goes via the Town Clerk, and there is a committee which scrutinises all the fund-raising arrangements: . collections, charity events and so on. Everything is properly accounted for and banked.

NOTES

1. *Journey so far:* this and the four following four chapters are the edited transcript of a lengthy conversation which took place on March 6th 2005.
2. *Mayoral visit to Micklefield Combined School on 6th May 97.* According to the Bucks Free Press, rumour went round the school that the Prime Minister was visiting, the children's political awareness having been doubtless awakened by the General Election a few days before, when Tony Blair succeeded John Major as Prime Minister.
3. *France:* the Mayor of a commune is directly elected by the people and is also a representative of the Central Government, hierarchically under the Prefect.
4. *Germany:* High Wycombe's twin town Kelkheim in Hesse is of this type. In some parts of Germany the role is different and apparently based on the English model.
5. *Church Service:* such an event, known as the Mayor's Sunday Parade and Service, takes place periodically in many towns across England and Wales.
6. *Chain gang:* it's true. My Dictionary of Phrase and Fable, ed. Nigel Rees, confirms that this is the collective noun for mayors.
7. *Reasons for weighing in the Mayor:* see also another explanation on page 7.
8. *Royal Air Force:* High Wycombe is home to Headquarters RAF Strike Command, self-styled 'teeth' of the Royal Air Force, and thus home to some of its most senior serving officers.
9. *Daws Hill:* this Air Force base used to be USAF headquarters in Britain, and is rumoured to have a nuclear bunker buried in the hill. It has now been sold for housing redevelopment.
10. *Jaguar aircraft:* the single-seat version is an attack and reconnaissance aircraft and the two-seat version is used as a trainer.

CHAPTER 11

The work of the local council

DO YOU HAVE TO DECLARE YOUR INTERESTS, LIKE MPS DO?
Directorships, consultancies, gifts received and so on?

Every councillor does. The members of the committee which oversees
the activities of the Mayor are called the Charter Trustees, and they make
sure everything is properly controlled. Not only this of course, the charity
nominated by the Mayor would have to be the one which gets popular support
from everyone, because many hundreds of people are involved both in giving
and voluntary activities. So there is nothing dodgy behind the scenes, it is
all very public and transparent. As a matter of fact you could say this about
what the council does in general. I am not saying that there might not have
been some kind of corrupt activities going on in the past, but these days
there is scrutiny from so many quarters, including audit, Government
auditors, risk assessments.

Not to mention the media.

[Laughs] Oh yes, there is no way that money can flow out of the Council
by fraudulent means.

I have already discussed with you the view that many people have
that politicians are untrustworthy and liars. It's not true. They are so
constrained by rules and guidelines and audits and checks and balances.
For example a councillor must leave the chamber when certain matters
are debated, in which the Councillor has an interest as previously
registered in Members' Interests. And it would be a serious offence to
have an interest and not register it.

*People may have an idea that Mayors get rich by money being passed
to them, let's say by property developers bidding for contracts. Were any
offers made to you?*

Well [laughs] no. But I think the people of High Wycombe understand
very well that our Mayoralty here is not at all like the institution of the same
name in Jamaica, Canada, US, France and so on. In those countries, it is an
executive role. Their mayors have the same kind of role as our Chief
Executive, Richard Cummins: my counterpart in Kelkheim[1] is an example
of this. However, when he comes on his official visit to Wycombe, he talks
to me as his civic counterpart. He might talk to Richard about some technical
aspects, for example trade or development: but then he would probably talk
with me about those things too.

*All right. Can we clarify the difference between Richard Cummins as
Chief Executive and you as Mayor?*

Richard Cummins is not an elected Councillor, he is a full-time salaried person. In central government he would be called a civil servant. But here he is known as a local government officer.

Who appointed him?

The council senior councillors would examine all the applications from candidates, as in any kind of normal job application.

OK now, supposing you are on the Development Committee, and I represent a firm of architects bidding for the new Western Sector Development. Could I approach you and say, "Mr Graham, I want to show you that our plan is the best. I have arranged a trip for you to fly business class to Italy, where we can show you the quality of a scheme we have done on the island of Capri"?

[Laughs] No, even the main planning officer for the District Council could not afford to accept any bribe like that. You have sixty councillors, some of whom will be on that planning committee. No matter what kind of cushy treatment anyone was offered, he would have to stand by while the plan was discussed and examined by everyone else on its merits. But he would have the dubious pleasure of seeing his name splashed across the headlines as recipient of those favours. That would be his only success!

So, let's get this straight. You are telling me that here in High Wycombe we have a system whereby corruption is impossible. Why can't we package this up and export it to other countries which need it so desperately?

[Laughs] Well, I did not quite use those words. We have transparency, guidelines and codes of practice. All I can say is that in ten years as a district councillor, I have not heard of any scandal in the terms we are talking about.

But going back to what you were asking before, it is certainly true that councillors are approached by members of the public to assist with their requests. Yes, it is a form of lobbying. But it would not be a big property developer. It is more likely someone who wants to get higher up in the waiting list for Council housing.

Let us suppose that there is a family living in two-bedroom accommodation, but they have four children. The councillor has every right to try and advance their claim for priority. Everyone on the waiting list has some kind of need and they are all different, so they are prioritised accordingly. There is a housing committee which is prepared to review the circumstances when they change, and a councillor is free to submit a case worthy of attention to the committee. A councillor might give advice to the householder, to get a doctor's letter for example, to support the case for rehousing.

So who rules? The Housing Committee [councillors] or Housing Department [officers]?

The Committee cannot overrule the Department, which consists of housing managers and highly trained people as well as clerks with less expertise. There is a very strict code of practice. Imagine everyone in a queue, each with their priority number. There are regular meetings to decide who is most deserving to take up council properties which become vacant: matching up the particular need—location, number of rooms and so on—to what becomes available.

Is it the Committee which determines the rules for allocation of housing, and the Department which executes those rules?

Yes, but this does not mean that the Councillors can just make up the rules to suit themselves. The Housing Committee would include representatives from the Housing Department. On the Councillors' side, there would be representatives from all the political parties. This ensures the rules would be balanced, fair and practical.

So you could only change somebody's priority on the Council's waiting list if the circumstances had changed in some way.

It's not a matter of exerting political influence or "muscle"?

That's right, it's not.

Now if a constituent comes to me as their councillor, it is my responsibility to investigate the truthfulness of what they are saying to me. The more honest they are, the better it is. Let's suppose they have overcrowding in their accommodation and their housing is in a badly run-down condition, perhaps with damp and mildew. This would have happened only because no one had reported anything earlier. Not everyone is very tidy and organised in that way. They let things get on top of them before they do anything about it. Or perhaps they have some problem, some disability that has made them feel less able to report things.

It is only when you go out visiting as a councillor, perhaps canvassing before an election, that you notice it, perhaps a damp patch or a crumbling wall. And then you would ask if they have reported it. Then they may make some excuse as to why they have not reported it. This is where the councillor has a responsibility. I would say to the householder, "Do you want me to take up your case?" And if they said "Yes," I would go to the officer responsible for housing in my ward, make my report and get him to come out and investigate my constituent's situation. I guarantee you that in those instances some action will be taken. There won't be any problem, because the Housing Department wants to keep its properties in good condition.

Or it could be that I visit the family and they have this problem of damp which is a health hazard and they say that yes, they have reported it, and they are waiting for something to be done. Maybe they did not keep pushing. They did not till now ask the councillor to help, and things are taking rather longer than they should. This is why you have councillors: to represent the people. That is why they are elected. The councillor can go direct to the officer concerned and seek for speedy action. Let's not forget, the councillors are the bosses of the paid staff, bosses of the local government officers.

The Mayor opens a bonfire night firework display in aid of charities nominated by Wycombe Round Table, including the Mayor's Appeal in aid of the elderly.

To be a councillor is a very full responsibility. People need to understand this. You shouldn't vote for someone just for their personality. They have to be fully aware of the regulations. They have to be someone who will make an effective representation on your behalf. For certain local matters, you go to your councillor, for other matters you can take your case to your Member of Parliament, and they may take it to the House of Commons. If you have problems relating to accommodation, the environment—for example rats running around in your area—take them to your Councillor.

And if you don't get satisfaction from your Councillor, I suppose you can go to the local Press. I vaguely recall some case where the Council acted very quickly after some bad housing conditions were published in the paper.

Well, I don't know about this in the ten years I was Councillor.

Maybe it was before your time.[2]

Well, the only case I can think of was with a private landlord who had a number of properties, all rather run down. When it discovers tenants living below an acceptable standard, the Council can do one of two things. It can either rehouse the tenants themselves or it can take out papers against the landlord in accordance with existing laws, asking for the accommodation to be renovated up to a proper living standard. If this is not done within a time limit, the Council would have power to close it down, preventing the landlord from letting the accommodation. More recently, Councils have been given powers for compulsory purchase of such properties so that they themselves can take them over, bring them to standard and add them to the Council housing stock. Left unimproved, such properties would become eyesores and even environmental risks.

If it was a local council property, then there would be no excuse. If it belonged to the County Council, the District Council would have very limited influence. And if it belonged to a private landlord, any compulsory interventions by the Council would be limited to the law of the land.

Well, it's my impression that things generally proceed very smoothly in local government in this country. I wonder what the trouble is in some other countries?[3]

Well, I can't speak much about other countries, but in the United Kingdom I think in recent years we have moved forward as well, in our own housing development.

Do you remember Rachman?[4]

I remember Rachman very well. It was in the early Sixties—

—when you were just recently arrived—

That's right. People like him were making a lot of money out of the discomfort of others and exploited a situation. Nowadays it is not likely to happen at least on any scale, as there is so much legislation to protect tenants, much of it in consequence of his notoriety at that time. But I think in other countries too the standard of housing is better than it was in the Fifties and early Sixties. Standards of living have increased globally.

You will have heard that there is now pressure to build more houses, in High Wycombe, Milton Keynes and Aylesbury[5]. And in fact there is pressure to increase the housing stock across the whole country. People want to move from London to the countryside, and the South East remains the most popular place to live. In 1970 it was hard to persuade people to move out of London. But now people are much more willing to move out, to the Midlands and elsewhere. Some have made their money, perhaps by capitalising on the high London prices. And now the road links are much better.

In your time as a councillor, what committees were you on?

Quite a few, including Environmental, Planning, Housing, and Transport, the latter in liaison with the County Council[6]. I was for example involved in the planning of changes to Daws Hill Lane, as it was in my constituency. I argued that before we started to build on the Abbey Barn housing development, we would need to get the infrastructure to be able to cope with the additional traffic. And I also would also argue that the houses built close to the motorway would need soundproofing for the comfort of the occupants. Those are the kinds of things I would be insisting upon, if I were still a councillor.

One thing I was involved with was to do with roads: on Bowerdean Road, where they have wide grass verges, they have made parking spaces, properly paved, so the cars can be kept off the road without churning up the grass verges into mud. This was at my suggestion. They ran out of money before they could do it completely.

Instead of the things they use now for traffic calming such as chicanes and bumps, which are nothing but a nuisance, what they need to do is to narrow the road every now and then.

And then you could allocate more on-street parking.

Yes, that is a better situation. But they just wouldn't listen. One of the other improvements that I did in Bowerdean Road, as well as the off-street parking, was to get a roundabout installed, to slow the traffic down and give people a chance to cross. And then, when I was living near the top of Arnison Road, I made a representation to have traffic lights put in at the junction with Amersham Hill Road. Since they installed them the traffic has flowed properly.

At one time the County Council wanted to put traffic lights on the Magic Roundabout[7]. I objected several times to such an horrendous plan, arguing that traffic circulation there is already optimal. The way it is built, it gives you choices. You can go either left or right to get anywhere you want, whichever is the clearest at the time.

And that's why it is never really jammed up. If there's a breakdown at one part, everyone can go the other way to avoid it.

Exactly. Well, if they got rid of the flyover as a part of the Western Sector development, then I might have to change my mind, because I have no idea what might be affected then, but the way things are working now, there is nothing better or more suitable.

I can't see why they would have wanted to change it anyway.

It's just that it gets congested at certain times of day. The rest of the time it's fine. If I was involved as a councillor now, I would want to discuss it with the police to get their view, and find out how many accidents they have there. As a traffic system it works surprisingly well.

I found the Environmental Committee a very useful one to be on. We have changed the system of dumping at the High Heavens[8] site. It has been improved immensely. There are segregated containers so that when you dump your household waste you must put bottles here, paper there, green waste here, timber there: everything separate to maximise the opportunities for recycling without employing an army to do it. When they introduced the wheelie bins[9], I think that was an excellent idea. And now you can purchase from the Council some special green bins into which you can put organic waste so that it turns into compost for your garden. And there is also a fortnightly paper collection for which they have given each household a special container. And in many parts of town you can dispose of bottles and other items for recycling.

Environment also includes the air we breathe and the cleanliness of the streets. These days the Council regularly keeps the streets clean with mechanical sweepers and washers. They measure the pollution coming out of the bus exhausts, going up Amersham and Marlow Hills.

Our town of Wycombe used to be a small market town, with a river running through the middle. But then in 1960 they built the Octagon[10] and the Bus Station, and built over the river. It was a shame.

Now they have done work to preserve the remains of the St John the Baptist Hospital[11] on the London Road. It's a listed Ancient Monument[12]. It is part of our heritage. So, even though there are new developments to keep the town vibrant and modern, there is concern for the ancient and archaeological. For example, the High Street was pedestrianised some years ago. The building which houses Woolworth's is not very old. But the historic statue of the lion[13] has been preserved. These all come under the Environment Committee. The Council has a high regard for the quality of where we live.

Yes, I remember how the town used to look on a Sunday morning, after the Saturday night revellers had left all their litter and remains of take-away food thrown down anywhere. It was disgusting. But now that it's clean, people respect it and want to keep it that way.

Yes, it's true. People follow a lead, either to be clean and tidy, or the opposite. And now you can be fined for dropping litter in the street. Council officials should report people they catch doing it. Even members of the public should report them. It's expensive to keep cleaning it, for example if it has just been cleaned on a Friday night after the Market has packed up, it's a shame if people make another mess later on the same Friday night, which means that the cleaners have to be hired for another shift early on Saturday morning. And then everyone complains about the high cost of the Council Tax: "Why is it going up?" These are some of the reasons. People deliberately deface buildings with graffiti. It is very expensive to clean them off. Then there are those fly-posters, sticking things up on shop-windows. We are the community, we make the community the way it is.

NOTES

1. *Kelkheim:* High Wycombe's twin town in Germany.
2. *Sebert's time as Councillor:* 1989 – 1999. I (Ian) arrived in Wycombe in 1988.
3. *Local government problems in other countries:* I was subconsciously recalling a particular dispute between the Municipality of Kingston in Jamaica and its refuse collection team. Some of the team had been made redundant. The next day a mysterious fire broke out at the waste disposal depot, burning acres of garbage and sending up plumes of black smoke to choke the neighbourhood. The redundancies were reversed and the fires put out, with neither side acknowledging that the matter had been "negotiated" in a rather characteristic way.
4. *Peter Rachman* became known as Britain's most notorious landlord. He acquired many slum properties in London suburbs particularly Notting Hill. He used to acquire squalid buildings with sitting tenants. He would use violence to evict them so as to make room for immigrant families from the West Indies who, without anywhere else to go because of a widespread colour bar, were crammed into tiny flats at rents which he would set extortionately high.
5. *Milton Keynes, Aylesbury and High Wycombe:* the three biggest towns in Buckinghamshire.
6. *County Councils* are responsible for maintenance of roads, traffic lights and parking controls.
7. *Magic Roundabout:* named after a children's TV programme, this is the nickname for a system of five roundabouts surrounding a central area of grass and trees, near Wycombe's town centre.
8. *High Heavens:* Wycombe's public site for waste disposal. The name evokes the well-known expression "stinks to high heavens", but the site doesn't smell bad at all.
9. *Wheelie bins:* tall bins in heavy plastic provided free by the Council for general refuse. The garbage

trucks have hydraulic devices to lift and upend these bins for emptying, so the workers need only roll them to and from the truck.

10. *Octagon:* a shopping mall in Wycombe town centre.
11. *St John the Baptist Hospital:* these remains, dating from 1180AD are with the All Saints Parish Church, the oldest surviving buildings in Wycombe.
12. *Ancient Monuments:* there are another 21 listed monuments in the Wycombe district. See http:// www.wycombe.gov.uk/planning/conservation/pdfs/archaeology.pdf
13. *Statue of lion:* Benjamin Disraeli and Winston Churchill both delivered political speeches from the platform on which this lion stands, when it was part of the Red Lion Hotel.

CHAPTER 12

The Labour Party and me

IT IS SUCH HARD WORK BEING A COUNCILLOR. SUPPOSE AN election is coming up, and that I have been nominated for Bowerdean Ward, as indeed I was. That consists of 2,500 houses. I have got to go and talk to those people, at least deliver to every household a leaflet showing official Labour Party policies and also my election address. So I will come knocking on your door: "Good morning sir. I am your candidate for the forthcoming election—"

I am imagining you doing this the very first time you stood as a candidate, in 1988.

Right, sure. "—and I hope you will be voting for me when the time comes." So he says with a big smile, "Oh yes, I'll vote for you, I've always voted Labour." That's a good start! It's also a pleasant start, because I have encountered one of my own. But then I go to a few more houses and someone says, "Sorry! I haven't got the time. I don't want to know." You start to feel there is indifference and there is opposition, as well as support. What do you do now? You keep on going, that's what you do. You don't weaken. You persevere. You keep knocking on doors, introducing yourself, handing out your leaflet, meeting some who do and some who don't like the look of your face. And then you go to a house where somebody comes out and says, "Well, why should I vote for you? Give me a reason." So when this happens I am under pressure. I have got so many houses to visit, but then I feel obliged to answer his question, explain why I am the best person, without wasting too much time. And you will get some that will try to derail you because they are Conservative voters: they just want to debate with you to waste your time. Time is of the essence. So, trying to keep it brief, I will say to him, "Tell me, what is your main concern?" So perhaps he will say it is the Poll Tax[1]. So I will tell him how dangerous and unfair the Poll Tax will be for his household budget.

So let's move forward to the time just before the election. I am canvassing and I call on you. I am going to be the patient listener. I will be learning from you what you want us to do. It might be that you have some complaints. Or you might be a supporter who wants to help. If I am convinced of this then I might ask you to do some work for me. I'll ask you to come out with me and help drop leaflets, and introduce me to your friends that don't really know me as yet. Most of these active helpers would be members of the Labour Party. Or perhaps they have become disillusioned with their previous party and they want to cross over to me. The campaign might go on for two or three weeks.

The day of the election, it is absolutely vital that in the morning you have a sufficient number of helpers to remind people it's election day, and in the evening, if they haven't voted yet, to ask them "Please vote now". Finally check the lists at the Polling Station to see who has not yet voted and go to see them—those who have promised you their vote—and if they have a problem to get there, make sure you have drivers who can offer them a lift, there and back.

On election night, I might have some spare tickets to enable you to come with me to the Town Hall while they finish counting the votes. So you would come and give me moral support. And then at the end of the night, we might all be jubilant, or at least relieved, to have our hard work rewarded with a win. After all the hard work, that gives a really good feeling.

And how do you repay your constituents for having put their faith in you? You have to be consistent in representing their interests in Council, keeping in touch with them so that they can tell you their problems.

For when you are on the campaign trail, they sometimes say, "That's the trouble with you people. We don't see you for three years, except for now, and that is only because it is election time". I want them to understand how difficult it is. Your councillor, unlike your MP, is doing all this work as a volunteer. He is unpaid, so he has to have a full-time job. He looks after a ward of 2,500 households, but he has a family of his own too. So in the three years between elections, the councillor does not have time to visit all those houses. But what I have done is to deliver newsletters, especially to my more active supporters. I also give them my address. Every Saturday morning, at least for the first five years, I would hold a surgery, where my constituents were invited to come to Townfield House[2] between 10 and 12 o'clock. It worked. After that, we distributed a questionnaire, to ask people what they wanted. Ninety percent wanted to stay informed. We could only do that by delivering newsletters, and that costs money. So I tried to increase Labour Party membership. And during my Chairmanship of the local branch of the Party my ward became the most strongly represented. This extra membership brought a flow of funds into the Party. To make it interesting, when we used to have evening meetings of the membership, I would invite them to come up with a question: not just something about Branch affairs, but some political concern for discussion, so that we might end up with some recommendations for the Executive Committee (EC) or the General Management Committee (GMC)[3]. And sometimes we would end the meeting with a raffle, to raise revenue and add a bit of interest.

Would the Labour Party still have meetings for a certain ward if it did not have a Labour councillor at the time?

They would. Since they could not pass their views forward to a councillor of their own, they would pass them to the GMC or the EC.

So this was the local scene. Why don't we look at how they put up a

Parliamentary candidate? That is where the EC and the GMC really come into their own. They have to organise interviews to meet the candidates.

Would Parliamentary candidates be selected from amongst experienced councillors?

No, not necessarily. They could be selected from anywhere in the country. It would be the regional office in Reading which would make the selection in conjunction with the GMC of the constituency Labour Party.

And what about the National Executive? Don't they sometimes insist on certain quotas of women or ethnic minority candidates?

Oh yes. At the beginning of the selection process, there must be at three women at least in the list. From there on, of course, they are selected on perceived merit. This has at times brought us into difficulties, as I am not sure that it has always resulted in the best candidates being selected. There is no quota for ethnic minority candidates, but they are very strongly encouraged to apply. Overall it is democratic, but sometimes not all the selected candidates show up on the night. Then you have to take the best of those who do turn up, and therefore you might not end up with the candidate you had hoped for.

So how would you propose it is done better?

I would select the candidate based on their performance on the night: those who turn up and those who show themselves to the best advantage.

If there is a quota of a certain number of women and then they choose not to turn up on the night, I would not think you should stop the process until they do come along. In fact I would not have those quotas at all. Everyone is free to join the Party. It is not as if there are exclusions on any grounds. Selection should be based on the merits of those who turn up to make their presentations.

And I suppose that whether it is a Council or Parliamentary election, if you are a beginner, they will try you out with a seat which is not easily winnable.

Exactly so. It would not be fair to put a new person, no matter how brilliant they might be, in a winnable seat, because they might not in fact win. So it means that you have to keep your strongest candidates for your existing seats—the ones that you already hold.

You represented the ward that you were living in, weren't you?

Yes I was and that made it easier, whether they knew me already or not. The very fact that they know you are local is a plus point. The ones who know you might decide that they like you and what you are talking about.

But the first time you stood as a councillor you did not win.

That's true. There was already a Labour councillor holding the seat in my ward, so I contested Keep Hill and Hicks Farm Ward. Nobody knew me in that ward. But in fact I ran quite close to the winner[4]. It coincided with a difficult time in the Labour Party, when the Left was threatening to tear the party apart. After Neil Kinnock and then John Smith came on the scene, the party began to gain ground again.

Before that it was Michael Foot as Labour leader?

Yes. I mean him no disrespect, he was a great guy, but not leadership material. This was the short-sightedness of the Left of the party. When I consider some of their behaviour in those years, I can't think they really wanted to be in Government. It made life very difficult. You would be on someone's doorstep and—how polite the British are! They don't want to vote for you and they don't want to see the Labour Party on their doorstep. They might be watching a soap opera such as *East Enders* or *Coronation Street* when you called, so they'd say, "Hello! Oh yes, I have always voted for the Labour Party." A downright lie. But they are too polite to say "Clear off!" [much laughter]

People are quite comfortable with the government we have now. The Labour government has been quite successful with the economy and with its overall management of the country. In general people are pretty much satisfied. The difficulty we have with support for Labour now, as reflected in the last local elections, is the situation in Iraq. Before that, the biggest issue was the National Health Service. People could see that a lot of money had gone in. it was not quite so easy for them to discern that actually the Health Service is also working better than before.

I would like to comment on what I see happening with the NHS in Buckinghamshire. My perception is that they are wasting government money on paying exorbitant salaries to "high-flying" managers, leaving us top-heavy whilst skimping on basic vital tasks like keeping the hospitals clean. There is even talk about reinstating the old-fashioned matrons who ruled strictly like sergeant-majors and insisted on inspecting for discipline and cleanliness. It's not Central Government who are to blame. It is the managers within the Trust[5] who need to be harried and if necessary kicked out. In some instances I am convinced they are pursuing a party-political agenda, I am convinced of that. Instead of spending money directly on doctors and nurses, they spend it on business consultants and managers who keep changing structures and manipulating the paperwork. I think it would be better if the Government put the onus on Trusts to manage their own affairs. They should submit their overall budgets to Central Government, and after approval the money would be handed over to the Trust. The Trust's performance should not be blamed on the Government but be judged by the local community. If managers fail then they should be kicked out. They should be accountable for whether they have carried out the Government's directives.

Do you think that the problem is the targets set by Government[6]?

No, from what I understand, and from what the doctors themselves have been saying, the targets are not the problem. Let me give you an example from my own experience when I was working at Norvik making electric blankets. When they introduced a bonus system the daily output of blankets increased from 10 to 20 per person. So in the hospitals by measuring performance they can increase their reputation and the money the hospital receives. I am assuming they take a pride in the quality of their work and would not compromise it, and that they would like their hospital to be top-ranking. I think the reasons for their targets not being met is political. Some of the managers and consultants are Tory party supporters who want the Labour Government to fail. Targets help motivate the hospital staff.

But surely there is a difference here. Factory workers may need an incentive. I would have thought doctors and nurses would already be self-motivated and dedicated.

Well yes, indeed they are dedicated. That is precisely the point. The extra money being allocated to the Health Service needs to be allocated to additional doctors and nurses rather than extra management and paperwork. If they are Conservative supporters they are reluctant to agree that things are running well. They want to blame the present Government. Especially as we are now in an election campaign.

But the hospital managers should be answerable.

What I am not clear on is who evaluates whether they have succeeded or failed. If this is done at a local level, then how is it measured? Won't it mean even more bureaucracy?

It is like this. The Government is pouring money into the Health Service in order to achieve its objectives, of reducing waiting lists, increasing cleanliness and so on. But what I see is that the Trust, which has a lot of Conservatives in it, uses the money to employ more managers—

I understand that. But just now you kept saying "should". That implies that you see the need for change. Is there a mechanism already which allows you to sack them?[7]

I don't think there is.

So you are asking for something to change.

Yes, central government should cut out the middle tiers. What I want central government to do is to ask the managers of the NHS trust in the hospitals, "What number of staff do you need to attain the four-star status?" They should know what staff they need to run a successful hospital, and what equipment. Then the Government grant them the money. They have the right to expect certain results in exchange for the money.

But I think you may be asking for an extra layer of management at the Trust so as to measure the results! In fact there would need to be more managers in the government as well, to evaluate the answers given by the managers in the hospital. You are creating a new bureaucracy.

Not necessarily at all. It can be done with interviews. These things come out through searching dialogues. The whole point of the Trusts, in fact is a mechanism to deliver the required results. The tools have been already given. There can be no excuse when a failure occurs, and the failure will be readily apparent.

OK, then let me just ask one final question. Who should have the job of firing the manager? Should it be done locally or by central government?[8]

****

When I was first elected as a councillor, I used to hear the complaints of my constituents under the government of Margaret Thatcher—about the Poll Tax, for example. Or maybe they would have a young man in the family who wondered if he would ever get a job at all.

And then in those days they were denying the concept of community. It was everyone for themselves. That concept of selfishness was really fostered in the Thatcher years.

She said, "There is no such thing as society."[9]

That was the kind of one-sided selfishness that was current in those days. How can you run a country when you don't care for one another?

So today, if there was no Iraq War to complain about, I am wondering what people would find to criticise about our present Labour Government. Relatively speaking, this country is at ease with itself right now.

It seems that way to me too.

Everyone is in employment who wants to be. People are not much worried about education. It has sorted itself out. The Labour Party in two terms has been clearing up the legacy of the Conservatives over the last seventeen years. This is something that takes time. As a Labour supporter, I am not saying that I agree with 100 percent of what they do. Let me put it that the 75 percent which I agree with is in the absolute best interests of the people in this country. Sometimes as a motorist I feel upset at their transport policies. I feel that they have been squeezing the motorists. But I have to be realistic. This is a small country. Traffic management is a big issue. I know there are too many cars on the road. It hurts me that I can't go to London and park where I want. I'm sure these exclusion zones will be extended more and more[10]. The Government could use a different method to force cars off the road, by subsidising and prioritising public transport. Transport has been deregulated, but in a way it needs to be re-regulated, so that people can be guaranteed a comfortable and reliable journey.

Another thing I am not happy with is their immigration policies. Why couldn't Labour have foreseen the way that the Conservatives are exploiting this at the present moment? Even Jim Callaghan at one point, I believe, admitted he could have done more with the immigration laws. With such a history they should have been meticulous in redrafting the laws. We are not a big country. We have taken on more immigrants than most European countries. All the countries in the European Union should share in the responsibilities for upholding human rights—I mean in relation to refugees. There is bad feeling in this country about immigration.

Which is caused by what?

Well, in this country we are very liberal-minded, very humanitarian. We do not want to turn away those who are fleeing from brutal regimes or persecution. But others come for economic purposes and this is where the government should take a firmer line. We should stop providing benefits to those people. It alienates the people who are here legally. It causes bad feeling amongst those who were born here and will do no good for race relations. That is one point, to tighten controls on illegal immigration.

My other point is specifically in relation to those who come from other European countries. As things stand they have the right to come and go freely, but my contention is that we need to take action, regardless of where Brussels[11] stands on this. There are still certain people with Fascist leanings in parts of Europe and we need to ensure that our good community relations are not jeopardised. I believe that everyone coming to the country should be required to agree to all the Race Relations Acts that have been established here. Anyone breaking those rules would be deported.

But why? What is the perceived risk? Why should we go to the trouble of making such a law?

It's a known fact. We have seen racist behaviour in Germany, and more recently in a football ground in Spain, where black players from the United Kingdom were verbally abused.

So other countries have Nationalists who would be against the values that after many years of effort we have established successfully in this country?

Exactly.

Yes, but if they are Nationalists, why would they want to come to this country? You can only have nationalist feelings about your own country.

[Laughs] Yes the French Nationalists, like those under Le Pen, might want to stay in their country, but they might have an interest in supporting the British National Party over here, and acting against black people in Europe. We have this great asset now that is worth preserving, of a highly integrated society. But those countries might fear the free flow of different ethnic groups from this country to theirs.

But blacks are in most countries in Europe. If they only wanted to see white faces, I am not sure where they would go these days. Whilst you could get those who apply for British citizenship to sign an anti-racism agreement, you could not do that with EU citizens.

Right, and this is why I want people not to fear the introduction of ID cards, which would at any rate allow us to track where people have come from. And we would not allow these racists to enter the country.

But if someone has not committed a crime, what can you do?

Well, it could be embedded on their ID cards, then we could keep an eye on them.

Border controls and immigration policy should be decided by the Westminster government. It is our own internal problem. Since we are surrounded by sea, we are in a different position to the rest of Europe. We should have the last say on who enters these islands. We should have pressured the EU to keep such a concession. I say this even though I am a paid-up member of the Labour Party. One day I hope we will have a leader with the strength to tackle this point.

Though I have areas of dissatisfaction, I am sure that none of us is feeling a hurt from the Government's policies. It is just that we feel that they could do more, which is likely to cost money, so are we prepared to go that far? For instance to saturate the roads with public transport, so that people hardly need to use their cars. If they could reliably reach their destinations in a shorter time than by car, there would be no problem. One day a government will have to subsidise public transport to an adequate degree. Otherwise we will be just tinkering at the edges of transport policy.

What should a voter do in the forthcoming election, if they are strongly opposed to our intervention in Iraq supporting the Americans? Should they support the Liberal Democrats?

The Lib Dems will not form a government so it is a wasted vote. It would be best to vote Labour. The Conservatives were strongly in favour of fighting the war in Iraq. If they had been in power, the rush to war would have been even quicker. Iain Duncan-Smith, if you remember, was strongly in favour of the war. It was Tony Blair who insisted on holding back as long as possible to get UN approval. People had reason to trust Labour more than the Conservatives on this issue. The Government went along with President Bush because of information received. We don't know the accuracy of the information given by the Security Services to Tony Blair, but it was all he had to go on. We may have to wait 30 years[12] before finding out to what extent the Security Services may have blundered, if any.

Isn't it the case that many Labour MPs were extremely disappointed with Blair's unconditional support for Bush, who went so far as to ignore the United Nations in the end, in pursuing his war?

Well, I wouldn't say he was a "poodle" of the Americans in the way that you are suggesting. I met Tony Blair before he was Prime Minister and I think he is the strongest and most visionary politician that I have met. If you are a strong believer in something, it is hard to walk away and do nothing.

OK, I'll accept that, but if our leader is a strong believer in his own cause, it works against democracy. This worries the British people.

Yes, but the elected government is responsible for our security. I hope we will recognise that Tony Blair would not have committed our forces knowing that there was no real evidence for weapons of mass destruction threatening our security in Iraq. I cannot believe he would have risked military lives for that unless there was a perceived threat. I do not believe he would have deliberately misled the British people on that.

And now there is a hot debate about the threat posed by terrorist suspects. A court has said they cannot be jailed without trial, so the Government wants to hold them under house arrest. It is perfectly credible to me that there are people out there who want a terrible revenge on this country.

Exactly. And that is why we are so distressed to have our Government support Bush against our wishes, making us more at risk from terrorist attack than we would otherwise have been. America's fight post 9/11 was theirs and not ours.

I agree with you partially, but for 50 years the United States, Britain and Europe have been allies. During this time we have seen the dismantling of the Soviet Union, and the Berlin Wall. The NATO alliance was for our own protection from threats. And I do not accept that our open support for the Americans has put us under a greater threat than other European countries. We Britons travel world-wide, we are major world travellers. I have not heard of us being under major threat anywhere. Now they are saying there are a certain number of terrorists in our midst, waiting to strike. Whether it is 200 or only 30 is not the issue, because even 30 would be too many. I feel very strongly about this country. I don't want us to be under siege any more than you do. You and I both have children. If we know there are cells of terrorists, we need to give authority to the police to take them off the streets and we need legislation to make it possible. It has to be done regardless of Parliament's objections[13]. This is why sometimes there are dictatorships, because people get impatient with discussions.

It's known that those terrorists are here. And this also gives responsibility to the media. A certain amount of free speech needs to be curtailed for security reasons. The media publish too much information that could be useful to an enemy, for example the movements of the Queen or members of the Government, or police plans. I have sympathy for the families of those who have been arrested without trial, and also with those people themselves, if they happen to be innocent. I don't want these terrorists putting at risk the way of life of the country. That is why the Government should act.

NOTES

1. *Poll tax:* the local tax, properly known as the Community Charge, which replaced the old Rating system and was in turn replaced by the current Council Tax.
2. *Townfield House:* Labour Party headquarters in High Wycombe.
3. *General Management Committee:* of the Wycombe Parliamentary Constituency Labour Party.
4. Results of election: Beale, Dolores Jean (Con) 690; Graham, Sebert Headley (Lab) 651; Rundle, Reginald Thomas (SLD) 237. Source: Bucks Free Press 12/5/89.
5. *Trust:* Sebert refers to the South Bucks Hospitals Trust. The NHS is now divided into a collection of regional trusts for the management of hospitals and general practices.

6. *NHS targets:* for example, how long a patient has to wait for an operation, measured in months.
7. *Questioning the use of "should":* I felt like a journalist interviewing a politician. It must have been something in the air. The General Election was imminent, and everyone was doing it!.
8. *Who should fire the failed hospital managers:* Like any expert politician, Sebert gave an answer which did not match the question. We moved on to a different topic.
9. *No such thing as society:* "I think we've been through a period where too many people have been given to understand that if they have a problem, it's the government's job to cope with it. 'I have a problem, I'll get a grant.' 'I'm homeless, the government must house me.' They're casting their problem on society. And, you know, there is no such thing as society. There are individual men and women, and there are families. And no government can do anything except through people, and people must look to themselves first. It's our duty to look after ourselves and then, also to look after our neighbour. People have got the entitlements too much in mind, without the obligations. There's no such thing as entitlement, unless someone has first met an obligation." Prime Minister Margaret Thatcher, talking to *Woman's Own* magazine, October 3, 1987.
10. *London exclusion zones:* part of the Congestion Charge scheme whereby in a certain zone motorists must pay a daily charge to enter it. Based on a high-tech system of cameras which capture the number plates of vehicles and enter them into a computer. Motorists who have not paid the charge or are not exempt are traced and fined.
11. *Brussels:* i.e. EU laws. These laws, designed mainly with land boundaries in continental Europe in mind, permit freedom of movement between citizens of member states. As an island, Britain has always seen things a little differently.
12. *30-year rule:* in general, Cabinet papers are released to the public archive after 30 years.
13. *Parliament's objections to new laws for suspected terrorists:* the big debating issue of the day in early March 2005 was the Bill authorising house arrest for suspected terrorists who could not be brought to trial for lack of sufficient evidence. The issue was a constitutional one as the new law clashed with the rights enshrined in Magna Carta of 1215 and more specifically the Habeas Corpus Act of 1679.

CHAPTER 13

Interlude[1]

HOW ARE WE DOING WITH THIS? I MEAN, SHOULD WE INCLUDE this sort of discussion, or edit it out?
Well, it is quite detailed, Ian—
Is it off the agenda, or what?
Well, as I said before, if I had gone to University and got a Bachelor's degree in Political Science, or had gone into politics at a higher level, it would have suited me. Or perhaps I might have been a lawyer.
Well, I think politics is right for you. For each of the crazy questions I have thrown at you, you have given me a good answer. I don't always share the same views, but in your answers you have always attended to where I was coming from and sometimes you have persuaded me to think differently.
Well, I watch television and—have you noticed?—I see that Tony Blair does not often get trapped in arguments. He doesn't give contradictory answers and that is the hallmark of a good politician. If you are successful, there will be always those who are curious about you and try to denigrate you and bring you down. When he first came on the scene they portrayed him as a prancing Bambi! But then the newspapers realised he was smart and they couldn't pin him down as some simple caricature. I have made a couple of trips to America and I listened to my black counterparts there and also to white Americans. They think he is wonderful. I don't want to sound too boastful about Britain, but for its size it still commands great respect around the world. People listen because they know that there is a clarity and a fairness in what people say here. It is because he is strong with a mind of his own that people criticise Blair. I think he leads Bush in certain respects, and has prevented the war from being worse. America has listened to some of his arguments.
You certainly give a persuasive case for Tony Blair.
We have to show more appreciativeness to the people around us. It's not only him. There is a body of people around Tony Blair. If he is guilty, every one of them is guilty as well. A Cabinet decision is binding on everyone in the Cabinet. And if it is too much for someone to bear—like Robin Cook[2]— then what he did was the decent thing.
Yes, I respect Robin very much for what he did.
Yes, I respect him for that too, but you don't hear of much dissension in Cabinet, and these days if there were any, you would hear of them through leaks.
But people might say that the other cabinet members are poodles and have to agree with Tony Blair.

But that can't be true. Each one of us has a mind of his own. They are elected by us. They are not just going to suck up to their leader. Even if they feel they must support a decision which they don't like, they have a very strong discussion first. Every one of them knows where the other stands. There might be a few who say, to preserve unity in the Government, "You know I am not really for this, I don't really like it, but better the Labour Government we have now than anything else which is on offer to the British people." So you come up with a consensus with perhaps 3 or 4 dissenting, but the majority are in favour.

[pause]

I think you should be in the House of Lords! You've missed your opportunity in the Commons.

[Laughs] I have no ambitions for that. What I do now is pleasurable enough. [Still laughing]

But would you be happy to go into the House of Lords, if it were offered?

Well, without a doubt, in those places of such magnitude and influence, I would have good fun there, and in any case some of those people there are much older than I am. My background has given me a greater insight than some of them have ever seen or thought of. Undoubtedly. The Lords is another thing that Tony Blair was going to reinvent. Maybe it has not gone the way it should[3]. It's foolish if they are only there because their father was a Lord before them, or they are only there because of their money. I think we need a mix of people, like we have with the jury system. We need to include people from the streets, shall we say, who were not born with silver spoons in their mouths. They have the knowledge of their own country and the feel of it, and the spirit of its people. They are not just the champagne drinkers but the lager drinkers and possibly the rough whisky drinkers too. Their experience is so wide because they have come from all strands. Take Robert Carr[4] who had been Minister of Employment at one time. He had been a shop floor worker, with a very humble background. His background made him good at his job—most of the decisions he made were right.

But so had Margaret Thatcher, hadn't she? Daughter of an ordinary shopkeeper.

Not so ordinary, I think you will find.

I thought it was a grocer's shop. Perhaps this was propaganda, to emphasise her humble origins?

[Laughs] OK, she was born above the shop. But there is a difference. Her parents had become prosperous. Her father had become respectable, was able to send his daughter to University. You see there is an advantage in politics in persuading the voters you are no higher than them, that you are at the same level.

I have found myself almost changing my political views, listening to you[5].

[Laughs] That's good, Ian, I hope all the others out there will feel the same, they'll read this and they will feel that these two guys—you and I—have done a good job. Every time we talk and then after you go away, I see more things. And as we go along, I understand you more clearly, and you are understanding me better. I think it is the same as we go through life. We can only express our true feeling, be ourselves. When you ask me a question, it's because there is a reason. You feel something strongly about it, you experience something which you want to put to me, and see what my reactions are going to be. As we share these visions and views, it becomes more interesting. So as it becomes interesting to you and to me, our readers also will find it interesting. That's because we have all shared in these experiences, whether in this community or in the wider world. Something of these experiences will have come across. And they may say it is true, or it is rubbish. But all of us will find some kind of a satisfaction because we have had a taste of it.

What I find so interesting about your experience is that you have come from somewhere entirely different and what you brought to the role of Mayor was a kind of spotlight. It had been going on for seven hundred years and yet had attracted little remark. It seems so unusual you taking on this role that it makes the traditions worth looking at. It seems to me that you bring fresh eyes to bear on age-old issues that have existed in this country. I feel that you speak with sincerity and, though you have defended politicians generally from my scepticism, I find you more ready to speak unrehearsed and from the heart[6].

Yes, there are several parts to your question there, it is wide. Firstly, I am open to any of your questions and happy to take them unprepared. Even as a councillor, I very seldom prepared my notes. If you are over-prepared, you still cannot know what your audience's questions are going to be. Because I am always ready to listen, I can address the actual situation that comes up.

My Mayoralty perhaps altered the institution a little. The phrase I would use was "Mayor of the people"—and "for the people" as well. I was one of the first to open up the office—known as the Mayor's Parlour—so that any of the public, and not just visiting dignitaries, could actually come in and see what the regalia looks like: the hat and the gown and the chain of office. There are two sets of robes. Some people would want to know the value of the Mayoral chain. It is made of gold, but its value was never disclosed, partly because I had no idea of the answer. But at least they were allowed to see it and touch it. A woman once said to me, "I have always paid my Council Tax, but no one has ever invited me upstairs, to see the Council Chamber." This is the place where the decisions are made as to how that Council Tax is actually spent. Normally the public is not invited there, unless for example there is a hearing about a planning application, where the public are invited to make their representations.

But there is a Visitors' Gallery? They are not excluded from ordinary debates, surely?

That's right, they could come but usually they don't. I invited the general public who had never seen it before, so they could come away with a new perspective on how things are dealt with. So yes, the Mayoralty has opened up and it gives an opportunity for more people to see my openness. If I had not been Mayor, I would not have been invited in some of the social functions and people's homes that I have been to. I am very humbled by that.

So? What is the point you are making here?

For instance, I have heard about Air Vice Marshals and—well, I will not mention names here. By virtue of being Mayor, I was privileged to meet the Air Vice Marshal at Naphill, and I was introduced to several senior officers from Europe. They were senior officers in Nato from France, Belgium and so on. If I had not been Mayor, there is no way that I would have mixed in such society. As I shook the Air Vice Marshal's hand, I said, "I have read about an Air Vice Marshal, I have seen one in photographs, but until now I have never met one!" I tell you, he laughed at that. So Ian, I think you may be able to imagine how fulfilling I found it from a personal point of view.

As you know very well by now, my background has been a humble one. I had to get into this by a certain route. First, the Afro-West Indian Association, of which I have been secretary for 14 years. Second, the Race Relations Council, which made me its chairman—this gave me the confidence to stand up in public and speak. Third, the Labour Party which nominated me as Councillor. I very much thank them for this, because without them, it could have taken a much longer time, or I might not have reached the goals that I have achieved. I am also most grateful to the electors, those who voted for me over the years, for their faith in me as their representative. I think it was because I represented them fairly and did not betray their expectations. I think I have covered your questions.

[Pause]

I'm running out. [Laughs] I'm running out of something[7]. I could listen more, but I don't know if I could ask any more questions. I know you are the one doing the talking, but listening is hard work too[8].

Well it's a good job you are running the tape. Imagine if I had to write my memoirs in longhand. This is where technology comes in. I am thankful for it. Takes some of the strain off. Less pen-pushing. Makes life a little bit easier for us[9].

Well, we have some teamwork. You are an accomplished speaker and I am quite experienced in writing. Between us we seem to manage.

The truth of it is, the first time you stand up in public, your knees are trembling, and you are not sure whether to keep your hands in your pockets, or whether to hold on to the table. If you look at various skilled speakers, you will see there are many ways that they deal with this. Yes, it was the constant work in small organisations that provided me with my long apprenticeship. Even the relatively lowly job as secretary of an Association enabled me to read out my minutes of the previous meeting, extract the gist of what had been said—it all helps with the building of confidence. Even things like making a speech at my niece's wedding, before two hundred guests, all these help give you confidence. The political platform is another thing. If you are at a Council meeting, and you stand up to make a point, it's got to be something properly constructed, short and crisp so that your points can be picked up easily.

As Mayor, I had an invitation to Wycombe Abbey School[10], along with our MP at the time, Ray Whitney, and one of the top Bishops in the land. As you may know, the first woman Mayor of Wycombe, Grace Reading[11], had been the Headmistress of the Abbey School. At first they had not allowed her to be a Mayor, because Wycombe in its entire history had never had a woman Mayor. In their speeches, the others had mentioned this lady, so when it was my turn, I spoke of how pleased she would have been to see me here. I think that was one of my better speeches. There were some very high-up people there at that meeting, many of them of the highest education and distinction—

Was this a prize-giving ceremony? Were the girls there too?

No, I think it was some other end-of-term occasion. The girls were there and some of their parents too. There was also a banquet. But it was tremendous. I came out feeling very good about it. Even Ray [Whitney] came over and congratulated me.

Surely it was a prepared speech.

I did not prepare the speech.

Really!

[Laughs] I used to find that if I had to do something written out a few jotted headings were best, but you see it depends on how it goes. I take my cue from the audience.

I have observed this, even though here you only have an audience of one.

If I say something and it gets a reaction from my audience, then I tend to go for it, and in those instances, having given a certain number of minutes to that subject, I would be glancing down at those headings to see what next I could come up with. I would see what topic might be worth throwing in, and if that goes well too, you are there. You don't need to write pages and pages. It may be different for a Prime Minister, who is going to be quoted or misquoted the whole time. In those circumstances it is better to issue the speech as a press release.

Those politicians who are concerned all the time about being quoted cannot speak from the heart so much. It's a shame, but they know that those who have spoken straight from impulse have sometimes made political blunders and regretted it later. I also wanted to acknowledge that you don't actually have an audience of one, you have a much bigger audience, but they are invisible! I am having to stand proxy for them.

That's right. I find it good that way. I'll be honest with you. I am talking sitting down. Sometimes I wonder if I give a better performance sitting down or standing up. Depends on the subject and the setting.

Yes, sometimes I feel that you are not addressing me personally. Sometimes I feel that you are addressing young people, with advice. Other times you are talking to your brothers, or the people in Bigwoods. I am right, aren't I?

Well, let me put it to you like this. We have been together on this journey, walking along, and I have been showing things to you. But there is one part of me you haven't seen. And maybe you would like to see that part of me, a part which is debatable as to whether it fits in to this scene that I have been depicting. Or is it going to be more suited for another time? It is a journey that I am preparing. I want you to walk along with me so that I can talk about it.

I think as you rightly say, that if this book comes out printable, and readable, that the reader will feel, "Yes, this guy is really talking to me, one to one, and nothing is being concealed."

As you said before, Ian, it's got to be interesting otherwise it won't get read. But I also recognise that the British people like a straightforwardness. They want to be clear about things, and whilst you cannot afford to hide anything from them, at the same time there are things that they don't want to know about. We go along, and if you like this one, we may go on another journey, to show that there is a lot more that I could deliver to you. But we don't want to waste your time as a reader. We want you to enjoy. The only way that we know you are enjoying it is by the number of copies sold.

Mmm, I like that. This could go in the Preface.

[Giggles, then laughs uncontrollably.]

Yes, we are going to put a lot of suspense into it. "And if you buy this book, you may get the chance to see Volume 2."

Absolutely! I don't think it's an unreasonable statement. You take up a book. You read the preface, the first page, the first couple of chapters. Something sticks. It's the story line. You can't just stop there. What next? You are compelled to read it. Because if you don't, you will not know what it's going to be about. I hope people will find it interesting.

Well I think so because what you say hangs together logically. It goes somewhere. It is not rambling. It is like your life, that has always gone somewhere. You could not have done B, if you had not done A first. It's—

—Interlocking. Yes. Looking over our transcripts you will see that sometimes I have deliberately stopped short, whereas other times we have spent longer discussing them. There are reasons. Compare this with politicians. Sometimes they stop short because they are not sure: they would have to do more research on those subjects. But here it is because we don't want to oversell, we don't want to lose interest with unnecessary detail. I just want to share my experience with people in a way that's positive, truthful and knowledgeable. We have dealt with things in a serious and an honest way.

Well, I have tried out bits of the draft on my teenage kids, and they didn't think it was boring, so that is a good sign.

[Laughs] Well, let's hope, because if the young people can find that someone from a different background, who's older, can say something that they can relate to, and see its benefits, then our time together—not that it's of no value in itself—will be so much more worthwhile. I am not talking about financial gain. We hope people will be able to follow, and enjoy, and heed.

I do think it is an educational project, in many ways. It tells us about the workings of local government, which I suspect many don't understand. The only understanding I had before our discussions came from a time when I worked for a County Council. Otherwise I would have known nothing.

Nowadays it is even more complex. It used to be just the various Committees plus the full Council meetings that were responsible for the overall running of the Council. But now we have moved over to a Cabinet style, where the senior Councillors take the decisions in conjunction with the senior Officers. This leaves the other councillors there more or less to rubber-stamp those decisions. They will still debate, but the decision has already been made. If I were still a councillor, I don't think I would enjoy that in the same way that I did.

You mean it changed after you left?[12]

Yes, I have yet to really get to grips with exactly how the Cabinet system works, but I am not very happy with it at all. I hate to rubber-stamp things. I believe every councillor should have an input from start to finish.

But not only that, it's the transparency for the public too. I don't suppose they can view the Cabinet meetings.

Right, but there is a bit of transparency in that all parties are represented in the Cabinet meetings. There would be representation in that the councillors could brief their leader who attends the Cabinet as to how they feel about issues. But as I understand it, once it has been through Cabinet, the decision has been already taken. Then they come back to inform the other Councillors.

It sounds like it is one more step removed from the public.

When it is time for the decisions to be made known, the public are invited to attend. The timetable of the open meetings is published. So in a sense the transparency is still there. It is not actually the Council's fault. It has come about from a Central Government proposal to make things more accountable. For myself, though I have long stopped being a Councillor, I still get information sent to me, and invitations to attend meetings as an observer, as a member of the public. I haven't been attending, but I have promised myself this year that I will. I want to see how they are doing, especially "my" members, to see how well they are performing, what questions they are asking.

NOTES

1. We were into our fifth hour of discussion on Sunday 6th March 2005. It seemed relevant to ask where we were going and to think about the content of the book which we were in the process of making. But we left the tape recorder running . . .

2. *Robin Cook:* Our conversations took place several months before the death of Robin Cook, on 20th August 2005.

3. *Reform of House of Lords:* the House has been partially reformed, with 90 hereditary peers still in place, and the remainder Life Peers or "people's peers".

4. *Robert Carr* (b. 1916) was elected to the Commons in 1950 as a Conservative. He was Secretary of State for Employment in 1970-72, Lord President of the Council and Leader of the House of Commons in 1972, following William Whitelaw, and Home Secretary in 1972-74. He became a life peer in 1976 as Baron Carr of Hadley.

5. This was no mere flattery. Conditioning in my (Ian's) early life had led me to vote Conservative, despite their policies being antagonistic to many of my views.

6. *The nature of the editing:* Sebert's words in this book have been lightly edited to convert them from an ad lib spoken format to written prose. Ian's questions on the other hand, have been rather heavily edited to reduce his long-winded rambles into something coherent. Editor's privilege!

7. *Running out:* my brain had gone temporarily blank (Ian).

8. *Listening is hard work too:* Our session had been running 4 hours continuously without a break. This was the way that we collected material for the book.

9. *Taping taking off the strain:* it would have been possible for me to leave the tape recorder with Sebert and let him talk into it alone, like Tony Benn and his audio diary. But the result would have been very different. The longer we went on, the more it became a conversation, not a monologue or even an interview.

10. *Wycombe Abbey School:* one of the top girls' fee-paying schools in England.

11. *Grace Reading:* Mayor 1956-7

12. *Changed Council Structure:* looking at the High Wycombe District Council Structure today (http://www.wycombe.gov.uk/council/default.asp?id=127&step=2) we see that even the committees are different from in Sebert's time.

CHAPTER 14

My ongoing roles

BUT YOU DON'T HAVE A ROLE ANY MORE ON THE COUNCIL. ARE you still a member of the Labour Party? Do you still have any position of responsibility within it?

Yes, I'm still in the Labour Party. I have been Chair of my branch recently but I'm still on the Management Committee (GMC) and the Executive Committee (EC). And I am their representative to go to the local Race Relations Council as well. I still have a role to play there. I still have a role to play in the Council so far as the community is concerned. It's very vital that we maintain the Hilltop Centre, which I am chairing. And another thing. About 80% of Wycombe is tied up in the Green Belt, and therefore the little bit of open space we've got will not last long. We've got to make sure that we keep and maintain those community facilities that we have. The ones that the minority groups are occupying are given to them by the Council. Those of us who are in charge of those have got to makes sure that the leases we have for them are more or less watertight. So for example if they have a plan to develop where the YMCA now stands, then the land on which the Hilltop Centre and the Badminton Club now stand might be needed too. If that happens, we want guarantees that the Council will put in a requirement to the contract with the developer, that a replacement for the Hilltop Centre is part of the new plan, built into it from the start. So what we want is assurance that if this is not agreed, then they cannot sell the land for redevelopment, or if they do, that they would have to find us alternative accommodation. Those things are vital to the development of the Afro-Caribbean community. Because of the constraints of the Green Belt, if they don't do that, there would be no other land that we could obtain. This is something that we have to fight for.

It seems to me that the only counter-argument that the Council could have would be if the community had not been making full use of those facilities.

Well, I don't think there will be any argument like that, because they *are* making full use of the facilities. In any case the Council cannot remove them just like that. The need remains and is greater than before.

But don't some community facilities fall out of use? What about that building that was used as an Arts Centre, along London Road?

I know the building you are referring to, the old school at Spring Gardens. What happened was that it was excess to Bucks County Council requirements as a school. Now it has been approved for housing. In between, it was indeed supported as an Arts Centre, but it remained a County Council property. They needed money and it was convenient for them to sell it off to the District Council for housing.

Did it not have vocal enough champions to try and save it as an arts centre?

No, I think the County Council in this instance had already made up their minds. They wanted the money. The only thing that could have happened as an alternative would be if the District Council had bought it as it was. They would not have done that. In the early Eighties we had proposed that we would have the Caribbean Elderly Day Centre there. We had also applied to use it for multiple purposes, so that several community organisations could take it over. But none of those arguments carried weight, because the County Council were able to realise millions of pounds from the sale of that site.

There was another derelict school, near us, called Lady Verney.

Yes, that site has now been redeveloped by the Guinness Trust. They could have done the same thing at the Spring Gardens site[1], by developing a mix of facilities, as we've seen at Lady Verney. But those are expensive projects and when I was a councillor, we rescued that Spring Gardens site and put a lot of money into turning it into an arts centre. We did want to keep it going. But since that time things have changed and the County have their own plans. This is not a reason to get despondent and as far as the Hilltop Centre is concerned I hope that whatever happens, the community will have somewhere. I have always argued the same way, with a consistency which everyone will acknowledge. I refer them to the issue of good race relations in High Wycombe. I also remind them that it is no use if a councillor representing black people makes promises to those people but then shifts his ground, or lets the goalposts be moved. The young people may end up frustrated, and one could imagine a time—this is what I tell them in the Council—when something happens, "and you, the Council, want me to go and pacify the crowd." Or I might even be in the crowd. If you make promises, you must try to fulfil them. Let me give you an example. I have been here in this country since I was twenty. When I reach the age of sixty-five, I want to have a place where I can walk in—

—as in the village shop in Jamaica—

and not just be wandering the streets with my walking stick, wondering where I can go. We need somewhere that those things can happen. There are also those who have prayed a lot. They want somewhere to assemble too. And then there are those who have a regular job who want to gather on a Saturday night and have a drink and a dance and enjoy that bit of leisure. Well, we are half-way there. We already have the Hilltop Centre[2], so part of my dream has been fulfilled. What I want now is permanency, so that I know that when I have gone, it will remain there.

When you were talking earlier about a crowd that needed to be

Betty Barratt (Chairman), Sebert Graham (Mayor), Ellen Hall (Deputy Mayor) greet Steve Cohen (Editor, Bucks Free Press) at the end of his half-marathon in aid of the Mayor's Appeal for the Elderly. A second later, they clapped him on the back in appreciation, nearly causing him to be ill all over their badges of office—or so he claimed later in his editorial column.

pacified, I assume that was a metaphor. You weren't talking about an actual riot, were you?

Well, it could be a riot. If you remember that incident in 1988[3], it was just a little incident in the multiracial centre, and there was the nonsensical accusation of a race riot in High Wycombe.

So you are saying you can be a detector of potential trouble? You could help nip it in the bud before it happens?

Or, we are the ones who could go and talk to the people and quieten them down a bit. If we keep on making promises, expectations rise accordingly. There must come a day when people see something tangible. People can see the Hilltop Community Centre as a permanent gesture from the Wycombe District Council. They do pay a rent, and they have a lease. If that had not happened, if there had not been something tangible like that, things might have become difficult. The younger generation could have become more impatient. Under those circumstances, who knows what might have happened? They are part of the society, so they have a right to have something which, like everyone else, they can identify with.

Do you see the requirement for Afro-Caribbean facilities going on forever?

Absolutely. This community in High Wycombe will always be here. They will still want community facilities, whether it is to pray or to dance.

Well, I am questioning that. You are an immigrant who spent the first 20 years in Jamaica. Your children were born here, even though they have lots of relatives there. Their children—your grandchildren—will have even less connection with West Indian ways of life. As time goes by they may intermarry and become paler.

The question of race—you are not suggesting that the black population are going to die out!

No, I don't believe in the idea of different races, really, only different cultures.

Yes, there will always be a mixture of cultures.

Yes, I accept that.

—and if you have a mixture of cultures, there will always be a need for development. When I came, I had a strong history and culture from my own personal background. It is the same with all West Indians who have come here. They have passed down that culture to their children, together with the relationship to their past country. So, I am becoming a grandfather, and some of my grandchildren will be lighter in colour than I am. Still, for the foreseeable future there will be a continuing need to cater for minorities, and that is what I am talking about. For that we need a building and that is expensive. There are various ways of funding it: support from the Council, lottery funding[4]. As long as black people, together with those white people who join with them culturally, want to be able to walk in somewhere just as they would walk into the Swan Theatre or the Town Hall for some fun, it would be there. The black people have their own white friends, whom they want to invite to have some fried chicken or some fried fish. [Laughs.] These are things we are not necessarily going to be able to do in the Town Hall or the Swan Theatre. So how are we going to be able to maintain our community standard, and pay the bills for the halls, for the purposes that I have been talking about? It's clear that we have to be pretty much self-sufficient, with a little help from somewhere else, to keep those things going.

But I will agree with you in one way. I do not see a need for a Race Relations Council going on indefinitely. The tolerance that we now have in our society should be enshrined in laws. We have travelled forty years to bring race relations up to the standard that we have now. We may need for a Commission for Racial Equality to remain there, continuing to monitor that there is fair play and opportunities given to everyone. But these small community relations groups that are scattered around the country, I don't see them as needing to survive. They wouldn't be there in thirty years' time. The first generation of this big wave of immigrants have been here as long as I have. They ought to be in the position to teach their grandchildren in the English language. And if they still don't speak English, there are places where they can go and learn.

This may be controversial and I hope when my Asian friends read this they won't feel insulted, but I feel that the schools should be strong enough to teach English to all children together, rather than make special arrangements for those who have not learned proper English at home. Even the West Indians born here now may still have a dialect problem, so maybe some Afro-Caribbean MP might ask for additional funding[5] for that.

Whilst the Commission for Racial Equality continues to monitor fair play and apply various yardsticks to measure what's going on, I see that the most positive role at the local level will be organisations approved by local authorities, rather than Race Relations Councils, which don't actually represent the people. The local voluntary organisations know where the people are, and the councils should know if the organisations are working,. That is the best way to distribute the funds to help the people. Those organisations could also be the ones to make reports to the CRE: for example in cases where they have been on the Council waiting list for housing for so many years, but still have not been assisted with housing. Another example is if someone had been unable to get a job because of discrimination, or wanted to tell the CRE that in a big organisation there are only two black faces. I envisage a link through the voluntary organisations at local level, backed up by the local authority and monitored centrally. This way the money would be better spent, and most likely it would also improve race relations. I have seen some people who came from a good position in the West Indies who could never do very well when they came here, and others who have found it hard to sustain a job for a long period.

NOTES

1. *Spring Gardens redevelopment:* outline planning permission has been given subject to public consultation to use the former school premises as a halfway house for former mental patients re-entering the community. A local journalist reports that neighbours are concerned about this plan.
2. *Hilltop Centre:* See Appendix A, "Multiracial centre is to be resited in town" and "Newsflash".
3. *Incident in 1988:* See Appendix A, "Police race riot methods provoke complaint" and "Comment on a riot".
4. *Lottery:* In the United Kingdom, the National Lottery funds much sporting, cultural, social and heritage development, on the basis of the recipient organisation matching the donor sum 50-50.
5. *Additional educational funding:* the reference here is to facilities provided in British schools to teach English as an additional language rather than as a base language. A number of children are brought up in households where English is not spoken, and the Government has made allowance for this, even where the immigrant families have been in this country for several generations. See for example: http://www.dfes.gov.uk/research/data/uploadfiles/RR184.doc

CHAPTER 15

Multicultural community

IAN, GOOD MORNING, WE START AGAIN[1], THE SUN HAS GONE IN, it was a pleasant morning before. We have been on this journey, and we have made a synopsis in our conversations, and now we need to go back and extend certain areas which were only touched on.

I was secretary of the West Indian Association for 14 years, and in that time, I have also been involved in race relations. That led me to being in touch with the Council and initially experiencing some frustration. That led me to join the Labour Party, and they encouraged me to become a Councillor. So in one sense that had a successful conclusion culminating in my becoming Mayor.

The other thing I have done which has been successful in benefiting my community—

Sorry, "my community" means what?

I refer to the community in which I live.

The community of West Indians?

No, all of us. I am referring to the Hilltop Community Centre which was a successful outcome for all of us. In 1991 I felt the West Indian Association was not moving as fast as we wanted it to. Some sort of renewal of strength and focus was needed. It needed to be re-formed. I discussed with some members of the community to see if they would agree that we needed a strong organisation, to reflect and further inspire the black community. We felt that having its own building, as the Irish and Polish had also done for their communities, would not be to keep the ethnic group separate but assist in a positive focus of their identity. Suppose we had some white friends visiting from London, or somewhere: we could take them there. That was my aim, now achieved, but at that time, in 1991, I kicked off the process by starting the Wycombe Black People's Association. It was very well attended, especially by the younger people, because its name had radical connotations. They were keen to identify with the kind of radicalism that it represented in their eyes. But after a year or so, the older members of the organisation and those with long experience started feeling it wasn't a suitable name. Because when they were talking to their white peers, they were told that it sounded racist and exclusive. I tried to tell them it was about black people's personal identity and development, to declare to everybody that they exist. We were not barring people who were not black. They too could become members. They would simply have to agree with the constitution, which did not have anything to do with race, except to say that there was no discrimination e.g. on grounds of faith or political leanings. But some of them still felt a little uneasy about it and therefore there was a debate, and the eventual outcome was to call it the Wycombe Multicultural Organisation, which embraces everybody, and everyone can join. Soon after that, we became a Registered Charity, and we have gone from strength to strength. The primary objective is education, and you may remember how we talked about the Tony Swann[2] report which discussed the under-achievement of black children. Since the years of the Afro-West Indian Association, we had been running a supplementary school, at the Green Street School premises. It was designed to help those children who had been identified as underachieving, and needing assistance via individual tuition. But then Green Street School closed down. We were given the Hilltop Community Centre, which was allocated by Wycombe District Council for the development of the Afro-Caribbean community; and again we established a supplementary school there. We had an average of about 30 children attending on a regular basis.

How did it work?

They came every Saturday morning from 10 to 12. It remains a flourishing organisation. And we also have panels for social welfare. If a member didn't show up for a few meetings, we would find out why, because another member would go out and see what had happened, for example if they were ill. That was the kind of social cohesion that we had. There would be a group supporting the bereaved. And we had a social committee to organise the dances and fund-raising. And there was a group with myself and Cojo who would look at the political situation to see if there was anything which would affect our community and we would make representations, to convey the feeling of the membership to the Council. We have become a very well-established organisation. We worked closely with the District Council which has spent a lot of money in developing the Hilltop Centre. We are presently in discussion with the Council to extend the present lease from 5 years to 25 years. And we are in the process of negotiating an assurance from the council, that in the case of any development on that site, provision would still be made to provide us with comparable accommodation. They would seek a contribution from the developers to provide something which would be suitable and allow for high-volume music[3] without disturbance to neighbourhood residents.

So I hope it will not be as it was in the days of the West Indian Association where the young people kept asking, "What have you done for us?" I think that argument is now dead.

That argument was expressed on the TV programme in 1988. The younger black people had felt that their parents had let them down, because they had accepted prejudice, had taken whatever jobs had been offered, had accepted the colour bar, with the result that their children were called names and so on. The younger people argued that the positive attitude had not been campaigned for till too late.

Yes, that is it. Now I hope that at least in my home town of High Wycombe, that argument won't stick any longer. Part of the way that we make sure it doesn't happen is to have two persons working from the High Wycombe Council offices. One is a development officer for the Afro-Caribbean community, with a brief to go out into the community and discover people's concerns and complaints, and to report it back to the Council; or to work with the voluntary organisations to do something about it.

Is this the same as the Race Relations officer?

No. The Development officers are I think subsidised by the Home Office. The other person's brief is to look at drug-related problems. Sometimes the perception is that the Afro-Caribbean community are handling more drugs than the others.

Very much so.

But it's not the case. The image that people have of the Afro-Caribbeans as the main drugs pushers is not the truthful picture. It may be true that they are users of drugs, but they are not the main source of supply.

I was talking about this perception with a friend the other day, and saying this to him; but he replied by asking me, "When did you last buy any drugs?" So I said, "1971". And he said, "If you go to London, blacks are the only ones on the streets that will be offering drugs to you." He said that the young black men—he excused the girls—were getting their revenge for slavery by bringing down the English.

[Laughs] Well, if it is a revenge, then it's a silly one, because not only are they damaging the other community, but they are inflicting great harm on their very own people and this is a tragic part of the scene.

And so, this person's role is to go out and find people who are caught up in drugs, and also to work with the schools, with consent of the teachers, to bring up the awareness of drugs, and the ways they cause us harm. These are the kinds of organisations we are working with—

And it would be necessary for these drugs officers to be trusted as not being police informers.

No, it is certainly not their business to report anything to the police, it is a question of cure, and if possible prevention.

We have also established links with Bucks County Council Life-Long Learning, which is an adult education programme. This is to teach new skills to the unskilled, for example in using computers, to re-equip them for new jobs. That is no longer in operation, because the take-up was very slow. So again we are looking again at the work of the Development Officer, to see if she had been successful in capturing details of those people in the community who would be in a position to benefit from this retraining.

Sorry, I am not clear what connection this has with what you were saying before. Is this another initiative?

Yes, this is another thing that our Committee has been involved in, to work with those two officers in the District Council. It was run through the Council and was subsidised by Central Government funds, to help people, perhaps older people, who wanted to go back to work but lack the new skills required today; and also the confidence to restart into a new job.

Was this restricted to black people?

Well, it could apply to any people. But because we had a building, it was easier for us to attract that money, because we had somewhere to bring the people to, for such a programme.

And because it is called the Wycombe Multicultural Organisation, there would be no ethnic restrictions?

Yes, and so we got the money and it was available for anyone.

I am still thinking about the original name, the Wycombe Black People's Association. That was an invitation for someone to start the Wycombe White People's Association!

Well we already had various associations for white people, in all but name. For example the Wycombe Labour Party. [Laughs] But you see if you had read the Association's constitution, you would have seen that it explicitly did not bar anyone because of their colour. It was given that name in order to give people more confidence, to believe in themselves, something to hold on to.

So the name "Black People's Association" was positive for its friends, but negative for its enemies?

Exactly. I think our trouble as black people is that more than any other race, we seem to take into account the feelings of the others. It's an inherent trait. The blacks will not go out of their way to make anyone feel uncomfortable. Some of our members felt that their white peers would feel a little uncomfortable about it, and we changed it.

I think you will find that in every aspect of black history, as far as I know, they find it very hard to make anyone feel uncomfortable. I am not talking about just the Jamaicans or the Afro-Caribbeans. I am talking about the entire black race.

Another aspect of community work is that it seems to take over your life, as if it were a drug, and this is what I have been saying to the members recently. You find yourself addicted to it. I mean, there are times when I want to give up. I have had enough. But then you go to bed and a new idea pops into your head. Or you get up in the morning and you find a situation in which you feel compelled not to give up.

So what makes it addictive? Can we analyse that?

Well, it seems to be connected with the fact that as we wake up each day we have a new experience. In 1988 I witnessed that so-called riot in High

Wycombe (See also Appendix A). The night before, I went to the Tuesdays Club in the heart of Wycombe. There were young blacks, Asians and whites, all together. I saw them with my own eyes, sipping drinks from bottles, hugging each other and dancing away. The next morning I got up to see a headline, "Race Riot in High Wycombe." Total nonsense. There had been a dance at the Multiracial Centre, which included people who had come from Reading. A few youths had got out of hand—there had been a disagreement.

Set right in the middle of—England
A little place they call High—Wycombe
Sixteen thousand West—Indians
Work and reside in High—Wycombe
It is Paradise Found, not Paradise Lost
On New Year's Eve they counted the cost
Now you would not believe there could be a prob—lem
Look all around all you see is green, man!
Now tranquillity seem so eas—y
When you walking around all de hills and vall—ey
On New Year's Eve was another stor—y
Frustration became a frightening reality . . .

Kendall Smith, rap poet (from the Here and Now documentary on Central TV (13.03.88) about the "race riot" in High Wycombe on New Year's Eve 1988). (See also Appendix A)

"When we do try to break into politics, the door is closed in our face. If you try to break it down, it just gets reinforced, and we give up."

"It's a stereotype we've got ourselves into. A typical black person is supposed to be rough, on the dole. There is no way we can change that."

"I tried to explain it [the riot] to my mother and she seemed to think it was us coming at you [the white people] and causing all the contention, and whatever else. But they're not out here seeing it for themselves, you know what I mean. I don't understand it."

"How did it start? It started with our parents. If they had fought like the Americans for their rights, it wouldn't be as bad as it is now. If they'd fought and not accepted the conditions over here, it would have been OK."

Expressions of frustration by black youths of Wycombe interviewed in the documentary. (See also Appendix A)

But the journalists have got to sensationalise it, to sell their papers. So that is what they did. I would never deny that there is racism in the town, or shall I say individuals with such leanings. It would be silly to deny it. But the reports, in blowing it up out of proportion, sacrificed truth for the sake of being provocative.

So that is one reflection. The other is that during my time as a councillor, I got to see the different needs of people. And with some, it is the experience of seeing those needs and doing something to make a difference which keeps them going. Sometimes it seems to me that there are only a limited number of people who are prepared to be volunteers. Maybe they are a special breed of people. I used to meet some people who were always out of work. It didn't seem to me that they were unfitted for employment. I thought that with support from Government, or the Council, those who were drawing benefit all the time should do some work in the community, like helping out in old people's homes. They might be able to do the gardening, or wash the windows. To do something in the community gives more fulfilment in life. And then everyone who pays for the unemployment benefits in taxation would see it as money well spent. The recipients would be putting something back into society. I suppose some people would say it was infringing on their human rights, or we were taking advantage of cheap labour. I think that attitude is short-sighted.

My son-in-law's job is to supervise gangs of convicted minor offenders who have been sentenced to community service, and they have to do just that, such as cleaning graffiti off the street, or decorating in care homes. In this case they are compelled to do these tasks otherwise they might be sent to prison. It works.

But some of these "unemployed" might find themselves too busy, because they are already filling their days with some kind of work.[4]

Yes, what you are describing is the Community Service Orders, which are supervised by the Probation Service. They are only allowed to do jobs as high as the hand can reach. They are forbidden to go up on stepladders. So in the Hilltop Centre, which has a high ceiling, they could only paint as high as their brush could reach. But if we are talking about unemployed people, working as volunteers, insurance cover might be arranged by the Job Centre for them—

—Or perhaps they would sign a waiver to say that they would do it at their own risk—

Yes, there is a lot that could be done. The questions are, how do communities work, how are they fulfilled? Think of the thousands of people engaged in their various ways in volunteering. They look after the elderly. They help out in care homes. They raise funds for good causes, disaster relief, the benefit of the world. Meanwhile, governments remain unable to raise enough money to fund education, roads and all the rest. Suppose there were no volunteers? What state would we be in then? Some people have never given a thought to the community. Some of those who have been to Africa and have seen the devastation and the way people live—some of them will be hooked on community work forever. What they have seen has touched them so deeply that they will never turn their back on voluntary work thereafter. They will know that it is a necessary part of their lives.

NOTES

1. *Start again:* this and the following four chapters are the edited transcript of a lengthy conversation on March 13th 2005.
2. *Swann Report* (1985), officially called *Education for All*, advocated a multicultural education system, and like the Rampton Report (see also Appendix A) linked underachievement of certain children to racist attitudes.
3. *High-volume music:* when I was staying in Jamaica some neighbours would have Saturday night parties so loud that the music seemed to be in our own house and would set our louvred windows vibrating, even though the sound source was more than a hundred yards away.
4. *People on benefits who work:* I was thinking of young musicians who manage to practise their instruments whilst claiming benefits. Where would our music industry be without this help from the Government?

CHAPTER 16

Why be a councillor?

I REMEMBER YOU SAYING IN A PREVIOUS CONVERSATION THAT one of the great joys of being a councillor was to be able to help people and alleviate their distress, for example when they were threatened with bailiffs. I have not forgotten that being a councillor is an important way to be a volunteer.

Sometimes people overlook the fact that councillors also have full-time responsibilities of jobs and family life. You might go straight from work into a meeting starting at 6.30 and finishing at 10 or later. They don't want to adjourn these meetings without having made decisions and tidied up the business. I think the public need to be more aware.

I imagine that many people assume councillors will have political ambitions, but it cannot be like that. Wycombe has sixty councillors but only one MP. So it's apparent that councillors will only do this very dedicated job if they get something out of it.

What I get out of it is a personal satisfaction. I never make promises, I just tell them "I will see what I can do". I can't tell the person who's pursued by bailiffs that I can get their debts reduced. But I offer to make an appointment for them with the local government officer concerned so that their side of the story may get its fair hearing. It is not that I will necessarily believe their story as against the officer's. There are strict guidelines, but the officers are also given a certain amount of discretion. Somehow we can usually manage to get something shifted so the constituent goes away happy. In fact everyone ends up happy.

I am thinking that it is possible to help people in similar, less demanding ways without being a Councillor. One could train as an Advocate[1], or to work for the Citizens' Advice Bureau[2].

Yes, but the councillor's role is quite different from the Advocate's. He may be engaged in advocacy, but as an elected representative, he works as someone within a structure of laws and administration. He is in fact the boss of the officials and therefore carries weight in the structure. On the other hand, he knows the rules and works within them.

I was wondering whether you were sometimes able to delegate requests for help from your constituents by referring them to advocates or the Citizens' Advice Bureau.

No. People only came to me with issues relevant to my role. In fact many of them had already been to the Citizens' Advice Bureau or advocates, and came to me for help on specific things, to do with housing,

Community Charge, delays in completion of Council works and so on. And as you gain experience over time, you learn more, and this means that when you deal with Council officers you know very well what rights the public have, and this enables you to give the best possible support to a particular constituent.

When you first start as a councillor you have very little experience. How do you cope then?

Your first year is a huge learning experience. You pick up a lot from your colleagues, especially the senior councillors. But they also give you access to lots of books and papers that you need to read. Being a councillor gives you a first-hand knowledge that I don't think you would get otherwise.

So you were already working full-time, say 37½ hours a week. How many extra hours would you be working on your duties as a councillor?

It must have been somewhere between 15 and 25 hours. It's the kind of work that is never done. You have to brief yourself for every committee meeting that you attend. There are constituents to meet or ongoing commitments to complete on their behalf. The job does not respect Saturdays and Sundays. And many councillors lose money. We wouldn't charge the phone calls for example that have to be made on Council-related business.

But surely you could claim that on expenses?

Yes, but I am not going to log every telephone call that I make. Overall it is a huge commitment of time, energy, money.

So, when an election looms, is there sometimes a shortage of nominations as councillors? Is there a balance of supply and demand?

That is a good question. There may be a lot of people interested, potentially, but it is frightening. You would not come to it with no experience of volunteering. In any case, you first have to belong to a political party, and then you have to be nominated. If you are successful in winning election, you will in due course be assigned as a member of various committees. And as soon as you are on a committee, you are called upon to demonstrate ability as a public speaker, at least to be able to engage in debate.

Wouldn't almost everyone who came in as a councillor have prior experience of some kind of voluntary service, perhaps as a school governor?

Well some have and some haven't. They have all sorts of different backgrounds and experience. But what I would think they would all have in common is a leaning towards belief in the community, and a feeling that they could make a contribution.

They might for example have come from a Church background.

It's true, some do have a Church background. Local government is one of the best places to make a difference. This is where decisions are made that affect your life, or things that you have got to comply with. For example, here is a perennial issue: how do you treat Travellers[3]? There are many living in rural communities who do not want travellers' encampments to be near to them. They have long campaigned with District and County Councils to get them moved on. In some cases an issue like this has persuaded someone to get elected as a Councillor, because they believe passionately about something.

I don't know if in your urban ward you would have had a Traveller problem. But it concerns me a bit if the only voices heard in the Council are on behalf of farmers, who pay council tax, as against Travellers, who don't? Does anyone speak on behalf of the Travellers themselves?

Yes, [laughs] we have had councillors who have spoken up on behalf of Travellers and there has been a little sentiment in their favour, not just because of the legislation which is there to protect them. On the other hand they are sometimes their own worst enemies. And in fact this has happened in my own ward. They were at Handy Cross. The police had to be brought in to move them off the site.

Well, I know that throughout this part of the County, any opening from the road that gives access to an unused piece of land tends to be protected against caravans coming in, by a large mound of earth.

Yes, when I was a councillor there was a place in Stokenchurch we were trying to get them located to. Sometimes they don't want to accept the sites we offer. And as you know, they are free-rollers. If they see an opening they may decide to perch there. It's a very delicate subject. I can see the merit of people wanting to feel free. But then I can also see that people with an established residence wouldn't want to wake up in the morning and find ten or fifteen caravans parked next to their house, with their clothes hanging out on lines and so on. If the government or the landowners provided specific designated areas for those people, then one could say that if they moved out of them to park somewhere else, then the harassment could legitimately continue. Otherwise it would be unfair on the landowners. These people who have not paid any taxes often create extra litter, with an effect on tidiness and public health. As someone who came to this country and made it my home, it makes me feel uncomfortable too. So I can imagine how it feels for those whose families have been settled here for more than a thousand years.

Well, these travellers have been with us for hundreds of years too.

Yes, so you can see from that the tolerance of our British society. [Laughs] Now, you have just stirred something up here! They are Europeans of different cultures and habits, and it demonstrates how tolerant British society is. And we have not stopped trying to accommodate these people with different tastes into our own communities. I am saying that if they have been given certain designated areas, these people have to stick to those, and treat them with respect.

Let us suppose you have some Traveller families that want to move from South Buckinghamshire to somewhere in Wiltshire. They would have the right to do say to their friends in Wiltshire, "A few of us are coming down to your area. Have you got enough room to accommodate us? Then someone can come to use this designated site after we have left the space clear." Government should be able to help them to plan their lives in that orderly manner. It would be a network of linked sites across the country, and it would need some co-ordination, which could be informal amongst the travellers themselves. But they cannot just on a whim go and occupy someone's land.

Because that would not be respectful of the land or the need for permission. And I could understand that if they had no facilities provided then ultimately they might find themselves forced to go somewhere, permission or not.

I am not sure but I believe there are some local authorities who have made these provisions, and others are moving rather too slowly. But I hope that the view I have expressed is one that could make a difference. There are plenty of potential places and this is where landowners can make a difference. I think John Prescott[4] is looking at legislation, though I have not looked into it too much. I can only hope it is something on the lines I have been suggesting[5]. If it's not, then I think we need to go back to the drawing board and say, "We know where all the open spaces are. We know the landowners are and where the gypsies are"—pardon the use of that word, but that is what they used to be called—

They are called Travellers these days in recognition of the fact that they are different ethnic groups.

"We know where they tend to travel, and we know the places where there has always been trouble."

Isn't there a problem here, because you are speaking from a sense of wisdom and humanity, but since we are a democracy, and the travellers are a minority, the majority may be unwilling to allocate enough resources to solve the problem? Democracies are not always kind to minorities.

Well, if we don't care, we will reach a point where our society becomes intolerant. If that happens, everything that we talked about before will break down. We will always have to care for minorities and there will be times when the majority may have to bear a burden on behalf of a minority.

These problems have been with us for a long long time but in the last few years it has been aggravated by the increase in development which has maybe taken away the lands which the travellers were using in the past, and unless we replace them, the problem will not go away. There is no point in shifting a problem from one place to another. We have to find a long-term way to deal with these problems. The travellers have got to understand that land space is getting less, and therefore when they are given sites they have to respect them and use them in a sensible way. There will not be any others available and so their travelling has got to be planned, as I explained before. It's a matter of well-organised site-swap.

They should be able to organise it themselves, I am sure they have mobile phones.

Yes, well many of them have enviable facilities on wheels. We are not to think of them all as poor people in that sense. They like to move and they like the fresh air of the countryside. They need to organise, if they have not done so already. Things cannot proceed as they have done in the past[6].

NOTES

1. *Advocates:* I was thinking of a local organisation called People's Voices, which supports those who by reason of disability, age, learning difficulties or other vulnerability may not be able to represent themselves in order to deal with various official agencies.

2. *Citizens' Advice Bureau:* a registered charity to help people resolve their legal, money and other problems by providing free, independent and confidential advice, and by influencing policymakers.

3. *Travellers:* more commonly known as Gypsies, but that appellation implies that the travellers are part of the Roma or Romany ethnic group. Actually Travellers are of several ethnic types and what they have in common is simply their preference for a nomadic way of life.

4. *John Prescott:* Deputy Prime Minister. His intervention on behalf of Travellers was in his role as Secretary of State for the Environment.

5. *Treatment of Travellers:* A Conservative party website announces that the Labour Government's Department of the Environment has issued new guidelines: "The new rules explicitly state that forced evictions of illegal traveller camps are banned if the land is publicly owned, that councils and the police cannot infringe any aspect of the Human Rights Act when dealing with travellers, that welfare checks for travellers take priority when dealing with illegal encampments, and that police and councils 'should be sensitive to different cultural perspectives' of travellers." The Conservatives seem convinced that opposing human rights will win votes.

6. *Local authorities' duty to provide official sites for Travellers:* the policy Sebert advocates was official Government policy until repealed in 1994 by the Conservative Government of John Major.

CHAPTER 17

My travels

NOW, I WOULD LIKE TO CHANGE THE SUBJECT FROM TRAVELLERS to my own travels. [Laughs] I have been travelling thorough Jamaica from Lennox Bigwoods, Darlaston, Kingston, Montego Bay and then I hit the United Kingdom. And I have talked so much about the United Kingdom, but my travelling did not just end there. I have seen various parts of the United Kingdom and parts of Europe too. I have had the chance to admire and get a feel of those countries that I have gone too, not in a political sense. I was interested in their behaviour. My first venture outside the UK was a trip to Holland. It was an experience. I certainly saw a difference in behaviour, for example in their drinking pattern. It is not that I am a big drinker but I was interested to see how it was there. It struck me how many places there were which offered prostitutes and sex shows. That kind of behaviour was up-front, in ways that you would not see in the United Kingdom.

This sounds like Amsterdam.

Yes, it was. This was quite striking. I will just mention titbits or highlights of my experience. And it was interesting to try out the eating places, to compare them with the UK, although to tell you the truth I was not in those days someone to eat out a lot and try much strange food.

What year did you go?

It was some time in the Seventies, just for a weekend trip. You could easily cross the Channel by Hovercraft from Dover to Calais. Then take a train.

The beer was different to what I was used to and people were more noisy in the bars. The friendliness was very open and jovial. I did not use the buses or trams but you have to be careful crossing the street, because they the drive on the other side. [Laughs] And then there were the canal systems: all very pleasant to look at.

I had work connections with my contacts who used to supply the Ford Motor Company, and some of them were in Holland. I had the chance to meet up with one of them there, and it was pleasant to have a few beers together.

I passed through Belgium too. The beers were similar. I found the place very clean. When you are travelling, you look for clean facilities where you can feel relaxed. Their public conveniences were quite pleasant.

Better than England at that time?

Well even these days, we had so much discussion in Council about for example public facilities for mothers who wanted to change their babies' nappies. The facilities were not to an encouraging standard. It is something that needs to be looked at, so when they do this new Western Sector Development, on the site of the old chocolate factory at Bridge Street and the big car park and so on, I hope they will build something in these complexes now that are going to be truly acceptable for mothers who want to take their children into town, and have somewhere fresh and clean, just as if they were at home. It would cost more but I think people would be prepared to pay for a service that they feel sure about.

Well some of the supermarkets have achieved this now, anyway.

Yes, the supermarkets are almost there and they can do it in Belgium.

The other country I visited was the old enemy country—not my enemy! [laughs] I mean the historic enemy.

Well, as in Fawlty Towers[1], some Britons are still fighting the last War.

[Laughs] I can understand it in a way. Suppose you had lost your son, or your family members in the bombing, it's going to take generations before you can forget that. Some can forgive very easily, some can't.

Well, I went to Germany[2]. As I have mentioned, High Wycombe and Kelkheim are linked as twin towns. And I have mentioned that the Mayor of Kelkheim is equivalent to Wycombe's Chief Executive. I went to meet him and then after that I went to look at the city with various friends and companions. I found it very similar to the United Kingdom in landscape, climate and countryside. I could understand the rivalry because they are so close, so similar. Their facial features are the same too.

Well, the Angles and Saxons in any case came from Germany.

Yes, apart from the language, it felt very similar. The beer-drinking was similar, except that they drink from larger tankards than here. OK, the eating habits are different. They eat more sausage and the sausages are bigger there, and more different colours. I feel that it's wonderful to go places and see how they do things in different ways.

It may be funny to say this but my first friends in the United Kingdom were policemen. I would be walking down a street in London, and if I wanted information that was valuable and reliable, I would ask a policeman and it was good. I went to Germany and I found it was the people themselves. They went out of their way to make me as a foreigner and my Mayoress feel at home. They were almost apologising for everything, the way that they were trying to make us feel at ease. I don't know if it would be the same for you, Ian, if you had gone there. Was it my complexion? Was it because I was a guest from the UK?

You were not dressed as the Mayor at the time?

Well some of them would have known that I was a Mayor. But other people that I met outside, who did not know who I was, were still as it were trying to make peace with the world.

Sebert Graham helps Bürgermeister Thomas Horn plant a tree in Kelkheim—High Wycombe's twin town in Germany

Well for one thing they would be practising their English on you. And you can be pretty certain that not many English would be practising their German when the Kelkheim people came here.

[Laughs] Well the English are like the French in one respect. We are so damn proud of our Englishness and our language, that we don't want to talk anyone else's. I have no quarrel with that. My quarrel is—but we will come to that. Yes, Germany has many things in common with the United Kingdom and I think it is a great country. I am aware that people in the Fifties and

Sixties still felt that a united Germany would have spelt trouble. I personally welcome the reunification and always felt the need for that Berlin wall to go down, for it divided people. I thank Mr Gorbachev and all the other people by whose efforts the wall came down. The united Germany is going to be good for Europe and the world. Coming together as a European Union is going to be a great force for good. There are of course things to sort out. I have mentioned before the example of Harold Wilson: laying a new foundation for Britain. This is what they are now doing in Germany when they are bringing the two separated halves back together. And it will make Europe all the stronger.

I found in Germany that the family structure still prevails. They have real communities, and they meet up on Sunday mornings. They get together—father, mother, children—they share food and they have family fun and outings. It used to be strong when I came to the United Kingdom in 1960. But now we no longer have that kind of really close communities. We hope to rebuild it again in the United Kingdom.

NOTES

1. *Fawlty Towers:* English TV comedy series starring John Cleese, a manic hotelier notorious for embarrassing his guests and generating chaos.
2. On a later occasion, Sebert told me of the time that his hosts in Kelkheim (Wycombe's twin town in Germany) took him to a beer festival, at which he made one of his extempore speeches. They rewarded him with their choral rendering of Harry Belafonte's *Banana Boat Song*: "Day-o, day-ay-ay-o! Daylight come and me wan' go home". (Belafonte was actually born in Harlem of Jamaican parents, but introduced Caribbean calypso to the European public.)

CHAPTER 18

Divided communities

WHEN YOU SAY "WE"—ISN'T THIS DIFFERENT BETWEEN THE VARIOUS ethnic groups in this country?
When I say "we", I mean people living in Britain. And when I came in 1960 as an observer I came into a sense of community, even though it was different from the kind of community that I experienced in Jamaica,. It was all the same a community feeling. Parents would say, "My John, my Jim". Families used to go out and enjoy themselves together. After Mrs Thatcher, no more community.

So why did it change?
Mrs Thatcher broke it up, by saying there is no such thing as community.

Why did that have so much influence? She said in an interview in Woman's Own *magazine in 1987 that there is no such thing as society. How can that have destroyed our sense of community in this country?*
It has influence because Conservatism under Mrs Thatcher had actually broken up the cohesion of community. The Poll Tax divided mothers, fathers, children. It made it into "each one for himself". That destroyed community, which should be a feeling of everyone working together, in unison with one another, in harmony. Community is that sense that everywhere we go, people have feeling for each other. That was destroyed.

Certainly she encouraged a fashion of selfishness. I was working as a consultant in a bank in the City from 88-91, with all the Yuppies, showing off with their red braces and their big black mobile phones on street corners. And they were admired, for some reason.

****

So, we have a bite and a drink. We are talking about communities. Wouldn't it be good if whilst we are talking we had the technology to have our conversation automatically typed up?

It would still have to be painstakingly edited.
It is so true about communities. Here we are, two individuals, but we are now formed into a little community. When I was talking to you, before our little break, I was feeling so passionate about what we were saying. About Mrs Thatcher. As I have said before, I was out campaigning, and I have seen the suffering of people who were trying to buy their own houses. People who were trying to help their sons and daughters rise in the world from the bottom. There is such upset in society if people feel that they are left at the

bottom, abandoned. It brings frustration and bad feeling. As I was talking to you I was getting inflamed with my memory of the poll tax. I could see how families were being destroyed. People were losing their homes. "I don't know when my son will ever get a job." "My husband has just lost his job." Communities were being broken up through the Community Charge, which was the official name of The Poll Tax. I tell you, when I arrived in this country we had communities. I remember very well how it was, arriving as a newcomer, joining this established country.

I feel very strongly about it, thinking about what was done to people's lives, adults and children alike. Then I went to Germany and I found that what we have destroyed in Britain still survives there: a real close-knit community. I also visited Bavaria whilst I was there. The wife of my counterpart, the Mayor of Kelkheim, was from those parts. There were real communities there. They were having fun in the park: families gathered for picnics. We've lost that.

I am not disputing what you say, but it still seems a mystery to me. If you are saying Margaret Thatcher did it, that makes her more powerful than I think she could have been.

She came in with a shopping list of philosophies. The public got to love her because she was a strong woman—

And she crushed the miners[1], and especially Arthur Scargill[2]. Everyone hated him, apart from those in the mining communities.

A very weak Labour Government had been defeated when she came to power. Margaret Thatcher was a very strong Prime Minister. The people of Britain were seeking someone with that kind of strength and as you rightly say, she had gone through the Falklands War, came through it victorious, and was able to push through some very strong new policies. She was able to destroy the trade union leadership as we knew it, almost obliterated the trade union movement, which does not make me jump for joy. It was perfectly true though that the trade union movement had made mistakes and needed to be reformed.

She destroyed the print unions which had kept a tight grip on Fleet Street[3].

What people must understand is that without the trade unions our standard of living would not be what it is today. Multinational companies[4] would not have paid the salaries and wages that we genuinely needed. Without unions, the standards of education and health would not have been as they are. Multinational companies would have only looked after their shareholders and higher management.

If our government under Jim Callaghan[5] had listened to Barbara Castle's recommendations, *In Place of Strife*[6], and the trade unions had listened to Barbara Castle, Mrs Thatcher would not have become as strong as she did. Mrs Castle's way would still have kept the unions in the Labour Party's bosom, but they would have been more controlled, as opposed to being destroyed. Callaghan's government was too weak to allow Mrs Castle to implement her recommendations.

So Margaret Thatcher came on the scene and destroyed almost all the good community provisions that previous governments had put in place: reducing the trade unions to impotence, privatising everything, like selling off the "family jewels" that had been left in trust for Britain by previous generations. She acted like a dictator, selling everything that the country had to be proud of. And then saying "there is no such thing as society".

So the people's fear was that it would be free education and the National Health Service that would be attacked next. The community feeling was closely connected to confidence in the Welfare State. In her reign of terror, nothing seemed safe any more, was that it?

You've got my feeling. That's exactly what I'm saying.

And you are suggesting that she had wounded the morale of all those who had fought for public welfare provisions so deeply that they were ready to give up the battle for good.

Exactly. This is why the Yuppies flourished with their motto, "Each man for himself". And the general government attitude was, "We don't make provision for you any more. You've got to fight for it, you've got to work for it, if you want it."

But it's not all of us who are able to be strong, and get riches for ourselves in the way that she was trying to foster. The way she saw it was limited to providing just one way, suitable only for the fit.

OK, let me play devil's advocate for a minute, and suggest that perhaps she took upon herself the dirty work that had to be done? Some of the privatisations have been damaging, like those in public transport perhaps. But the privatisations have not been reversed because they have introduced mechanisms for greater efficiency, wouldn't you agree?

I would say that not all privatisations have had bad outcomes. But some that ideally ought to be reversed are now quite irreversible. It would be far too expensive to contemplate. The transport system that we have now is a shambles. Government cannot reverse that kind of policy now. They cannot now take it over in order to make a proper train and bus system that will deliver you to your work in good time.

To let the weak be abandoned by the selfish, that was quite abominable, frankly. When I first came here people would refer to their sons and daughters as "My Jim, my Sarah" because they felt so close. But then when I went canvassing in the time of the Poll Tax, they felt quite different: "Why should I pay his poll tax? He lives with me, but why should I pay it for him?"

In relation to their own child?

Yes, that was the feeling. It hadn't been like that before. Prior to the Poll Tax, we had a rating system. You would pay one single rate for your home. Parents would be helping their sons and daughters to acquire their own homes.

So you might have had a family of various generations living together, grown-up sons and daughters, grandparents and possibly an uncle or aunt. *You're saying that the Poll Tax had the effect of splitting up families because the householder did not want to pay for other family members?* Yes, that's right.

So they let them clear off?

There were people who left High Wycombe in the time of the Poll Tax, and some who decided they could not vote in the elections[7]. They fled. They moved around so that they could not be located to pay the tax. The thing to do was to be in transit. The Poll Tax has been abolished now of course, and replaced by the Council Tax. But now when you fill in your electoral registration form, you have to give your present and previous address. Now, there is no hiding place. Your records will follow you like your medical record.

Well, I think I have exhausted that one on community.

And you have persuaded me, again.

In hindsight, though we had a long setback in those Thatcher years, I can say that we are regaining the ground that we lost. But anyone who was involved in local government in those days will tell you the tales they heard on the doorstep, of jobs lost, children could not find a job, bankruptcies, shops closed down. Everyone over the age of 25 will have a story to tell about those years.

And all this was due to government policies?

Yes. Yes. Yes. Interest rates up to 15 percent. I don't want to keep harping on the differences, but right now I would say that this country is at ease with itself. There are two things now which bother the country, not that the Government in my view is blowing it out of proportion.

I still feel safe when I am out. But I must be truthful, I must confess that when I go to London I am always cautious. For example, I would not stand near a litter bin. I would avoid anywhere that I thought might have a concealed bomb. I am very concerned about going on the Underground trains[8]. It is obvious that our bridges and water supplies are very vulnerable, if any terrorist would want to attack us. I am prepared to say that the first priority of the Government must be to protect every human being in this land, and consequently all the installations—for example generating stations, reservoirs—on which we depend. It is their responsibility to ensure that no matter what the cost, these are not maliciously interfered with. Whoever is suspected of such malicious intent should be arrested first, questions asked later. Some of the nonsense that is being touted around, I can't tolerate[9].

Well, is it nonsense? People are defending freedoms.

Yes, well freedom comes at a price sometimes. We have always been nice to everyone, but there are some who don't want to be so nice. So this legislation says, "We are still nice, but if we find that you are intending to hurt us, we're going to do something about it. We're going to move you."

That sounds fair.

You are hinting that this is an issue of human rights and civil liberties. We are all concerned about civil liberties. The trouble with those civil liberty people—I was listening to them on television—is that they are not responsible for our security and they don't have access to the secret intelligence which the government is being given.

But don't you feel happy, as I do, that the government in the last week has been given a very hard time? It makes me proud that together the houses of Parliament have been alert to the dangers of weakening our constitution. I feel they are saying that even though the Prime Minister may have reason to act like a dictator in times of perceived crisis, they are not going to let him act in such a manner. I thought in fact that the objections of Parliament resulted in exactly the right answer. I rejoice at that. Don't you?

I will say merely that I am happy that there was a full debate, and that a pragmatic decision was reached. Everyone put their case in the Commons, and it was thrashed out. Then it went to the House of Lords, where there are many learned men, perhaps at a higher level of learning and wisdom than most of the MPs. Again they debated without being restricted to the dogma of their own parties. I felt that they ended up with the best outcome in the circumstances, given that they had to rush through the law before the men were otherwise released from jail[10] to be free to roam our streets.

Of course there is the factor of the Election coming up—

And therefore political point-scoring.

—And political point-scoring does not help.

Which is why the House of Lords is so valuable because its members are not having to fight for re-election.

Yes, well it was a good debate and the outcome was satisfactory for the government with the additional bonus that it will be looked at again in a year, with more time to debate. But you know I sometimes wonder if the British public is a little naïve in such matters. I mean, look at what happened in Madrid[11]. The Spaniards did not believe that something of that scale could happen to them. France has not had any real problems in that way. France—well the Americans have been describing them very rudely.

So you are saying that France is less at risk because they are not aligned with the Americans?

[Laughs] Well the Americans—

Now this is precisely the point I was arguing last week! I am anti-American because I feel we would be safer if we were not their allies[12].

Well, I don't think it would be so nice for us to sit on the fence and let America defend us out of the goodness of their hearts.

Well, OK, and I am surprised you did not make another argument about France's position, that their opposition to American interventions in the

Middle East was less for humanitarian reasons and more to protect their own trade with despised regimes[13].

Well the Americans certainly had been calling the French a lot of names[14]. And they have done corrupt deals with their former colonies in Africa. If I am an odd one out here in speaking up for Britain, I want to say that it has a way of doing things that most people will accept. We do things out of a strong belief, from conviction and integrity. The Australians, even though they are so far away, did their bit too. They went in with the British, and the Spanish too before they had their change of leadership, based on the principle that you cannot allow terrorists to impede your daily life.

There are some of the nations of the world that you can look to and know that they will always be there for you. France's attitude now reminds me of Switzerland's neutrality in the two world wars, profiting from both sides but never putting herself at risk.

They are not upholders of high moral values?

There are a few countries like that, sitting on the fence and letting others go through the fights on their behalf.

But historically, Britain has had a terrible record on moral values.

I have always been a supporter of the United Kingdom.

But surely not historically. Take slavery—

But I said right at the beginning of our conversations, that on slavery, it was not Britain's fault alone. There were people in Africa who captured and sold the slaves, and they were as guilty and corrupt as any of the white men. So in this generation I am not going to hold anything against them and I would not encourage my children to hold anything against them.[15]

But now it is different and we can hold something against those who are causing what is happening in Africa. Governments need to re-educate their people. We have the communications media to reach the world. They have a mission now to wipe the slate clean of all the wrongs done in the past. Now is the time to do things differently so that the world can see, "Yes, we are humanity, a world community. There is no reason to allow what is happening."

And that our interventions will be for the right reasons and not just for economic gain.

Exactly. Exactly. I could not put it any clearer. I don't hold any malice against any countries, though great wrongs have been sometimes done, which hurt me as well. I was reading an article in which the historical Irish sufferings were being compared to Black sufferings. And I would add to that the sufferings of the Jewish people. The sufferings of the African slaves took place over a longer period. They were beaten, tortured, burned, raped. There is no monopoly of suffering in this world. Britain has suffered too.

Yes, I was talking to a Yorkshireman the other day who reminded me that young children were forced to go down the mines and pull carts along rails, like donkeys, never seeing daylight. It was not only the black slaves, that was his point.

Yes, but regardless of that, there was no cruelty to compare with the treatment of black slaves. The terrible brutality started before they had even left African soil. And then there was the Atlantic crossing . . . and then generations of slaves. Even their children were slaves. But they are such a tolerant, kind, long-suffering people. Some forgot—

That's why they were taken as slaves! The Spanish tried to enslave the original inhabitants of Jamaica, the Arawaks. But they just refused to work. They lay down and died, or allowed themselves to be slaughtered. Same in South America. Which is why they had to import Africans, who in any case were bigger and stronger.

Well, to close this chapter, I am glad I was not around in those days. I would be one of those who died on the first day, because I would not have worked.

This Yorkshireman I was mentioning, he is not without sensitivity, but in relation to the black history of slavery, he echoed what many white people think: "Why don't they get over it? It was terrible but it was so long ago." Well I told him what I thought—not that he wanted to know—but I wonder how you would have answered. He thinks it is used as an excuse by black people for all kinds of special treatment.

He is wrong and misguided. They can forgive, but they cannot forget.

Even today the African lands are still being ravished by those of European origins. Each day they wake up, they can see the exploitation of African produce. I heard yesterday that they use a black wood from Africa—

Ebony?

No, it is a special one, *mpingo*. They make oboes and clarinets with it, as well as some saxophone mouthpieces. The trees are in danger of extinction. There is no good substitute for this wood in making those instruments: no other material gives the required tone. Now some African botanists are taking on this problem and replanting them. Each tree will take seventy years to mature. The world-wide classical music community, which is so dependent on these instruments, accepts that it must put some money in to regenerate the planting of these trees. It is a delicate matter because the fields have to be burned at certain times to clear the land for other reasons, but without damaging these *mpingo* saplings. Till now they have exploited this wood and made great profits which have not been ploughed back into Africa, to make this crop sustainable. That's just one example. Copper and gold are other examples.

People are more educated now and we have world-wide communications media. We do lots of trade with Nigeria and South Africa, which are relatively well-off, but why don't we put investments into other African countries, so that they can be placed to supply more of our needs?

So, what are you suggesting? That Africa as a whole exports finished goods rather than raw materials?

Yes, I am suggesting that development aid should be targeted on that. Help those African countries that are already more developed to do more and help their African brother states which are less developed.

Then the question will inevitably arise, what are we going to do with those countries with bad, corrupt governments and autocratic leaders whose policies do not help their people? I know we have talked about this before.

Yes, but what I am saying is that the reason black people can forgive yet not forget, is that they can see things happening today, at this very moment. They cannot even get adequate benefit from their own land and produce. Whose fault is that? It's our fault in the West. There are so many trade barriers. These really inhibit development. It is not as if we are likely to see Africa develop so fast that they will become a threat to the West[16]. [chuckles] So why don't we help them?

One of the reasons I am suspicious of the European Union project is that it exists only for Europe's interests. If Europe is strengthening itself relative to the rest of the world this seems to me bad for Africa. Why can't we have a plan not to stop at Europe, but gradually include Africa in our community?

This is a good point here, Ian, and we may have touched on this earlier. The initiative taken by Gordon Brown[17] should be taken seriously by the rest of Europe and the United States, so that they can follow with similar proposals. As I have said to you before, if the United States is so afraid of terrorism, then the best protection against that is to feed and educate hungry people, help them use their own land so that it sustains them. Let them produce the commodities that we will want to buy. Our market is limitless in that respect: we in the West will always want more and more. People cannot claim that there is nothing they can do.

You mentioned about the corruption in Africa. This is one of the sticking points which made America reluctant to cancel their debt payments. But I also want to see American or British governments do government cleansing, where we take over a government, if it has been behaving corruptly. We could have regime change.

But don't you think that this will cause much resentment? Would it be better done by a unity of other African nations?

If Africa wants help, and they do—the world needs help, the Caribbean needs help [laughs]—

Yes, you need regime change in Jamaica!

[laughs] We are going to have regime change in Jamaica shortly[18]. [Ian cheers and claps.] In Jamaica we have 2½ million people. We are friendly both with the United Kingdom and the United States of America. We should not have the high unemployment rate that we have there. We grow only a

third of the bananas that we used to grow. That is partly because we have diversified our crops. We have real problems in Jamaica—and you have just pulled me away from the thread of our conversation by the way—in that country, if you throw down a seed anywhere, it will grow. Here in the United Kingdom, we want winter vegetables. Whatever it is, we can grow it there. There is too much land going to waste in that little country. All the governments of the United States and the United Kingdom need to do, to stop the trade in ganja and other drugs, is to give the Jamaican government money to subsidise their agricultural output, give them the machinery to work the land—people will gladly work it.

That kind of action will stop this pretence.[19] Everything else they are doing is a pretence. They know and I know we can't all become rich, especially all at the same time. But there are some of the people who need to be moved up. The rich countries know from a poor country's history that they will not be terrorists. They are very law-abiding people. They know the temperament of the people. People are not going to become terrorists or dictators overnight.

But if you let the country go down and down and do nothing about it, that is when you do breed gunmen and no-go areas, like what is starting to happen in Jamaica.

Exactly. This is the big lie. So if the United States and Europe, which is becoming one of the largest markets now, if they want to be truthful now, they, more than anyone else, know the benefits of assisting Africa. The Dutch, French, Spanish, Portuguese, English, Germans, they have all been there. If Band-Aid[20] can raise £36 million—I know that is only a small token amount of what is needed—

What about Red Nose Day[21] too? They think they will raise a record amount this year.

That's right, and all this is from private people, not government money. If all the European countries were to say, "We will match what you raise,"—

That would be good. But then of course the public would be paying twice because for every pound they donated another pound would come out of what they pay in taxes.

But it's less painful.

Especially if the government is able to save on something else to pay for it.

Exactly, and all human beings, I believe, regardless of colour shade, when they see little children rotting on their beds, or their limbs stick-like through starvation, something must come over them, even for a few minutes. They must recognise that this is abhorrent. I don't think there is a human being in this world that wouldn't feel something for those children, at least I hope I am right about this.

Yes, but I think there is a problem, and I wonder if I mentioned this to you before. If the only pictures of Africa are these starving children, so emaciated and remote from what we can imagine, I wonder if that is a barrier to people recognising that they are our brothers and sisters. Don't you think we also need to have positive images too? We need to go beyond merely being sorry for them and see them as just like us. The black people may see them as brethren but I am not sure that all the white people do.

[Pause] We are all guilty of that. Each one of us who has contributed to year-on-year fund-raising has a responsibility. My simple way of looking at it is to say, "How many farms have we tried to cultivate? How many have we helped to irrigate their lands? I want to see the results. Show me the wells you have built with the money."

You are talking about participation. I don't think we have enough of that.

Exactly. You see, we are constantly putting in money as private individuals, and so are governments. But what for? I spoke earlier that we should contribute money to help the Africans irrigate their soil. To show them by example what practical agricultural initiatives they can take. It is not impossible. So many things were done that seemed impossible at first, like when they laid cables across the Atlantic on the seabed. But we are talking of Africa, laying pipes across land. We can irrigate that continent. It is not all barren or drought-ridden.

So you are saying that we are able to do almost miraculous feats of technology, when we have the will to do so?

Exactly. What I am saying is let the United States or the EU do some substantive engineering work, that will not go away tomorrow. Irrigate the soil, teach the people—then they will always have food. It will actually cost us less than the aid, in the long term. The reason we are not doing it is this. There is no such thing as give-away, in aid terms. All the governmental aid that has gone to Africa has been paid for. We need to stop the lies[22] and get down to the core of the problem. Now I have not done any research on this, but I am not aware of any part of Africa where this has been done, in a real substantive way.

This reminds me of a book I read as a teenager. It is out of print[23]. The author proposed that the Sahara Desert be flooded to create a Tchad Sea, which would help irrigation. Its evaporation would increase rainfall in the entire region.

If we can go to the Moon, and we are looking now to go to Mars—

—And they have designed an artificial moon, a great satellite mirror, which would reflect the sun's rays at night across Siberia.

It seems to me that with a bit of determination most things are quite possible. The only reason why it is not happening is that there is no real economic gain for any one individual state.

But there is today a push from the caring population in many countries to do something. People could, if they wanted, force companies and governments to act more altruistically. Even the shareholders can put pressure on their companies.

That's a good point. I would not rule capitalism out, though I dislike its greedy motivations. We take so much out without always putting back in. Even here in the United Kingdom we are prepared to destroy jobs for our own people to get things made in East Asian countries where they can be made more cheaply. I am not happy about our factories being pulled down here so that the same goods can be made in China. What's happening there is almost frightening, though given the history of China I don't think we have anything to fear.

Well it is frightening if we imagine they might take over all the manufacturing in the world.

NOTES

1. *The Miners' Strike of 1984* lasted a year, as both Mrs Thatcher and Arthur Scargill (see note below) were equally determined to fight to the end. It seemed almost like a civil war. Not many were hurt physically: the casualties were the relations, traditionally co-operative, between police and working-class families.
2. *Arthur Scargill:* president for life of the National Union of Mineworkers.
3. *Destroying power of print unions:* It was notorious that newspaper proprietors, for all their power in the land, had not been able to break the unions' hold on the printing processes, whereby certain shift jobs which were not particularly skilled were yet highly paid and over-manned. This was the kind of challenge that Mrs Thatcher relished.
4. *Multinational companies:* E.g. Ford, where Sebert worked for more than 20 years.
5. *James Callaghan:* Labour Prime Minister from 1976. In the General Election of 1979 he was ousted by Margaret Thatcher. He died a couple of weeks after our conversation and his failure to listen to Barbara Castle's warnings about the unions was widely referred to in obituaries and reminiscences.
6. *In Place of Strife:* Government White Paper written by Barbara Castle in 1969 which proposed disciplines and legal penalties to limit the power of the unions, which fought the proposals bitterly. The following year Harold Wilson's government was toppled by the Conservatives under Edward Heath.
7. *Poll tax:* eligibility to pay the tax was based on the electoral roll, which itself is based on residence at an address.
8. *Going to London:* our conversation took place months before the London terrorist attacks of July 7th, 2005.
9. *Locking up suspected terrorists:* Sebert refers to the stormy passage of legislation through both Houses of Parliament in March 2005 to put suspected terrorists under house arrest without trial.
10. *Suspected terrorist house arrests:* The need to release them from jail on a certain day was in obedience to a directive of the European Court of Human Rights. (to be checked)
11. *Madrid:* reference to terrorist atrocity in which a train was blown up with great loss off life. This occurred before a Spanish election and influenced its outcome. The previous government tried to blame the bomb on the Basque separatist group ETA, with no supporting evidence, though the likelihood is that Al Qaeda perpetrated the outrage because of Spain's support of the US Coalition in Iraq. In the subsequent election, the people voted for a new Socialist government which promised to withdraw Spanish troops from Iraq.
12. *France less at risk from terrorists:* this was my (Ian's) brief moment of triumph. I had been waiting for the opportunity to demonstrate that Britain's support for America created an increased security risk from terrorism. See page 151.
13. *France: compassion or commercial interests?* Oddly, when I felt I had won the argument, I did the gentlemanly thing and offered him some ammunition to fight his way back! Odd, but the audio record does not lie.
14. *Calling France names:* E.g. "cheese-eating surrender monkeys". The phrase, from an episode of the American satirical cartoon, *The Simpsons*, struck a chord with many patriotic Americans when France opposed its invasion of Iraq. Americans felt poorly treated after their part in liberating France from the Nazis.

15. *Legacy of slavery:* it was odd to find myself (Ian) outraged by slavery in the colonies and all the cruel wrongs of the Industrial Revolution in England and the Potato Famine in Ireland and the slate mines in Wales etc, whilst Sebert remained staunchly pro-British throughout. Perhaps I am what in America they would call a "card-carrying Bleeding-heart Liberal".

16. *Africa's development not a threat to the West:* a veiled reference to the fears in some quarters of China's rapid technological and industrial development.

17. *Gordon Brown's initiative:* Mr Brown, the UK's Chancellor of the Exchequer, offered a package of debt relief to Africa worth £1 billion, agreeing a deal initially with Tanzania, but extending to 70 other poor nations, mostly in Africa, in the hope that other countries will follow suit.

18. *Regime change:* referring to impending national elections in Jamaica.

19. *Pretence:* See page 254.

20. *Band Aid* got its name because musicians, led by Irishman Bob Geldof, leader of the Boomtown Rats band, got together to produce charity recordings.

21. *Red Nose Day* is a biennial event organised by Comic Relief, an organisation started in 1985. With active support by many stars of show-biz, its main method is to urge viewers to donate by telephone whilst watching a 6-hour "telethon" of comedy interspersed with appeals. Red clown noses are also sold in the weeks prior to the main event as a fund-raiser in their own right (especially amongst children) and also remind people to donate more substantially. Two-thirds of the proceeds go to good causes in Africa, whilst the remaining third is directed to good causes in the UK. It has raised £337 million between 1985 and 2003, an average of £35 million per Red Nose Day.

22. *Lies:* I asked Sebert to explain what lies he was referring to. He explained that they were the same as the pretence (see page 253) that the rich countries were giving to the poor countries, whereas in reality their aid is motivated by self-interest, and has often left poor countries in crippling debt.

23. *Engineers' Dreams*, by Willy Ley. Viking Press, 1954 (US) and Phoenix House, 1955 (UK). One of his projects was the Channel Tunnel linking England and France. That has been realized. I (Ian) worked in its operating company Eurotunnel, when it first opened.

CHAPTER 19

Global challenges

YES, SO WE NEED TO BE VERY WATCHFUL AND ENSURE THAT our people have appropriate skills as I say. Maybe we can export some of our people—

Not forcibly, I hope![1]

—[Laughs] well, to acquire some of the skills and the working habits that other countries are successfully adopting.

In fact many thousands of young men and women used to go from the British Isles to all the corners of Empire: soldiers, administrators, engineers, and hone their skills and hopefully doing some good.

Yes, and then the money used to return to the United Kingdom.

Nowadays, we have students coming from all over the world, who take back their expertise. We import nurses, teachers and doctors. You are saying we should export some people too?

Well, I have been saying earlier in our discussions, we could re-educate our own people, get their skills up to a higher standard. In some ways we are still behind—we have shortages. We don't have enough scientists, for example. Our manufacturing is so reduced now, we are depending on tourism for much of our income from overseas. They come to see our London Eye[2]— we are famous for our innovations. We need to keep on being innovative.

We seem to be overstuffed with service industries—

—And some of those will not last more than five years.

In 1981 I went to Malaysia as a management consultant. But then Mrs Thatcher upset Mr Mahathir, the Malaysian Prime Minister, and he kicked out the British consultants[3]. Then Malaysia employed Filipino consultants, who offered their services more cheaply. British skills cost more. What can we now export?

[Laughs] There is education. We still have a very high prestige there. We must be very careful not to chop and change too much with our system of education. Of course we are not the only ones to be exporting skills and education. If people come here to study and find that the calibre of education here is no better than their own country, or other countries, the supply of overseas students might reduce.

I still think, though, that this country is a breeding ground for genius. This is where I think teachers should have the right to teach in a way that suits their children best, and have the right to monitor how they are progressing, to harness those brains towards the field that will most suit them and will secure them gainful employment. We will continue in Britain to produce people with innovative ideas. This is what Britain has always been about.

This makes me think of the two areas[4] in which both Britain and Jamaica excel. Can you think what they are?

[Laughs] You better tell me.

One is music. You had Bob Marley, we had the Beatles. This kind of innovation has made money for both countries.

It has indeed, but again, whereas the Beatles made millions, in so many ways—

—Including tourism, but then I think Bob Marley has done that too for Jamaica—

But again, the Western countries have got to be honest. Not only government but the businesses who manage music. I must be one of the few Jamaicans who can't sing. [Laughs] But Jamaica—

But you are famous for your karaoke performance[5].

Well, it did not make me any money. The Beatles made millions. The Government appreciated it here, because it fills the coffers. In Jamaica, because the Jamaican dollar is so different, that money is almost useless outside Jamaica.

When big money is concerned, people want American dollars.

That's right. Bob Marley's estate should be worth billions, but I doubt if it is worth much. All the royalties for what he has done are going in somebody else's pocket. I am not saying he got nothing from it, but compared to the Beatles and Michael Jackson, the well-established singers in Jamaica—let's not look at the individuals—are not comparable. Everywhere you go in the world, you can hear music that reflects a Jamaican or reggae influence. I have travelled a bit—United States, Canada, Europe—Tunisia. When I was in Tunisia, I rapped with those people, or shall I say, they rapped with me. I was amazed that they'd recognise me: "Bob Marley country?" In other parts of Africa too. Jamaican sound, from Blue Beat to Reggae, is what you hear everywhere. How much do they get for it?

It's not that I think the Government should be scooping in money for it, but the people who are in charge of the music scene, they are not giving the just rewards to the artists themselves.

But some people are saying that money, in the form of big business, destroys creativity in the music industry.

That's right. I have talked many times about dishonesty. It is the dishonesty and the greediness of people that causes the problem. Whereas Bob Marley's music was different in that it was music of peace—

He was prophet of unity and peace as much as he was musician.

Exactly. Or look at Jimmy Cliff too. An outstanding Jamaican, started before Bob Marley[6]. His message is one of hope, of people recognising who they are and how to get on. Every one can rap with that music, black or white, because it tells you whoever you are, you can make it—

   —*If you really want. I am thinking of his song, "You can get it if you really want".*

   —but then nobody promotes them. And who should do that? Well, all the people at the top, with no disrespect, are white people.

   And one thing I want to say to African people, if they really want to progress, then they have got to start creating their own employment, having control over finances,—

   But if I may interrupt, I think one good thing France has done for African music is to give them a world-wide platform. Musicians who make it to Paris often stay there, and they are doing Africa the service of telling the world about its culture. And many African musicians are doing something comparable to Bob Marley for their own countries and world unity. Sorry to interrupt the flow.

   No, it is all right. And I reiterate, with no disrespect, the finances of the world are mostly controlled by those of European extraction. There is no doubt about it. And this means that these people have the biggest influence in the creation of wealth and jobs. The developing people, for example the Jamaicans and the rest of the black world, that are coming up and developing their skills, they are really dependent on these white people. You mention France in some ways benefiting the Africans. Jamaica has benefited from America in the same way. Jamaica's musicians are very influential and not confined to Reggae.

   But the huge income does not redistribute to Jamaica in that way. What they get is a small proportion of what the white people in the music industry get. They are not promoted with their fair share of air time either. And what they play over here is not the best Jamaican music in any case. But the music with the most quality and the most meaning in the lyrics, it's not considered commercial. But if it were marketed professionally, who

---

It's most unusual!

Steve Cohen, who later admitted he did not know the song very well, joked afterwards that Sebert had been miming for most of their big duet. But Sebert's voice could be heard loud and clear by the audience . . .

From *Bucks Free Press*, 08.11.96

Mayor's karaoke has chain reaction

High Wycombe mayor Sebert Graham's karaoke performance in a local boozer has prompted requests for him to 'cut a disc' of special hits. He joined *Midweek* editor Steve Cohen at the Anchor pub to croon the Tom Jones smash, It's Not Unusual ...

From *Midweek*, 12.11.96

Sebert Graham and Steve Cohen sing "It's not unusual" in a pub Karaoke contest in aid of the Mayor's Appeal.

knows how many other reggae artists we might be hearing about in the United Kingdom?

Marketing is what requires heavy investment, so this is why music promotion is done by the rich[7]. . . .

Sorry to have diverted our conversation so much into music, but when you were talking about education towards fulfilling one's skill potential, I wanted to broaden it to arts and culture. These after all are the ways in which a vision of the world is propagated into people's imagination.

Exactly, the encouragement has to be at source. In this instance that means whilst children are at school. The teachers have a huge role to play in the world. It is a great gift. In the course of a single day a teacher has to consider so many aspects of a child's development. It is a great gift to be a good teacher.

So when I talk about monitoring children, I know there are people in my community who don't want that. But in my view you have to measure, so that you can bring out the potential. It is almost like being a scientist. There is so much evidence available of what the child is capable of. It is for the teacher to pore over it and extract meaning, to keep a constant watch[8]. I am talking about monitoring in a truthful way. To evaluate each child individually. If you do this, let's say from the age of eight or nine, and continue until he or she has left school, there should be no doubt where he or she is going to fit in.

But this is very revolutionary. You are going way beyond mere grades.

Are you saying, in effect, "We believe that every child has wonderful talents. Our aim is to bring them out and identify them?" And then you are looking at society—in a very un-Thatcherite way—to see what roles are needed, to try and match the supply to the need. And if you discover that more mathematical ability is needed, and children are not doing well enough at maths, then you will suspect that there is something wrong with your teaching methods?[9]

Absolutely. When we look at educating children, we must consider not just their needs but also skill shortages. You remember that I mentioned the uselessness of much of my education, and the irrelevance of the books we were given to read.

Well, yes, but please explain again, because I am not sure.

Well, we were given these reading books, Brer Anancy, Mother Hen and so forth—

I remember.

Totally useless.

Mind you, I have discussed this with Karleen[10] and she was shocked by you.

[Sebert laughs]

Brer Anancy is a celebrated folk tale of Jamaica, and here you are rubbishing it.

All right, I am coming back to that. Everything they are doing now, of course they are doing it for a reason, and especially from ages 7 to 10. When they get to 12+, there should be no need for this formal test[11], because they would have seen a pattern over a number of years through their method of monitoring.

Yes, and those with enormous talent, for example in dancing or music, start extremely early.

Yes. Every child should have a history which follows them right through their schooldays. Even when they go to their pre-school nursery or playgroup, teachers know even then their capabilities.

But it is not formal at present, is it? It could be like one's medical record. Ever since 1948, and the birth of the National Health Service, everyone has a medical record, and wherever you go—

—It follows you. When I came here in 1960 and started working, I was given a National Insurance number, which has never changed.

And that links to a record of your payments. And now with the technology, your education record could be kept on a smart card, for example—

Oh yes, it's not impossible to do. Then we will have less unemployment, people will not be mismatched to the job—

—Which is what happened to me—

People should be trained to develop themselves in the best way for them. You may call it an elitist society. But it won't be that. Because we will each be at the level that is appropriate for us. Not that we are stuck there. But it goes beyond the pigeon-holing of how many A-levels you have. It reveals the unique natural ability that resides in everyone. If a child says, "I want to be a teacher," then their own teacher may sit down with them and look at whether they have what it takes. Now in the past with West Indian children, because of their athleticism, being so good at sport, there is no doubt that in the past they were strongly encouraged to go into sports and physical things like that, but only the lower levels of the more literate occupations. It was rare that they would be encouraged to become a doctor or a lawyer. I could go to any West Indian family and ask them if their children in those days had been encouraged by their teachers to be doctors or lawyers. Don't take my word for it, ask them yourself whether any of them received such encouragement.

In our very first conversation, you were mentioning the Swann report on underachieving children[12]. We are talking about self-fulfilling prophecies.

Yes.

There could be an error in the assessment. You gave the example of a child who wanted to become a teacher, and being not encouraged to pursue it—

No, what I'm saying is this. No teacher or careers officer used to give encouragement to a black child to aim high.

Well, yes, but Karleen's sister, born in this country, is a barrister. She managed to make it.

OK, don't move away from what I am saying. I am speaking of the system. For black or white children, monitoring will be a good thing. Now let me talk about career structure. I know there are some black high achievers. I am saying that there was no one when they were young at school who told them that they could be these things. People had low expectations of them. And I believe that teachers still have low expectations of Afro-Caribbean children.

I have to ask why.

Well [pause], many things. Some children are brought up only by their mothers, in a single-parent family. In this country, that doesn't wash very well[13]. Society tends to look down on that. You might have a brilliant child but the parent is in a low-status job. It is not that Afro-Caribbeans are less bright than other people. In this country your background, the job your father does, the area you live in, will have an influence on your aspirations and achievements. Because of their athleticism, plus all the other things, the expectations are that they will not go to university or achieve high academically.

Well, I used to see all the West Indians in the Sixties working as bus conductors and therefore I assumed that is all they were capable of doing. I see that prejudice is born this way.

That's right. Some of them could have been teachers in their country of origin, but then they found they were not able to get a job as teachers here. And in any case you had to have many skills to work on the buses, including being able to count quickly and give out the right change. *In which they were more highly skilled than John Major!*[14] That's the truth! And some of those West Indian bus conductors were former policemen. Some of those immigrants have had a very hard time. Their expectations have not been fulfilled, through no fault of their own, but because the society in which they found themselves was unprepared for their arrival. There is a social structure, with its traditions of expectations and standards. And in this society, if you are below that standard, then God help you.

NOTES

1. *Exporting people:* a foolish interjection by Ian, but I could not help thinking of slavery, convicts being sent to Australia and the idea of repatriation of immigrants, as encouraged by Enoch Powell.
2. *London Eye:* otherwise known as the Millennium Wheel. Owned by British Airways, this is the largest observation wheel in the world and very popular with tourists.
3. *Upset Mahathir:* Britain used to offer the same subsidised university education to Commonwealth students as to British students. Prime Minister Thatcher stopped the subsidy, inciting Prime Minister Mahathir to take revenge by kicking out British consultants.
4. *Two areas in which Britain and Jamaica excel:* we got round to discussing music, but not the other area: I can't remember what it was. If I'd had cricket in mind, that would have been an error because it is the West Indian team and not the Jamaican one which is famous.
5. *Sebert's karaoke show:* fundraising effort by a pub for the Mayor's Appeal.
6. *Jimmy Cliff:* born 1948, reggae musician, latest album *Black Magic* (2004).
7. *Music promotion:* poignantly illustrated by the 1977 film *Rockers*, which shows how a young Rasta buys a small motorbike in order to travel round his country with a bunch of vinyl records, trying to place them in local outlets, whilst hampered at every turn by poverty and petty Mafias.
8. *Monitoring children in classroom:* Sebert did not say this explicitly, but I believe he means that monitoring is based on the teacher's direct observation of each child, rather than statistics of marks in tests. Qualitative monitoring in the round, rather than quantitative monitoring in a single dimension.
9. *The "Monitor and Match" method of teaching:* since Sebert had referred to these ideas in previous conversations, my question was intended as a summary of his position.
10. *Karleen:* Ian's wife, born like Sebert in Westmoreland, Jamaica. She had once typed the manuscript of a book about Brer Anancy for Jamaica's celebrated folklorist Louise Bennett (Miss Lou).
11. *Formal test:* In the County of Buckinghamshire, but not all over Britain, there is selection of secondary education for children based on the "Eleven Plus" examination though in Bucks it used to be a year later, hence 12+. Those who pass go to "grammar" schools. Those who do not, go to what used to be called "secondary modern" schools. Since the qualification for what now seem to be called "other secondary schools" is to "fail the eleven plus", the whole subject is treated as delicate, rather like "race". However, it seems that the people of Bucks do not want their test abolished or to establish the "comprehensive" system of secondary education which operates across most of Britain.
12. *Underachieving children:* see also Appendix A, "West Indians do as well as whites at our school – head declares".
13. *Single parents:* In Jamaica and African countries, a child might be partly looked after by grandparents, or even great-grandparents, so that the effect of an absent father might be less.
14. *John Major, would-be bus conductor:* after leaving school at 16, he applied to be a bus conductor but his application was rejected, allegedly because of poor mental arithmetic. This supposed shortcoming did not prevent him becoming Chief Secretary to the Treasury, Chancellor of the Exchequer and Prime Minister from 1990-1997.

CHAPTER 20

One people

IAN, GOOD MORNING AGAIN, WE'VE HAD OUR LITTLE BREAK for a couple of weeks, over Easter, and now we resume our journey[1]. I hope you won't be fed up with me calling it a journey. This morning I would like to look towards the future, having spent some time recently with a group of young people, highly educated young men. One of them as it happens was born in the Caribbean, on the island of St Vincent, and has come to the United Kingdom to pursue his law degree. I was very moved by our discussions and I would like to share with you my pride in meeting these young people last night, on the 2nd April, 2005. It seems like a good occasion to look at how the future lies for the people of the Caribbean, those small developing countries.

Like many developing countries in the world, they are much hampered by international trade tariffs from making greater progress, and finding their economic strength. These barriers to free trade make things extremely difficult for them. But there is reason for hope, as the young people in those parts have had access to higher education and now they are starting off on a more level playing field.

It does not really matter what the propagandists may be saying about black people not achieving. I know that here in the United Kingdom there is a tendency to say that the educational system is failing black children. It might be a failure on both sides, but I must admit that I am more concerned about the failures or underachievement of the black minorities. There have been suggestions recently by Trevor Phillips[2] who is the Chair of the Commission for Racial Equality. I am in great sympathy with some of what Trevor has put forward. But I don't want to see some kind of apartheid within education in this country. My experience of race relations is that black people are not asking for any special treatment, just a level playing field. If the education system here is strong enough and fair enough, if children are given the same start, the same opportunity, and the same treatment, black children will be able to achieve as much as their white peers. But it's got to be seen to be fair.

My issue is not about whether we should have grammar schools or comprehensive schools[3]. Whatever system we have it should be level enough and good enough, with parents having the choice, knowing that whichever they choose, their child will have the best chance of emerging with good recognised qualifications. And if this is not achieved by normal means, then I am fully in agreement with Trevor Phillips that there should be funds allocated for schools with black teachers. They would follow the same curriculum as all the other pupils in the country but with more attention to their own black cultural heritage. These black teachers would be more familiar with the patterns of gesturing for example; something that a white teacher would not find so easy to recognise. It is true that a white teacher will have had a certain experience of black behavioural mannerisms, but he will not fully comprehend fully the significance of their behaviour and what they say.

You said something about gesturing.

Yes, for example certain movements of the arms and the head. If I acted like that and you were the teacher you might think I was getting excited. But it is not that. It is their way of expressing themselves with all of their body, a bit like the Italians perhaps, and other Mediterraneans. And sometimes [laughs] they can be misunderstood for that kind of thing. It is something for the education system to recognise.

But let us come back to the main point of education of those who live in the Caribbean. I spoke in earlier sessions about the education I received in the Nineteen-Fifties in Jamaica. Well that is no more. It is now much better there. It is excellent by comparison with what it was, though there is still room for improvement. Now, it is mainly a question of a rather poor economy finding enough extra money to put into education, to raise it still further.

You are talking about Jamaica.

Yes but this applies equally to all those Caribbean countries which were formerly protectorates of the United Kingdom. There has been aid from the UK, US and Canada, sometimes through the World Bank. But in such cases, the agenda has been set. The money is made available for certain restricted purposes, such as road development. There might be a small allowance towards education, but they don't leave the recipient government any discretion in how it is spent. And that is not really fair.

I am wondering if the Caribbean countries would be stronger if they were more politically united, like the European Union.

Well, this is a subject that we are coming to. When we started our Federation[4], which if my memory serves me right was about 55 years ago—

—Which was before independence?

Yes, Jamaica, Barbados, Trinidad, Grenada, and others. Had we pursued federation in the true sense of a supra-national government, we would have been much better off now. We have the European Union, which shows what that Federation could have become like. When that federation was formed, there was no European Common Market[5]. The European countries were still at loggerheads with each other. Had the Caribbean countries stayed with it and developed it, they would have been better placed today. There might be a difference in the approach in the banana trade with the eastern

Caribbean for example. All of the countries would now be planting bananas, cane, taniers, and the various fruits.

Taniers?

Yes that is a food, a kind of provision, we have baddus, we have yam, we have taniers, dasheens[6]. And there are also winter vegetables, which are purchased by the United States, Canada and Europe. The Caribbean's wealth of sunshine and fertile soil renders it gifted to produce the kinds of produce prized by the world. Then there is Trinidad with its asphalt, and Jamaica with its bauxite, used to make aluminium. They could have been in a dominant position, had they got together. However, it is not too late. Now we have the CARICOM[7] States, pursuing a similar course, trying to knit things together. That's good but we need greater co-operation from some of the countries concerned. It's no longer a time that we should all be growing the same crop with each country trying to sell it to these huge markets. I would like to see it being organised co-operatively so that say Jamaica, Barbados and the other countries would each produce an agreed quota of sugar. The resulting tonnage of sugar would be marketed as a unified Caribbean product. Therefore you would have a better chance of getting a good price for it, by putting them all through one channel. By coming on the market with a bigger volume of commodity, you have greater bargaining power and more chance to determine a fair price.

So I see that the future will be determined by those who are now the young people, like those whom I met last night, with their high level of education and fresh thinking. They will be the Caribbean leaders. There, like anywhere, you find a class structure. You will be looked up to if you had completed your education overseas. It doesn't make you the best person. In this country, I would not say that the best brains are the ones who end up in politics, and it is no different in the Caribbean. Family background has tended to influence an individual's outcome just as much as the educational grades that he or she may have attained. We need to sweep those traditions out of the way.

Now, I am talking especially about Jamaica when I say that in our two dominant political parties, we have strange people who stay leading them for years and years—too long, they never know when to step down, even when the people are saying it is time for them to retire—

Why am I thinking of Edward Seaga?[8]

[Laughs] Well, that's you! Well, he is a good man, but there comes a time when you say, "Yes, I have done my bit. Yes, there are brighter young people coming up, and this is their future."

So I hope that sometime soon the Caribbean which consists of about 33 million people—I am not including Cuba or Haiti—will realize that it is time to bury national pride, and take a step that will help bring prosperity for the next generation, and a greater recognition of ourselves as one people.

Let's have a Caribbean government, and then you can imagine in so many years' time Jamaica holding the presidency, and let us say Trinidad holding the Finance Ministry. Let us co-ordinate our best minds in the Caribbean, and have a single state.

They are already doing this with the Caribbean Court of Justice, isn't this the same kind of thing?

Well, there is still a question mark over that. Yes, it is a similar kind of thing. But I am hoping that the business people in these countries will see sense, and set the pace, rather than the politicians. And then I would welcome it if the politicians would listen to the voices of business, and indeed to the voices of the people. And then the political parties could set their agendas to take account of those arguments. It is the business people who will be able to bring money into those countries, through the cultivation of excellence. Politicians should recognise that policies which help business will be for the benefit of the country as a whole. Economic improvement will help education, police and all kinds of development. I am hopeful for that.

I remember attending a meeting in Westminster Hall, listening to Sonny Ramphal, who was at one time the Commonwealth Secretary-General. Some of these arguments had been put. In the Caribbean there is a tendency at times—or indeed I can say this about black countries in general—for other people to tell us what's wrong, what we need. But then, knowing what needs to be done, we shelve taking action. We let the plans gather dust on the shelves. Then five years later the subject is discussed again: the very same topics which were brought up five years earlier. This is the kind of stupidity and nonsense that we need to stop. When we see a positive way forward, that is when government ought to act.

So I am hopeful that the younger people can take over the reins in due course. It is going to be their world. It could be like in the Sixties when the students were strong. They were activists and showed a lot of courage, by demonstrating in support of principles which they felt strongly about. We have seen in a few countries lately where people-power has been the spearhead for change. People get fed up of waiting for redress. If there is no action, then people should take action themselves.

Are you thinking of the Ukraine[9] and Kyrgyzstan[10]?

Yes, and I am thinking that it can't be long before they take similar action in the Caribbean. They are not what you would call corrupt governments comparable to some others in the world, but still they are not altogether straight. The people have suffered and if a party has been in power for more than ten years, and the people are not happy, the government of the day should be answerable to them and make a case. If they win the argument and the people agree with them, then by all means the elections should be accepted as fair and transparent. But it is not just transparency in the election process. What we are looking for is truthfulness from the politicians. They have not reached where they are because they are the best and most deserving people of the day to hold that office. Politicians should feel obliged at a certain point for the country's sake to admit that they have done their bit and should move over for someone else who is as bright or maybe brighter. There is probably someone else in the Cabinet who is ready to be a better leader. They should be prepared to take a backward step, not to disappear from politics altogether, but to take another role.

I believe you are saying that politicians should act out of public-spiritedness more than at present. To my perception, their own survival is all too often their first priority. You are saying their first priority should be the benefit of their country. I suppose they may be egotistical enough to think that the one leads to the other.

Absolutely. You see, power is sweet. People find it hard to relinquish it without a struggle.

Politicians who are ready to relinquish power[11] are in fact the popular ones, for example Nelson Mandela. The most unpopular ones fear the revenge of the people and the worst refuse to stand down until they are offered safe havens.

Nelson Mandela is a real example to all black political leaders: someone who spent 27 years or so in jail. He suffered. Then he came out, triumphantly gained power, never took revenge on the people who persecuted him, always did his best for his country, and then when it was time for him to go, he went without a struggle. He did not want to get in the way of anyone else's leadership and he remains as respected now, or even more, than when he was in jail or in power. That is the mark of a man who cares for his people. In fact he is not just caring about African people. He is caring about the world. This is his genuineness.

A lot of political leaders do put themselves first. They treat the country as if it is their bank. But the best ones know what it is to suffer and they have not forgotten. They have compassion.

I want to come back to the Caribbean. What I have expressed is what they should truly be fighting for. Unless they can create jobs and foster economic development, what use are they?[12] They must give the young people the chance to get involved in politics. The available technology needs to be harnessed, such as e-commerce. We need to give priority to using our own native products in the best possible way. We have a tendency to export more than we should. It's only happening because of the economic situation that we find ourselves in. What we have to do is create the atmosphere where whatever we produce, the people of the soil will be the first and greatest beneficiaries.

Can you give an example of this—exporting things that should have been kept for home consumption?

Yes, there are several examples. Let's take aluminium[13]. Why couldn't aluminium be used extensively in house-building within Jamaica? It is waterproof, it is not going to rust. It could be used in a lot of ways to help development, such as in low-cost housing schemes. Some years ago the mining industry was at its height. Perhaps we could have eliminated the poor housing—people living in shacks—if we had been sensible. We could have used the resources we had for our own direct benefit.

Or consider the import of Japanese and European cars[14]. We could have insisted on a deal with them to say that "We will not buy your cars unless you put some infrastructure in place so that the growers have some good roads to get their produce out of the mountains". As things stand, the producers have to sell their goods somehow and unless there is an excellent infrastructure, the exporting of surplus product at a good price cannot take place. Their need to export is so that they have the money to buy, for example, imported foodstuffs such as corn flakes. We are exporting things from the Caribbean that could have been used domestically.

So what are you proposing? That importers and exporters work more closely with Government, so as to act in the best interests of the country?

Yes, the coffee industry is now taking up more land, for example to satisfy demand from Japan. Whether the producers are getting the right price is another question. Which comes back to my earlier point, that Caribbean governments should form their own consortium to pool resources and establish co-ordinated prices for the commodities they are selling to the world. This would improve the economies of the member countries. This in turn would allow them to improve their education standards. These are some pointers for people to follow. We are looking for the new generation to improve things.

But there are so many coffee-producing countries in the world that it will be hard to raise prices in the Caribbean, won't it? Buyers will simply look elsewhere.

No, it is the quality of the coffees, they are all of different types. We in Jamaica are gifted in having some of the best coffees[15]. And of course coffee is just an example. The whole outlook for the Caribbean has got to change. We have to move beyond the thinking of the last thirty years. Markets are global now and we have to position ourselves strategically as the people of the Caribbean under their governments to capture some of the benefits now available. We need to stay on top and be in with the best of the world, not lagging behind—there is no need for that. Education there is of a good enough standard. They are also in a good position. Many have gone to the United States, the United Kingdom and Canada for their education, even to other parts of Europe. The Caribbean people, 33 million of them, have a wealth of education of the highest international standard. They should be riding high. There is no reason for them to be outsiders. They should be at the front. They have the right calibre of people and should be well equipped.

All right, but to the extent that we may be referring to expatriate Caribbeans who are the ones who have most benefited from this international education, how are they going to help the Caribbean countries? Or let me put this more personally, what kind of a role can you see for yourself? You are full of energy to support the situation and I am wondering what organisation you might want to join—or start—in which to make this input fruitful?

[Laughs] You can't catch me out again. If I was to say anything else to answer any part of that, other than what I have already said, it would be to say that the future is for the younger people. And also I would say that the Caribbean has got to move away from the influence of the older people. My contribution is here. If it is readable and it makes sense, I hope it may even get read by some leaders, who can take it to their governments. That will be my contribution. That is the contribution that I can make as an expatriate. And I am also making my contribution in working with the young, and encouraging them to go back to their father's or mother's country and make a useful contribution to those developments.

I don't want to offend those who live in those countries, when I talk about expatriates coming home with education. I do recognise and I have said it before that the people in the Caribbean are well-educated, and indeed well above earlier standards, and there is still room to make it even better. It remains the case that the expatriates going back home may have certain experience and skills that those at home don't have. Together as a team the expatriates and those who were born and educated in the Caribbean could make a definite difference to the way that those countries develop.

So this is my contribution [laughs]

Well I do feel inspired by that. One of the things I did whilst in Jamaica was to type up MA students' dissertations. I was struck by the focus which they all had on promoting benefit to their own country. Over here I think you would generally find something different in academic circles—elitism and self-aggrandisement. There, they were working on topics like the development of tourism. Or even philosophy. It is very important to understand not just the European philosophical schools which started with the Greeks, but to understand that the roots of philosophy go further back, to Egypt for example. I think philosophy is important in regenerating a country's identity. Why should it look at life with a Eurocentric perspective?[16] There is indeed much to undo. Even in my lifetime, in the Fifties, Africa was seen as a resource to be pillaged by the whole of Europe through colonialism.

Yes you are certainly right. I am not sure if it is just in Jamaica that they have this special direction that they want to go. I know that in our conversations I normally talk very strongly about Jamaica. It's not that I am leaving out the rest of the Caribbean, and at this moment I am considering the full picture across the Caribbean. They have to look strategically at where they want to go, and adopt as you say their own identity and philosophy, to make the transition from our inheritance to the clearer vision that now emerges, of how to pool resources and advance the countries in the Caribbean. It can be done and one of the things I found in the early Sixties when I came over here, was the indifference which those from different islands had to one another. They would call one another names, "Smallie" if they came from one of the smaller islands. Today I see that there is less of that nonsense-talk. There is a more positive feeling between the different sets of people. It's wonderful to have a loyalty to the nation that one comes from. Being black people from the Caribbean we should recognise that we have a common cause, to achieve certain goals, to get a position in the world by a set time. There is only one reason for those goals. It is for the upliftment of our people.

I wonder if I could repeat an anecdote I heard on Desert Island Discs. Yvonne Brewster[17] came over from Jamaica in the Fifties from a rich family to study drama, when there were few West Indians in London. One day at Tottenham Court Road Station she saw a man she recognised who had worked on the family estate. He was so glad to see her that he came up and hugged her, feeling perhaps that their mutual exile overcame the class divide that would have made this act unthinkable in Jamaica. She said "How dare you!" and he went off in shame. She has remembered and regretted her words for more than fifty years.

Yes, you see this is a weakness in some of us, to preserve such distinctions. If only they had read the teachings of Marcus Garvey[18] as spread through his Universal Negro Improvement Association. He did things to prove to Jamaicans, "If I can do it, then you can do it as well." He provided many examples of that. His teachings were that you should recognise who you are. I do sympathise with that man that she met, whose self-esteem perhaps had gone. And had he been a confident person, that kind of behaviour could have been reversed.

Yes, that is like that earlier instance, that I was telling you about, when I left the Army and was seeking employment. You get those patronising letters, knowing very well that for a black African Caribbean person applying for those job positions that were available, someone of a fairer skin would have been given the first refusal. I was of the second-rate, as far as they were concerned. The class system out there was partly based on colour.

But when you were applying for a job by letter, they would not have known what colour you were.

[Pause] No, well, you see in that country it was not hard to work out. Our names may be as good as anyone else's but where you are writing from, what you put in your letter, all these things can be easily interpreted.

And of course they scrutinise these things very carefully for clues.

And if you phone up, they will listen to the accent, and try to draw conclusions from it.

[Chuckles] Yes, it is the same everywhere, nothing changes. Yes, this business of personal self-esteem. But we all learn. I am sure that in the story you just told, he reflected on it. And she obviously did too. We do things in the heat of the moment, then we walk away and there is time for long reflection. We have a conscience but sometimes we do or say something which seemed right at the time. But afterwards, you have to make peace with yourself.

I would like to wrap this up by summarising that the Caribbean is a single region, even though we are many nations with our different dialects and so on. We all recognise each other's abilities and our African origins. What hurts one, hurts all. When a hurricane hits, it does not matter which island. We are in awe, just hoping it will go away. But whichever island gets it, we all feel it. That is when we recognise our brotherhood. I have been talking about how we can come together and be even closer, working for a common goal. It is driven by business, the need to capture overseas markets. It needs politicians to be honest with themselves and recognise the need to organise a single market. I hope that having recognised it they will not deviate from it and the quicker they can do it the better.

I know you are trying to round this off, but I still have a question.

[Chuckles]

We are talking about the Caribbean as a single region but there are some artificial boundaries, which I think are mainly set up by languages. Outside the English-speaking group of nations there are Haiti[19] and Cuba[20]. From one point of view they are brothers because they all came from Africa under similar circumstances. It is not their fault that they are separate. They were under the control of different colonial powers. I think it is a shame they are not closer. Or maybe they are closer than I think.

They are close. Cuba is in a different category from the other countries I have been talking about earlier: Trinidad, Barbados, St Vincent and the Grenadines, and all those English-speaking islands. When you look at all those places, and I include Dutch Guyana amongst them, what we have in common is our African ancestry. The black Cubans are also of the same ethnic group. I don't think you will find a single Jamaican family which does not have at least one relative in Cuba, or I will be cautious and say that at least 75 percent of Jamaicans have such connections—perhaps with someone who went to work there for a time. We still have that feeling for Cuba.

The 33 millions I was speaking of, I don't think they include Cuba. They might include Haiti. And what we must note is that in Haiti the structure of power is uncommon in the Caribbean. All the same we still look at them as our brothers. Jamaica welcomes Haitian refugees, though we are a poor country ourselves. Other countries operate border controls, but Jamaica just welcomes everyone's refugees.

So I have really been talking about the English-speaking Caribbean countries. If they were to focus, so that their economies get right, we would be in a position to help Haiti. We could supply some oil more cheaply to those countries. Haiti is one of our poorest sister countries. If we get some economic strength, they will also be benefited. We might want to pull them along. At the moment it would be difficult for an English-speaking common market of Jamaica, Trinidad, Barbados etc to say, "Come on and join us," because they couldn't sustain that. We have some good neighbours, Venezuela, for example. They have some difficulties with the United States, but still they have been helpful to Jamaica. I am thankful to see that the co-operation between Jamaica, Venezuela and Cuba is still going.

The United States is doing and has done a lot as well. There are those countries in the Caribbean that you could call democrats and those you could call conservatives. None of them are what you could call socialist, in our European sense (I am not talking about Cuba of course). Jamaica, I would say—especially the churches—is what you would call conservative. *Very conservative.*

NOTES

1. The remaining chapters are the edited transcript of a conversation on April 3rd 2005.
2. *Suggestions by Trevor Phillips:* "Black boys may have to be separated from classmates to help improve school performance, the head of the Commission for Racial Equality has suggested. Trevor Phillips also suggested black fathers not living with their sons should be denied access if they refused to attend parents' evenings." (from BBC website, 7th March 2005).
3. *Grammar, comprehensive schools:* "Grammar schools" are the basis of the selective education system retained in Buckinghamshire and a few other counties in Britain. In the non-selective system, traditionally favoured by the Labour Party, all children go to comprehensive secondary education without selection at age 11+.
4. *Caribbean Federation:* started in January 3rd1958 and lasted only till 1962 when Jamaicans voted against it in a referendum.
5. *European Common Market (now the European Union):* In fact the implementation of the Treaty of Rome on January 1st 1958 predated the Caribbean Federation by two days, though Great Britain did not join until 1973.
6. *Taniers, baddus, yams, dasheens:* varieties of staple foods grown in Jamaica.
7. *CARICOM:* the collapse of the Caribbean Federation in 1962 led to many initiatives to join in common causes across the English-speaking (ex-British) Caribbean countries, for example a Meteorological Service, the University of the West Indies, the Caribbean Development Bank, and in 1973 the birth of CARICOM, the Caribbean Community and Common Market. Surinam and Haiti have also joined.
8. *Edward Seaga:* an MP since Independence in 1962, Prime Minister from 1980-1989 and leader of Jamaica Labour Party from 1974 to 2005, giving the impression even then that his resignation was reluctant.
9. *Ukraine:* In November 2004 Ukraine held an election widely reported as flawed and it was later discovered that the losing Presidential candidate, Viktor Yushchenko, had been poisoned. Peaceful street protests forced a re-election the following month and Yushchenko won.
10. *Kyrgyzstan:* In late March 2005 Mr Akayev was deposed from his presidency by spontaneous peaceful protests by the people, though at the time of writing this (April 4, 2005) there is competition between two possible successors.
11. *Popular politicians are prepared to stand down:* I could also have given a Jamaican example in the person of Hugh Shearer, who stepped down as Prime Minister in 1974. At his death thirty years later,

in 2004, he was greatly mourned and praised by everyone, regardless of political allegiance, for his humanity as much as his political skills.

12. *Superfluous politicians:* when I (Ian) was in Jamaica, I was astonished at the attitude of the main political parties with an election less than a year away. There was little evidence of a vision for the future. It did not seem that the Government were in control of the country. Politicians pursued their own internecine agendas and the Government of PJ Patterson appeared generally dignified but helpless.

13. *Aluminium* is produced from bauxite, which occurs in a mud that is widely present in Jamaica. Mining started in the early Fifties and at one time Jamaica was the world's largest producer. However, its production is no longer very significant in the world commodities market. It has been blamed for deforestation in Jamaica and its contribution to employment is small. Bauxite and alumina production accounted for 9.2% of Jamaica's GDP in 1996. (Source: http://minerals.usgs.gov/minerals/pubs/country/1996/9515096.pdf)

14. *Japanese cars:* Jamaica, in common with other developing countries, imports many of these cars second-hand.

15. *Best coffees:* e.g. from Jamaica's Blue Mountains.

16. *Caribbean philosophy:* I (Ian) also had the privilege to type manuscript articles by the Jamaican poet, short story writer and philosopher Earl McKenzie, who has drawn together philosophical threads from a variety of Caribbean literary sources.

17. *Yvonne Brewster* is a prominent theatre director in the UK and has been voted one of the top 100 Black Britons. In Jamaica she founded the Barn and Talawa theatre companies, in 1970 and 1985 respectively. Both are still thriving.

18. *Marcus Garvey:* (1887-1940) Jamaican-born publisher, journalist, entrepreneur, crusader for black nationalism. Championed the "back to Africa" movement and considered a great prophet of the Rastafari movement.

19. *Haiti:* the original populations of Arawaks and Caribs were wiped out by the Spanish. The French took over and made it prosperous at the cost of importing African slaves, who were treated in the usual horrible way. The French Revolution inspired these slaves and their descendants to seek Liberty, Equality and Fraternity. The colonists and later Napoleon had different ideas. Haiti became the first independent black-ruled republic, in 1804.

20. *Cuba:* its early history resembled that of Haiti, but the Spanish held on to this island and it did not become a self-governing republic till 1902, though it remained dominated economically by the United States. Fidel Castro has remained in power since 1959 after wresting control from Batista. His Leftist government has been in economic conflict all that time, and in 1962 the USSR's military support for Cuba nearly caused nuclear war between the superpowers.

CHAPTER 21

Truthfulness

SO IF THE UNITED STATES, BRITAIN AND EUROPE, REALLY AND truly want to help—this is the hypocrisy, when we look at poor countries and talk about what we can do to help. This is a question that I raise again and again. Truthfulness. If the politicians want to be truthful, and regain our respect for them—When I first came to the United Kingdom, there were politicians I admired. If you looked at them and the way that they spoke, you would feel good. I remember there was one called Quintin Hogg[1]. He was very fond of saying "The law is an ass." [Laughs] Now Harold Wilson, there is an example of a politician who stepped down when he had had enough.

Wasn't that because he was starting to get Alzheimer's disease?

No, I don't think that is a known fact. People were more comfortable with politicians in those days. The only way that they can really seize the initiative is by acting truthfully and showing real leadership.

Now there is a point which you have brought up a number of times in the course of our conversations. It has to do with pretence.

Yes, the pretence of governments, especially of the United States and the United Kingdom. If you look at the situation of world poverty, it is nonsense in my humble opinion that they cannot intervene to alleviate hunger in the world. If the United States and the United Kingdom were really serious about it, they could. Take Jamaica, which is almost in the backyard of the United States, a super-rich nation. The people in the developed world could have helped the people of the Caribbean back in the Nineteen-Thirties, knowing that there was so much poverty on that island, people living in shacks, by giving them a cheaper loan. Or they could have given them what we call aid, to build proper housing. They could have assisted those governments in the development of their agricultural land by lending enough finance to purchase tractors and bulldozers. We have 14 parishes[2] in my country, 15 if you count Port Royal[3], but those fourteen are food-producing parishes, for example St Elizabeth, which grows a lot of cassava and pigeon peas and red peas; or Hanover, where we cultivate yam in large quantities on very fertile land. It would not have taken more than 2 bulldozers and two tractors in each parish. They could do a big acreage each day and then move on to another farm. This would have helped create employment and food product that could be exported. We were a United Kingdom protectorate. The United States used to offer our people jobs to pick oranges and so forth. Why not create employment in the islands of Trinidad and Jamaica and so forth, instead of inviting migrant workers?

So this is what I mean by the pretence. If they really wanted to, they could help the people in the developing countries, by teaching them skills, helping them maximise the yields from their own land. But they have not done that. The so-called aid that they have provided to countries is not given free. The recipient government pays for years and years after the loan has been taken out. The high interest payments then weaken the economy of the recipient country.

The pretence is to say "We're helping you" when actually what they are doing is helping themselves. And from a Jamaican perspective what I am referring to is those two countries that we have been closer to than any other countries in the world.

I think there was quite a different consciousness, in colonial times. There was not a sense of all of us being equal. The colonies were to be mined and farmed for their riches. All you had to do was to make sure that the people didn't starve. It was not thought that their people were equals deserving of the same chances in life. In fact I have heard that the education in places like Jamaica did not even aim at the highest standards. Because though slavery had been outlawed there was still the idea that they only need to be educated to the level that is required to make them useful. I find it shocking but I realise looking back that there has been serious prejudice, in my own lifetime.

Well, yes, and when I think back to my early years of education, what you have said is absolutely correct. In 1944 we had an Act giving universal suffrage in Jamaica. Before that people were—as you rightly put it—maybe people were given just enough education to fit in to their employer's needs perhaps, or to a certain part of society. In one of our earlier sessions I spoke of Norman Manley and Dr Eric Williams, those men of such stature in the Caribbean who came up through the normal system, not any particularly rich family background. Then they came to this country and obtained degrees with such high honours that they must have been absolutely brilliant. Even in my lifetime, education for girls was considered by some as rather less necessary by some people.

But that was true in Europe too, in the old days.

[Laughs] Well, if even the girls in Europe were suffering from this, then you can imagine what the Africans were going through. You will recall what I said to you about the sufferings of the Jews[4] and the Irish[5] and the other oppressed people. But the African slaves in the Caribbean were not allowed to communicate with each other. They were not permitted to be seen holding conversations. This would be enough to bring down floggings, incarceration and possibly death[6].

We have travelled a long way. There is something that I would particularly like to point out to young people. There is a tendency of our government to point out the advancement of one part of the community in comparison with others. This is a dangerous precedent. Let me make it clearer and clearer now for my African brothers, and in fact for all the young people in school. They ought to be absolutely proud of who they are. In those times of slavery the Indians in those Caribbean communities were given the chance to be taught commerce, but the Africans were not even allowed to talk to each another, never mind having the opportunity to learn commerce, which of course involved learning to read and write.

So who were these Indians? Are you talking about the indentured labourers?[7]

That's right. However they got there, they were treated differently. They were able to communicate. They were able to train in commerce and trade. Africans had no such privilege. All that was demanded of them was to be good strong sexual beasts. They were able to do the hard work and reproduce their kind, to produce another generation of slaves. Very little was given to them. You can see that those African people, who have survived such a long line of suffering, have done extremely well. Now we are the equal of anyone today. We have designers. Who was it who invented the traffic light? I think you will find that it was a black person.[8] Who made the shoe last?[9] When you look at the processes that they use to extract sugar from cane, I think you will find that a black man[10] made a big advance in that.

So I say to young people this: that African people have as good a history as anyone else. They are to be proud of it and never allow themselves to be put down, or to feel inferior to anyone else. But they should know that we are all achievers, all of us, black and white in this world. Every kind of person has made a contribution to the world that we have today. Maybe the Africans, through the legacy of Egyptian civilisation, made an even better contribution.

[Pause]

Well, I think so, yes.

So, [laughs] I want to say to the young people reading this. Here is something, and you can always go and do your own research. What I am saying is this. We are great achievers, and we have achieved through suffering.

[Pause] So, that puts the cap on that topic.

Good. OK [laughs]

I think I have covered your question, and I have pointed out the shortfall of politicians in their "pretence". There is a lot more to that pretence as well.

Yes, I think so.

Right now there is a pretence going on. You see it on the television. There are things to make you think. If we are going to spend billions of dollars, to create a shield of defence against attack from the air, to stop one country attacking another country, if we are prepared to spend massive sums of money to develop the Star Wars project, and cause massive pollution in the world; why not spend the money sensibly and create irrigation in Africa? Flood the waters of the Zambesi with a dam: you can dig the trench beforehand, so that the water will go a different way. The rain will always come again, to refill part of it.

I think I have grasped the essence of the pretence. Can I suggest to you what I think it is? International politics has always been conducted in terms of power. Historically, no country has wanted to encourage other countries too much, for fear that they become powerful and threatening. So in the poor countries an interest in world brotherhood may start to flourish, but the foreign policy of the richer countries remains to keep other countries at a lower level. They even have a rationale to support their view. The rich countries have already endangered the world with pollution. They don't want the poor countries to develop too much and make it worse. The poorer countries request the rich countries to stop polluting so much.[11] America refuses.

True. Pretence. What you say is exactly right. Big countries, big businesses, they want to stay in control. Looking at it more locally, we cannot afford to make everybody white-collar workers. There has to be someone to sweep the streets and do those kinds of jobs. Limits are established to keep things under control. And they are applied also in the world order. If Jamaica and the Caribbean were helped to become sufficiently powerful and self-sufficient, where would the rich countries look to sell their goods to? So it is economic considerations which really predominate. There is a pretence that we want to help the poor, but it's a lie. The United States wants to export its excess goods. And here in the United Kingdom it is the same. Therefore we have to have that kind of control,[12] that kind of order, in relation to the world. But then we may ask ourselves, does China have atomic weapons? If they haven't got them, but decide they want to get them, are the United States going to say, "You can't have them?" Would they therefore attack China? The answer is "No!" They could not afford to do that. The population is too large, and China's resources now are equal to the United States, in a way. They are looking at what they have achieved in the last thirty or fifty years. At the rate of accelerating growth that they are currently achieving, they are going to overtake the United States. They have already overtaken Britain. What are we going to do? Are we going to stop them doing what they are doing? Before long it will be their cheap goods that will be flooding the poor countries. Because the control that we in the West have over our smaller Western brothers will have to be loosened. We alone are not going to stay as the sole providers of what the world has now come to perceive as necessity. There are things that everyone will be wanting. This is why I say that we in the West, the big players, have got to redefine our strategy, where we are going. What are we going to do with China, and with India? India is now a big player in our life in the West. These days we are exporting jobs to India.[13] It is such a populous country which has a high respect for education. Here we are in the West, the United States, France, Germany, Britain and all the rest, making our lives comfortable. We will really and truly have to be thinking where is this going to end? How is the world order to be controlled and developed? Who will be the key players?

Yes, there is a pretence. We have only just outlined a few of the aspects of why it happens, why the aspirations of humanity are not being allowed to gain fulfilment. But they will not be truthful about it to the people. They won't tell them, "You've got to remain as you are, at the bottom of the heap." [Laughs] The world should know the truth. There is no doubt about it. [Laughs]

The question for me is this. Now there is only one superpower. How can you express opposition to it? Obviously terrorism is one weapon, which on moral and other grounds we reject. What else do we have? I can only come up with something vague, called people power. People have a conscience. They have a sense of what's right, a sense of brotherhood, and I am not even sure how much leadership is required. As in Ukraine, as in Kyrgyzstan, they seem to rise up spontaneously.

Well that was the answer I was going to give you! It's the people. Regardless of how powerful the United States is, it's been played out as I was saying to you before. There comes a time when they will be overspending. In order for the United States to continue as at present it will always have to squeeze its military budget. By increasing its military budget by a certain amount it will also have to raise that amount of money in taxation. Some of the world's resources are running out. I know they said twenty-five years ago that by now we would be running out of oil and that has proved untrue. But if they continue going on like this they will run out of resources. Their economy will get weaker and as that happens people will grow disenchanted. The United States would begin to decline and give space to the Chinese to grow more. There is no stopping them now. There is a free market. Everyone can try and sell their goods in this global village. There may not necessarily be another cold war but there might be an economic war, a trade war. This is the most likely scenario, a real tussle between East and West. Korea, China, India, with all their goods coming here, so cheap. There is nothing you can do to stop it. Meanwhile, you can't forever waste valuable resources on weaponry instead of valuable things to give us all a better life. A long time ago when they showed footage of China the streets were thronged with push-bikes. And recently I saw more recent footage and you could compare the highways and the houses with those in the United Kingdom. Nowadays their streets are full of cars. Now they are acquiring the comforts of life that everyone wants.

Pretence. Governments should really let the people know what is happening. If people have been prepared, it is easier for them to accept.

One thing that seems plain today is that with our modern communications that jump across national boundaries, like the Internet and satellite TV, it is no longer possible to limit the information they get, or impose on them a

one-sided propaganda. For much of the Cold War, the people in the USSR
believed they were better off than in the West. That could not happen today.

Yes, people are better informed and maybe that played its direct role in
the downfall of Communist governments in Russia, and the pulling down
of the Berlin Wall. Television showed them how their cousins were faring
on the other side. And politicians like Mikhail Gorbachev could see it
coming. He ushered in a campaign of truthfulness[14], to stop the pretence in
his country. Once the floodgate had been opened, there was no looking
back. But sadly I learned in last Sunday's *Observer* that some of the East
Berliners are hankering for the way it used to be[15]. I think it is partly due to
impatience. As you know things have not moved as fast as they had hoped.
The West German economy has been under some pressure.

I could understand if some people in Iraq said that it was better under
Saddam Hussein. There was some sort of order in the country, terrible though
it was. For some people the chaos since the invasion has been worse. And
this may also have been the case in Russia, where they feel that at least
there was less crime before and everyone had the right to a job.

Well let's take Iraq first. I think you will find that the Iraqis will gradually
appreciate the enormity of the human suffering that had gone on to some
extent undetected for years and years. When it has all quietened down—it
won't go on forever. They all have television now and as you say the
communications systems are so good now. Education will be better and
they will appreciate the freedom of speech where before it was all
indoctrination about the greatness of Saddam Hussein. Now they can hear
and see and speak the truth. They will notice the change. [Continues about
the different factions of Muslims Sunni and Shiite. Can they work out their
differences? etc. Expresses hope that a fundamentalist government does
not take over and that the new governments of Iraq will be more diligent
towards the benefit of the people.] Listen to what the people are saying and
give them free speech. Then Iraq will be good.

Russia has changed. I am not sure to what extent the corruption there is
something new. I am not going to go down that road. We have gangsterism
even here in the United Kingdom. My suspicion is that it is no worse in
Russia than in other places with gangs in big cities. The Russian people
now have freedom of expression now and are able to demonstrate. Maybe
sometimes it is better not to have too much loose ends or too much
government—[pause]

Too much democracy?

Maybe not. [pause]

Well sometimes from what you have expressed it seems that you may be
too impatient with democracy. You would like to get things done without
too much debate.

Not only that. Here we have central government, and two tiers of local government (leaving out parish councils). Sometimes I think it is a nuisance. Central government's programmes sometimes get humbugged or stopped by bureaucracy in local government. If you had a centralised system with one subordinate tier, let's say the County Council, then the central government would give the orders to the County and say "this is what we want to get on with." I think it would be easier to monitor: a direct order given from the centre, for example to implement changes in education and ensure consistent standards across the country. "This is the model that you are going to work from. Period." It is not for those at local level to subvert the government's wishes and fiddle around and do what they want to do.

What you are describing sounds more like the French model of government.[16]

Well, I did not know about that, but it makes sense. From my experience of seeing local government in action, I would say there is nothing too wrong about a centralised system. It seems appropriate that the Prime Minister has a lot of control. I would not ask three or four people what is happening. I would look for a single responsibility for a given department. It's easy to follow and there is no argument about accountability. It is the same thing in schools and hospitals. There should be clear-cut direction from the top and a reduction in excessive administrators and bureaucracy.

[Laughs] And that would be a reduction in democracy.

It would save money, which can only benefit the country.

Yes, but we have a different tradition here. France had a revolution, and then they had Napoleon. They reinvented their administration from scratch. May I give you an example? The high-speed rail link through the Channel Tunnel required new tracks on both sides to accommodate the fast new trains. France simply decreed that they be built, there was little question of democratic objections. In England it took years of plans and objections at the local level before the route could be agreed.[17]

NOTES

1. *Quintin Hogg:* Conservative politician, academic and barrister. He renounced his hereditary peerage to enter the House of Commons, but later re-entered the Lords with his original title, Lord Hailsham, as a life peer.
2. *Parishes:* equivalent to counties in the UK.
3. *Port Royal* was at one time a significant town in Jamaica, made especially famous by the privateer Sir Henry Morgan.
4. *Sufferings of the Jews:* in the Holocaust from 1939-45.
5. *Sufferings of the Irish:* in the Irish Potato Famine from 1845-50.
6. *Sufferings of African slaves:* Sebert's point, as I recall from previous conversations, is that the Irish and the Jews remind the world of their terrible sufferings, inflicted by their fellow men (for the Irish Potato Famine did not inspire assistance from the English). The suffering of the slaves was worse and went on for hundreds of years, generation after generation being treated inhumanely.
7. *Indentured labourers:* "Following the emancipation of slaves in 1833, and the period of unpaid apprenticeship that followed, many liberated Africans left their former masters. For the owners of sugar-cane plantations, who required a regular, docile and low-waged labour force, this appeared to spell economic disaster. Britain was forced to look elsewhere for cheap labour and turned its attention for a brief period to China, and then to India.
    "The solution came in the form of a new system of forced labour, which in many ways resembled

enslavement. Indians, under an 'indentured' or contract labour scheme, began to replace enslaved Africans on plantations across the British empire, in Fiji, Natal, Burma, Ceylon, Malaya, British Guiana, Jamaica and Trinidad."
From http://www.nationalarchives.gov.uk/pathways/blackhistory/india/forced.htm

8. *Inventor of the traffic light:* Garrett Augustus Morgan, an African-American, filed the patent for the traffic light in 1923. See http://www.princeton.edu/~mcbrown/display/morgan.html which also describes several other inventions and honours received for them and also a medal for bravery. See also http://www.sciencemuseum.org.uk/on-line/garret-morgan/page4.asp for more details of the life and work of Garrett Morgan.

9. *Inventor of the Automatic Shoe Last:* Jan Matzeliger (1852-1889): Matzeliger invented the Automatic Shoe Last Machine, which shaped the upper leather of the shoe and attached it to the sole. The machine could manufacture an entire shoe in one minute and dramatically cut the cost of shoe production. (Information from http://www.sciencemuseum.org.uk/on-line/garret-morgan/page6.asp)

10. *Norbert Rillieux, inventor and sugar chemist* was the son of a French planter/inventor and a slave mother. "It was stated by Charles Brown, a chemist in the U.S. Department of Agriculture, that [Rillieux's invention of the sugar processing pan] was the greatest invention in the history of American Chemical Engineering." See http://www.princeton.edu/~mcbrown/display/rillieux.html

11. *America refuses to stop polluting:* I had in mind the Kyoto Protocol, which America and Australia have refused to sign. It is now in force by those countries which have ratified it. For some useful information see http://news.bbc.co.uk/1/hi/sci/tech/4267245.stm

12. *Exports:* Sebert or I could have mentioned at this point the trades in arms and tobacco conducted by rich countries at the expense of the health of everyone. There was a 1997 treaty to ban the sale and use of landmines for example,

13. *Exporting jobs to India:* modern telecommunications have created jobs overseas for India's large number of highly qualified university graduates whilst they remain in India. They undertake roles intimately connected with the UK economy such as developing computer systems for banks and large corporations. Others staff call centres in which they are trained to speak English like the English themselves, and to understand British culture, slang, weather and so on.

14. *Truthfulness in Russia:* for instance Gorbachev's policy of *glasnost*, "openness".

15. *East Berlin today:* see http://observer.guardian.co.uk/international/story/0,6903,1451109,00.html for the article Sebert is referring to. Though the Berlin wall is down, it still exists as an invisible divide, and the East Germans have not integrated with their Western brethren.

16. *The French model of government* remains more centralised that that of Britain though laws passed in 1982 and 1986 have marked slow steps in a process towards a greater decentralisation of democracy. For more information see http://en.wikipedia.org/wiki/France

17. *High-speed rail link:* the new railway line from Calais to Paris was completed in 1004 to coincide with the opening of the Channel Tunnel. On the British side and act of parliament authorising the construction of the link was not passed till 1996. The line from Folkestone to London will not be fully complete till 2007. However, the route from the tunnel to the capital is more densely populated on the British side, and I believe this has been the cause of so much delay in design and construction.

CHAPTER 22

People power

IAN, I WILL NOT CONTRADICT MY EARLIER STATEMENTS. I appreciate the United Kingdom and I would not swap it for any other country. What I expressed to you was my personal view. But I still see merit in the way that the Westminster government operates, and that is to let the people have a say, and to bring the government closer to the people. Hence, we have the three-tier system.[1] It has a problem—slowing down the implementation of beneficial change, and an advantage—avoiding a dull uniformity.

Yes, I see this impatience in Tony Blair. He would like to be the kind of dictator that you indicate.

[Giggles]

But his dictatorship is swayed constantly by public opinion. This week it was the business of the school dinners. Now Jamie Oliver[2] has had an audience with him at 10 Downing Street. Instant policy change. If you listen to the people like this, it's a sign of being unprincipled, though it is a form of democracy.

[hesitates] . . . I've been told that my attitude is similar to Tony Blair's. I have supported Tony Blair and Gordon Brown from day one. I have met them both and I have seen them grow. I won't blame Tony Blair for this. Politics and law are fun. They are like playing chess. Politicians are there to think quickly and take advantage of the situation if something is good. You pick it up, make your swift move, because there won't be a second chance. Probably the opposition would have done the same, and if Tony had slipped and missed it, the opposition would have seized on it and made an election promise[3] out of it. It's not Tony Blair, it's not the Labour Party that we have to blame. We the people simply don't pay enough attention to things. What about the parents? Why did they not make complaints before? They could certainly have found out what was on offer for school dinners. They could ask their children for example. We talk about people power. One individual can get on television and proclaim that the nutritional value of school dinners is rubbish. Why didn't the parents get together and say that their children would not go back to school until better meals were offered?[4] In the United Kingdom, we do not protest enough, we do not pay enough attention to the things that we ought to. That is the problem.

But there is an underlying class war in British society, coupled with a cynicism. I tend to think that parents were inhibited from taking direct action because diet is a kind of class distinction. It would have been the middle-

class mothers interfering with a working-class diet. What class of parents would try to get their children to eat salads? But Jamie got acceptance across all classes.

It was whilst looking at your press cuttings this week that I realised our English tendency to sneer at other social classes. I was reading about the Mayoress's presidency of the Townswomen's Guild. I used to feel it was an institution reserved for a certain class of woman that I refused to take seriously. We create class stereotypes as a way of avoiding issues. I feel that your presence on the public scene has helped to break down this bad tendency. Britain has been a series of "closed shops". I think of you in the Officers' Mess at Naphill, mingling with the top brass in the RAF and NATO.

If I had not been a Mayor, I would not have been there. Let me come back to this topic of school dinners.

I am sorry. I had side-tracked the conversation into something else.

No, it is all right. We can follow up the very point you are making. On the news today, it was pointed out that a three-course meal for a Member of Parliament in the Commons dining room costs £5. That worries me.

That's the cost of the ingredients?

No, that is what they pay. £1.50 for a really nice sweet. If they earn £140,000 a year, with all the subsidies and privileges they receive, and I am still subsidising their lunch, why cannot they subsidise my children's school meals so that they spend more than the average of 53 pence on the ingredients? France spends £2 or £3 on their school dinners. We are at the bottom. I would suggest they give more to the children, and from their pockets pay £10 for their meals in the House of Commons Dining Room. They should pay the extra as a gesture of solidarity with our children who have been given such poor nutrition. They can afford it. They have high salaries, guaranteed for five years. Some of the parents have no jobs, or at any rate no job security. This is an example where politicians should be honest and straightforward. It is a chance for them to show humanity.

You are attacking what's left of a class system that was once a hundred times worse.

Yes, we understand that. But Tony's a good Christian. A lot of them are Christian now.

I am wondering whether Christianity helps in this. For two thousand years Christianity has propped up the prevailing class systems. They were not traditionally in support of equality. I can remember as a child that in church we still sang certain verse of "All things bright and beautiful" that is omitted today: "The rich man in his castle / The poor man at his gate / God made them high or lowly / And ordered their estate". For hundreds of years they believed that God meant the black man to be a slave and the white man to be a master.

Well, I am not going to contradict myself. I criticised the parents before for not standing up for better food for their children till recently. OK let's say that regardless of the ideal of Christian love, and regardless of there still being a class structure which benefits some more than others, we are supposed to be now in a classless society, where there is equal opportunity for all. I am saying that the MPs should have been shamed into giving up their subsidies for food—

Look, you know that I agree with you. All I am doing is pointing out that you are calling for a revolution in this traditional society of ours, which runs on privilege.

[Laughs] I—well, this will be a bloodless one.

I am very glad to hear it.

Well no matter which side the MPs are on it could benefit their party if they made that sacrifice. It could win them votes.

But even in Russia, after the Revolution, the Party members and top people used to enjoy many privileges that were denied to the rest. My fear is that the more you move towards centralised government, the more you create the climate which continues to foster privileges for the few.

Well, I did not go all the way for centralisation, but it is just that in things like education and health, I feel—and this applies to both parties in office—that central government had abdicated some of the responsibilities so as not to be blamed.

Aha! Well I have got you here. You were saying the other week—and we have it on record[5]—precisely the opposite. You were saying that the hospital trusts should be decentralised more, to prevent the government from being blamed. You were saying they should sack the managers—

Exactly. There is nothing wrong with what I am saying.

That is the opposite of what you were saying before.

No! What I am saying now is the very same thing. Because we have this tier of government, some of those people sitting in County Hall, with their Conservative majority, are the ones who are blocking the Government. Now if at the local level the Government had its agent pledged to work directly with the government, then things would get done and there would be no argument. Then, if the person in charge at the local level did not carry out the government instructions, he would be sacked. At the moment, with the system that we have, they are able to hide away from that.

Now, let me give you the example of Handy Cross. The issue of redevelopment has been hanging for a long time.

The big roundabout over the motorway, or the sports centre?

The roundabout. For example should there be a flyover? Because of the Carrington[6] land involved, that was a hot potato in the Conservative days. For central government, it was nice to shift it off to Aylesbury [where County Hall is situated] and let them, as agents, take all the flak.

Because it is County Hall who manages the roads.

That's right. This is an example of shifting the blame, a case where we should look for more truthfulness. If government want to get something done, they will do so, especially if they are the ruling party at the County Council level. You follow me?

Mmm, I'm following it but I am wondering if you would have taken this view if the County Council were Labour-dominated.

Certainly, when I was in local government, my concern was for Wycombe people and how the best outcomes could be reached. There are some things which should not get snared in party politics. One reason I lost an election once may have been to do with my strong support of pedestrianisation in the town centre. I believe that people should be able to walk freely along the High Street, without being at risk from traffic. I stick to my principles whatever the government. For example I consider the present Labour government the most anti-motorist that I have experienced. Well I have to accept it and admit that there is too much traffic on the road. You have to do something about it. But whether it is the way that I would have done it as a Minister of Transport, that is another matter. In many respects I am at loggerheads with Westminster policies. If it doesn't work, knock it out. If it works, keep it. That's my politics. [laughs]

OK, the tape is going to finish in a minute. Perhaps it is time for a break? Well, we have reached the end of a—

—a milestone. [Laughs] Yes.

Yes, it's been good, it's been very challenging today.

Yes, today has been full of detail, because when we started off, we were wondering where we would go, and thought we might fill in some gaps left in our previous sessions. But I find today a bit fresh in a way. It has covered a lot of details.

And so in conclusion to today's session, I think it is only right that we talk about the future. We were talking about the future of the Caribbean earlier. Then we got on to the topic of the future of what our children eat at school. Then we looked at how MPs in Parliament should behave. That is also future. We looked forward to a future in which politics at all levels is conducted with truth and without pretence.

So it comes back to young people. The future is theirs. They have the power to put politicians in place, and to remove them too. You put them in power because they have promised certain things, or you have given them your agenda: what you want them to get done over the next five years. You can tell them what changes you want them to implement. They have the right to see that the future for their own children is not neglected, in terms of education and welfare. There should be no need for a celebrity to come on television to point out that your children are eating rubbish food. You as a parent should be asking your children every day what they are having to eat at school. And if you are not happy, then you should be able to wave your own flag and do what Jamie Oliver has done. And on that note I would like to end today's session.

OK, great. Um, can I ask a question?

Of course, go ahead.

Where are we? [looks at watch] I thought that—[realises that the session has been going a long time]

[tries to put something in words] To me, this is very vital stuff, because what we have been talking about has been striking at the root of traditions in this country, and if you just take school dinners and compare them with MPs' dinners, the mindset ties up with colonialism. Both are based upon a hierarchy, a class system. The people up there [gesturing] get the best, and the people down there should be very grateful—

—for the pittance they receive.

The whole world is like this. Almost every country that has an army, divides it into officers and men. The officers of course dine in the very best way, with the regimental silver and the servants attending. The officer used to have his own batman to look after his uniforms and so on. As if they were higher beings, probably closer to God. This attitude of difference remains in the world. I think much of what you are saying clashes against this ancient hierarchy of class. I thought before we started these discussions that we no longer have a class system in this country. The ruling classes always resist being pulled down from on high, but simply by being Mayor you have gone to places which were the cliques of the white traditionalists, like those officers' messes you were invited to. Perhaps no black face had been seen there before.

Well occasionally there would be another black face. I was never deterred from going to those places but I must say there was a feeling of surprise on occasion. I would go accompanied by my Mayoress to many places, not only Naphill, where we would be the only two black faces there, and we would always find that we had a ready audience. They would start an enquiry. They would want to investigate your background, and find out how it happened. It was the curiosity of meeting us.

I used to call myself the Mayor of the People. It is true that what I did, I did not do for myself, but for those children at schools, especially the black children. When they saw someone in my position, also black, come to their school, you could see the glow on their faces and the appreciation. I don't think the black community as a whole has had enough exposure to people from their own background who have got involved in things. We have a few politicians. What about in prisons, prison visitors? I would be interested to know how many black people they have in there.

Inmates?

No. Not inmates but prison visitors. They have certain quangos[7] you know. I would be interested to know how many are going to the places where black people are locked up as insane.

I have heard that a disproportionate number of black people have been diagnosed with schizophrenia and such illnesses.

Exactly. According to statistics there are a high proportion of them in institutions. But who are visiting them? Who are talking to them? Who are trying to find out what they are going through?

I have a friend of Jamaican roots who is a nurse in a mental ward. I could ask her.

Yes, it would be very interesting. Even though I have been involved for many years in community work, I can only remember prison visits on about two occasions. It is not that I was asked to make those visits. The community relations officer, Alf Webley, was making the visits and on these two occasions I came along too. There were a lot of young black men, who needed someone to talk to, they needed counselling.

And it would be so much better if it were someone they could more easily relate to.

Yes, I've seen it a number of times when we have put the call out for people from the ethnic minority groups to become JPs.[8] There have been adverts for them to join the Police. The Navy is interested to recruit them, whether it says so directly or just implies it by including black faces in the advertisements. But I cannot recall any advertisement for people to volunteer as visitors to institutions. Or perhaps there are paid positions to do this. And it is my perception that where they are paid jobs, blacks don't usually get picked [laughs]. I am just curious as to how you get on these committees and how it works.

Well there are various levels of committees, I suppose, with school governors at the bottom end and Royal Commissions at the top end, where you would be selected from a list of what they call "the great and the good".

And it is not all unpaid of course. Sometimes they say "You won't be out of pocket." In various circumstances out-of-pocket expenses are refunded.

Well, what about non-executive directors of companies? I would not suppose there would be many black faces there.

Yes, these are the kinds of situations where with all the British openness that I have found, there are still areas in which the power is kept rather exclusively by small groups.

I feel that it is a characteristic of British society in particular that there are cliques of the like-minded. Membership is defined by whom you wish to exclude. Take for example clubs which had always excluded women. Why? Well one reason was so that the men could tell certain types of joke, or more generally feel at ease with one another. Whoever is excluded is an outsider group that you can tell jokes about, whether they be a different class or a different ethnic group. I can remember when such structures were unquestioned. I was in a work team in 1970 when a woman member joined the staff, and there was some dismay about how we would still work with the same cohesion as before.

It has been long understood in this class-obsessed society that the Mayor, for all his pomp and dignity, might be a local tradesman and "not as educated" as those in the circles in which he participated as Mayor. With these kinds of traditions, I feel that a black Mayor is something else and will have made an impact upon the expectations and the cliques.

Yes, it has made a big impact. As you rightly say there is a cultural tradition which goes back more than seven hundred years. And what must be remembered is that even though he may have been a tradesman, he must have been a special kind of person to attain this rank. He must have done a great deal of voluntary public service over many years. It is one of the areas which bring on those privileges which you have described. Without being Mayor it would have been impossible to penetrate so many closed circles within society, and to hear and share the jokes which go on within them. The Mayoralty already has a tradition of breaking down some barriers.

I want to be personal and say that in your case the impact is not just that you are black but that you are who you are with your special integrity.

Well, I would hope so.

I could imagine a black person who manages to get into the circles of power in this country because he is ready to compromise, to follow the—the—

—the status quo—

—*the status quo. Like they say, Margaret Thatcher was our first and only woman Prime Minister. But people said that she did not stay true to femininity. You have stayed true to your agenda.*

The Mayor's position is different. You have to be a councillor to get there and that means that you represent your town. You have to live in the town area. You have to be elected by several thousand people. You have to be a councillor for a town ward for some years and then you may be nominated as Mayor. You are selected by your peers and this means that they judge your character to be sound. There has been no protest against me, either in the newspaper or from any other source.

But it still does not stop a Mayor from becoming big-headed.

No! Certainly not. Oh yes, there are plenty of opportunities for a sense of self-importance.

I am not suggesting there has been anyone like that in Wycombe.

Well, it is something that happens in life. But for me personally, my ambition was achieved when I became Mayor. This was my fulfilment, to be able to help people, to look at those schoolchildren's smiles. I mean all of them, across the board: black, white, Asian. They gave me some of my happiest moments.

I was looking at some of the press coverage, especially at a particular visit to Micklefield Combined School.

Yes, I visited that school twice I think, and another at Cressex, so many schools.

This particular one was the occasion when you asked them how many would like to be Prime Minister. The reason was that a rumour had been spreading across the school that the Prime Minister was going to visit. It was five days after the 1997 General Election, so even little children would have known that we had a new Prime Minister.

Yes and there was one at Cressex for children with learning difficulties. Recently I encountered a young woman in town who recognised me. I don't know what school she had been in, but she recognised me from one of those visits. Now she is 21. I was surprised!

Yes, in that year, I made sure to keep my feet on the ground. I remembered where I had come from and where I would return. I certainly knew it was important to remain the same to all the people I already knew. They could still call me "Sebert" of course though I was now "Mr Mayor". It was an elation to me, to make sure I was not above them and would not make them feel that they were inferior. In fact that is why I opened up my office, the Mayor's Parlour, so that everyone would have the chance to see it and understand all the functions and traditions. And I held some functions for the old people at the King's Church, called "Wycombe remembers", where they could look back over thirty years and remember what it used to look like. People came there who had not seen one another for up to fifteen years. Some of them were brought from care homes in various parts of town, and they were given a good meal, and performances, and teas and so on.

Yes, I feel good about what I was able to achieve in that year.

And I feel that it is magical in a way that you were the one who was giving back to the people their own heritage. I would like to write that from a perspective outside your own. I want to go through the press cuttings and talk to Steve Cohen.[9]

Even my peers appreciated my mayoral year. It was an extremely good year. I would not find it easy to leave Wycombe for good. I travelled from Jamaica and lived in London for six years. I had time to see what the London scene was about. It seemed more selfish, more that you were living alongside strangers. Then I came to Wycombe. I don't know how people will view it, but my involvement, for me, is an achievement. I know I am repeating myself, but to share in the heritage, to be elected by the people, all those times, and tramping the streets delivering leaflets—I could not bring to mind anything that has happened badly. How shall I put it, no mischief was done against me. I don't think any of them had regrets about it. High Wycombe has been a really nice place for me. I know about prejudice and racism, and what is going on in some parts of this country, according to reports. But in my years of going around to thousands of houses, dropping leaflets, knocking on doors, introducing myself, offering my services, I cannot speak of any bad thing that ever happened to me on that campaign trail. I have had the utmost respect for people and I think I have gained their respect as well.

And this is without compromising any of my real beliefs and my strong feelings about certain things. And people know who I am. [Laughs]

First Wycombe, then the world!

[Laughs]

Well if it works in Wycombe, why will it not work in a wider arena? Just follow the same principles.

Yes, people understand me. When I speak about politics and politicians, in fairness to them—I went into Boots[10] last week. A gentleman from the Pakistani community saw me. He said, "Mr Graham, are you standing for election this year? I haven't seen you." I said, "No, I'm not standing. I'm leaving it for younger people now. I don't have the feeling for it now. I don't like the way that the ward has been cut up.[11] He said, "When you were with us it was good. Now people don't do anything. We don't see them." [Laughs] He said, "When you were our representative you were always available. Now the place is different." I used to go through the ward and sort things out. Where I saw that people had been parking on the grass verges, cutting them up, I got on to the County Council, and had it fixed so they had proper parking. I used to walk through the ward, and note where they had dumped old mattresses, or where it was clogged with dead leaves in Autumn. Or there was a place, Sussex Close, where there is an alleyway at the end that is sometimes blocked by overgrown hedges. I would make sure that the Council would come along and clean up my ward. I used to be there for the people. They appreciate that. They know where to find you. That is what the old gentleman said. And he is not the only one.

NOTES

1. *Three-tier system:* Parliament, County Council, municipal council (City, Borough, District etc).
2. *Jamie Oliver:* TV chef and author of cookery books, who started a series on TV entitled Jamie's School Dinners, in which Jamie visits schools and persuades everyone including the children that healthy food is also tasty. On March 30 2005 He visited the Prime Minister to hand in a petition as part of his "Feed me better" campaign to eliminate junk food from schools.
3. *Election promise:* At the time of our conversation, the General Election campaign had got well under way, even though the date of the election—May 5th—was not announced by the Government till two days after.
4. *Direct action:* In Jamaica, direct action is often used as a rapid way to get publicity and change. Television news cameras would always be glad to report road blocks, angry parents with crude placards and similar local demonstrations.
5. *Shifting the blame:* It was my (Ian's) recollection that he did not like the Government being blamed for hospital Health Service shortcomings but—see page 94—there is no inconsistency in his argument.
6. *Carrington land:* The Carrington family bought land in Wycombe in 1795. The present holder of the hereditary peerage was foreign Secretary at the time of the Falklands War, which triggered his resignation. "Lord Carrington has had an extraordinary political career, serving in the Lords as the impeccable courtier to six Tory prime ministers, starting with Winston Churchill. The original Lord C was a banker but, as the ancestral line continued, the family distanced itself from that dirty business and was forced to sell the ancestral pile, Wycombe Abbey, to a girl's school." (From http://

www.mychelsea.net/chelsea/celebs&gossip-lord-carrington.htm) He lives locally and still owns extensive acreage in the area.

7. Quango: An organisation or agency that is financed by a government but that acts independently of it . Derivation: qua(si) n(on-)g(overnmental) o(rganization).

8. *Justices of the Peace:* the role in the United Kingdom is not the same as that in Jamaica. A Jamaican JP is someone who is authorised to sign documents and generally give guidance in the community. In the UK the main duty of a JP is to attend court for perhaps 26 days a year as a lay magistrate (unpaid) to deal with minor offences; also to deal with applications for liquor and other licences.

9. *Steve Cohen:* editor of the three local newspapers: Bucks Free Press, The South Bucks Star (distributed free), Midweek.

10. *Boots:* Well-known pharmacy chain.

11. *Wards cut up:* periodically the boundaries of wards and Parliamentary constituencies are revised in order to keep the populations in each roughly equal.

APPENDIX A

Community Relations in Wycombe 1976-1999. [A selection of items over the years. Those from local media are framed with a double line.]

Police alert as school feud puts boy in hospital

Vigilante groups were formed and police carried out daily patrols when a long-standing feud between pupils of two schools in High Wycombe ended in a severe assault on a 12-year-old West Indian boy. . . . Joel was at first thought to have a fractured skull. He also had severe internal bruising and stomach injuries. . . .

Afro-West Indian Association secretary Sebert Graham said: "It seems to me it would be advisable for teachers of both schools to get together on this. They have to be seen to be doing something constructive."

A senior police officer said investigations proved that the continuing tension between the schools and the assaults were not racial.

Excerpted from *Bucks Free Press*, 01.10.76

Breakdown not break up

At the annual meeting of Wycombe's Community Relations Council the Asian community took over all seats on the executive committee except one which went to a white man. In consequence, the West Indians have decided to withdraw support from the council.

The West Indian community have fallen a victim of their own apathy. They stayed away from the annual meeting, whereas young Asians increased the numbers attending and were able to vote in their own representatives.

Excerpted from *Midweek*, 05.05.81

West Indians do as well as whites at our school – head declares

The truth of the matter, at Castlefield Middle School in the heart of one High Wycombe's largest and oldest council estates, is that West Indian and Asian children perform as well in tests as any other pupil, claims headmaster Laurie Taylor, who is also a member of the town's Community Relations Council educational committee.

Condensed from *Bucks Free Press*, two weeks after the publication in June 1981 of the Rampton Report: West Indian Children in our schools, which claimed that black pupils' underachievement in school was due to racism.

West Indian calls for fairer education

A call for a radical change in the education system has been made by Wycombe's Afro-West Indian association. Secretary Sebert Graham told the annual meeting: "The system is . . . geared against the black people of Britain. Schools have failed to monitor and provide the West Indian parent and children with statistics to show just how many are sent to educationally subnormal classes unnecessarily. How many are sent home from school through some form of bias or prejudice? How many have been talked down to by head teachers? The West Indians in the USA, Canada and other parts of the world have achieved great heights in their chosen professions and are still achieving. The reason for their achievements is they are given the chance and the opportunity for their self-advancement."

Excerpted from *Bucks Free Press*, 20.11.81

Race Report Fails to Impress

There has been a cool response all round from minority group leaders in High Wycombe on the Home Office report on racial attacks published this week ...

The report looked at racial attacks across 13 police forces, including Thames Valley, which is responsible for High Wycombe, and concluded that specialist police units were not the way to deal with the issue. . . .

Secretary of the Afro-West Indian Association, Sebert Graham, added that this was likely to be yet another government study that would be looked at then shelved. . . .

Wycombe has been hard hit by racial incidents this year. Even the community relations office in Desborough Road has been attacked. . . .

Excerpted from *Bucks Free Press*, 20.11.81

This frail bridge between the communities

(From report on Annual General Meeting of Wycombe's Community Relations Council)

Incumbent Sebert Graham had held office for just a year, having been elected by acclamation. The election of Ghulam Rasool Mirza swings the balance back towards the Asians. . . . It is certainly true that the Multiracial Centre was flooded with Asians last week so that Mr Mirza's election was nothing more than a formality; yet also true that Mr Graham showed no sign of grief or bitterness, and to the contrary passed kind words about his successor.

This was not the diplomacy of the vanquished, afterwards and in another place to wail and blame anyone responsible for his fall. His praise for the character of Mr Mirza was genuinely meant, the good wishes too.

Excerpted from *Bucks Free Press*, 13.05.83

Police race riot methods provoke complaint

. . . An official complaint will be lodged today about the way a few police officers handled the disturbances.

Hundreds of youths were involved, the Anchor pub was besieged, a shotgun was found in the multiracial centre, and police brought in reinforcements in riot gear.

Afterwards they searched the Multiracial Centre. Cupboard doors and drawers were wrenched off in the centre's kitchen. Alf Webley, community relations officer, says this damage and locks smashed on other doors was done by police officers searching for weapons and drugs, though he himself was in the centre with the keys until 6 am.

"This is the sort of thing which makes not just young people but adults angry," Mr Sebert Graham, former chairman of the local Council for Racial Equality said.

On the morning before the riot the local free newspaper carried an interview with black youths warning that the town could become "another Brixton" if relations with police did not improve.

The Anchor's landlord, Mr David Britnell, said he and his family were fighting for their lives against black youths trying to climb in trhough the shattered pub windows.

There is bitterness amongst the blacks that hours after the last white youths had gone all those in the Multiracial Centre were still being searched and having their names and addresses taken.

In 1981, the inner city riots were copied on a smaller scale in High Wycombe.

Excerpted from *The Guardian* (national newspaper), 04.01.88

"When we came here we were strangers. We tried to fit in within society. Jobs that were given to us we took. We never argued about it. Because we came to work, because we'd families to send back in various parts of the West Indies, and therefore we take things willingly. The difference between us now—maybe I have been using the wrong terminology with 'black youngsters' and all that— the young *black Britishers* born here, it's a different situation. This is their country. They were born here. They were educated here. And they expected to be treated fairly. This is their country. They were born here. They were educated here. And they expected to be treated fairly.

"I would wish and I would sincerely hope that the authorities will now sit down and look seriously at the kind of facilities that they are providing for black people until the year 2000 because they are here—not as immigrants any more. But we're here to stay. We're not going anywhere. We are all citizens. We are ratepayers. We've got the same right to services like anyone else. So I hope that they will take that on board."

Sebert Graham speaking about Wycombe's "New Year race riot" on 01.01.88, on the 'Here and Now' magazine programme presented for Central TV on 13.03.88 by Zia Mohyeddin.

TOWN IS A 'SOCIAL DESERT'

Councillor Sebert Graham is pressing for more nightlife in High Wycombe to help youngsters with nothing to do.

Cllr Graham, a Labour member of Wycombe District Council, is concerned that young people could get into trouble if they became bored and frustrated.
...

Excerpted from *Bucks Free Press*, 07.09.90

Multiracial centre is to be resited in town

A new centre for ethnic groups came one step nearer this week when councillors agreed to replace one sited under a flyover. ...

Cllr Sebert Graham (Lab, Bowerdean and Daws Hill) said the council's £50,000 grant would not go very far. New venues would cost around £250,000, he said.

Excerpted from *Bucks Free Press*, 12.02.93

'It's our town too. All we want is something back'

Retired labourer Wallis Janes, 68, left his island home of St Vincent in 1959. His wife died during the one brief visit they ever made back. High Wycombe is his home town and he is staying. The town's Caribbean community now numbers about 5,000. Many have reached or are now approaching retirement age and say they need better state care. They want their own day care centre ... Pressure to find a new home for the existing tiny Multiracial Centre has dragged on for more than 15 years but it has been a slow process to get things moving. ...

Cllr Sebert Graham (Lab, Bowerdean and Daws Hill), the only Caribbean on the Council, waves Conservative criticism aside as an attempt to sabotage Labour's new alliance with the Liberal Democrats. "It is pure, undiluted political engineering," he said.

Condensed from *Bucks Free Press*, 17.11.95

NEWSFLASH

Wycome Multi Cultural Organisation

Dear Member and Friends,

You are invited to the opening of the newly refurbished Hill Top Community Centre on Saturday 22 February 1997.

Doors will open to all at 7.00 p.m.

The bar will be in "full swing" so don't be late as the beer will be selling at £1.00 per pint during the first hour, thereafter at £1.50 per pint.

Children are welcome!

W.M.C.O Members look forward to welcoming you. See you on the night!

Ex-mayor calls for MP apology
Lidington in trouble over his visa
for Jamaicans comment

David Lidington, MP for Aylesbury suggested visa controls in response to yardie-style assaults and murders in Britain.

Mr Graham: "I think Mr Lidington owes Jamaicans an apology. They've contributed a lot to life at home and in this country. They're law-abiding decent people. The Jamaican government is working with the US and Britain to tackle crime.

"Criminals, whatever their colour, have no respect for class or colour. Anyway, how does Mr Lidington know that these so called Yardies are Jamaican?"

Excerpted from *Bucks Free Press*, 23.07.99

APPENDIX B

Linking High Wycombe with St Vincent & the Grenadines. These excerpts from local media and Sebert's own archives refer to the creation of the High Wycombe St Vincent and the Grenadines Linking Association, in recognition of the thousands of Wycombe residents who were born, or whose parents were born, in this part of the Caribbean.

High Wycombe's paradise twin

St Vincent is 18 miles long and 11 miles wide, with a population of about 117,000 .... it is famous for its clear sea and sandy beaches ... It is known as the Land of the Blessed ... its main industry is the banana trade ...

Excerpted from *Bucks Free Press*, 01.02.97

BLACKS EARN PRAISE

The High Commissioner of St Vincent, Richard Gunn, praised Wycombe blacks for their artistic talents when he visited the town's Multiracial Centre on Sunday

Mr Gunn said he was pleased to see Vincentians still using the furniture-making and other skills learnt in their island homeland. . . .

It was a very good evening and Mr Gunn ... made the point that Vincentians could use the skills they learned in this country to help the economy of St Vincent if ever they went back," said association secretary Sebert Graham.

Mr Gunn also assured Vincentians – there are about 5,000 in Wycombe – that the Government at home was performing well.

Excerpted from *Star*, 14.04.89

Dear Sebert

Thanks for coming to see me on a couple of occasions to discuss the merits of trying to establish links with St Vincent. I believe that there is potential for interest in this, but having sounded out a few Members my personal view is that at this stage it would be probably be too early to take anything to committee without being sure that it has broad backing from at least two Groups. I have raised this with the two group Leaders and with the Chairman of the Strategic Policy Board. It would clearly be unfortunate if we were to take it to Strategic Policy Board too early and actually lose out on the issue because sufficient preparation had not been made. . . .

Extract of letter from Richard Cummins, High Wycombe Chief Executive 01.02.96

Dear Councillor Graham

Many thanks for your invitation to the St Vincent Independence Day Celebrations and Service on 20th October. I am truly delighted to be asked and you are quite correct that I am hoping to build up my contacts with St Vincent to the level where I will be working in the Island as a surgeon, perhaps doing locums when their own surgeons need a break. To this end I have exchanged letters several times with Mr C- FRCS, who is one of the two Consultant General Surgeons at present on the island. . . .

From a surgeon working in the Wycombe area, 07.10.96

Thank you for your letter dated 8 January 1997 with the information that the Honourable Minister of Foreign Affairs of St Vincent and the Grenadines has indicated that he is supportive of promoting the idea of linking St Vincent and High Wycombe. . . .

Extract of letter from European Officer of Wycombe District council to the High Commissioner for the Eastern Caribbean States, 18.02.97

MAYOR AIMS TO TWIN WITH ST VINCENT

. . . The town, which is home to some 5,500 St Vincentians, has boasted strong links with the Caribbean since the first immigrants arrived more than 40 years ago. Mayor Sebert Graham, who left Jamaica for England in 1960 and has lived in High Wycombe for 30 years, revealed plans for the linking now being debated. "I believe we in this country can play a very useful part in the Caribbean.

Excerpted from *The Leader* (undated cutting)

Mayor sets up link with tropical isle

St Vincent's main industry, the production of bananas, has been hit by the European directive which requires the fruit to be of a certain shape and length.

One of the hopes is that in fostering international co-operation between the two communities, St Vincent could become High Wycombe's main supplier of bananas. Sebert Graham added that he did not want the link to become an excuse for council members and employees to visit the Caribbean.

Mr Graham said electrical equipment we take for granted like photocopiers and computers, could also be sent over there, if it became surplus to requirements.

He would also like to see educational links.

Excerpted from *Bucks Free Press*, 01.02.97

Photocopiers for mangoes may see an unlikely swap.

But if proposals to link High Wycombe with the Caribbean island state of St Vincent come to fruition, supporters claim that residents on both sides will benefit. . . . The High Wycombe area is home to the largest percentage of Vincentians living away from the island.

Excerpted from *The Leader* (undated cutting)